The Greasy Thumb Automechanics Manual for Women

written by Barb Wyatt
illustrated by Julie Zolot

ISBN 0-918040-00-0

Second Printing	January 1978
Third Printing	January 1979
Fourth Printing	August 1980
Fifth Printing	March 1982

ORDERING INFORMATION

Price: $8.00

40% discount to bookstores or individual women ordering five or more books. Postage paid by orderer and to be included with prepayment.

Postage and Handling:
Postage is paid on orders of one book.
On all other orders, add 10% of total
price after discount. All first orders
must be prepaid. Credit will be considered
on subsequent orders.

Order from:
Iowa City Women's Press
529 S. Gilbert St.
Iowa City, Iowa 52240

INTRODUCTION

I wrote this book for a couple of reasons. One is that I was real tired of trying to use the available automechanic manuals--written by men for men-- for information on how to do repairs on my car. After spending a lot of time trying to figure out what terms in a repair explanation mean or deciding to fix something and getting no more help than "remove the old part and install the new part", I realized there is a real need for an automechanics manual that assumes no previous mechanical knowledge on the part of the user.

The other reason I wrote this book is that I wanted to pass on the knowledge that I have about cars to other women in a way that would be useful and helpful to them. I feel that women teaching other women what they know is real important to our present and future survival in this world as women separate themselves from men. Because I wrote this book, I don't want to be seen as some kind of authority on automechanics. Nor do I think any book should take the place of individual women exchanging their knowledge about cars. There are many women around who know a lot more than I do about cars and who probably had to work a lot harder to get that knowledge. Women mechanics everywhere teaching women what they know about cars is, to me, the most valuable transferal of skills.

ABOUT THE MANUAL

The Greasy Thumb isn't a manual for a woman who wants to learn automechanics as a trade, but rather it is for the woman who wants to learn something about how her car works, how to maintain it, and how to fix at least some of the things that might go wrong with it. Most importantly, it is a manual for a woman who doesn't have a man around to turn to when she can't get a bolt loose or doesn't understand how to do something.

When I first started thinking about writing this book, I had a hard time trying to determine what information to include and what cars to direct it towards. There is so much that I don't know, and so many different makes, models, and years of cars.

I decided to do two things: First, to not get into explanations of complicated repairs or repairs that go beyond the normal maintenance of a car. My hope is that women who want to get into doing more major work on their car will have the confidence to do so after doing all the repair procedures covered in this manual.

Second, the repair and troubleshooting procedures are directed towards 1970 or older american cars without airconditioning or extra power equipment. This is because: 1. There are some pretty good foreign car manuals around but I haven't seen any good ones for american cars; 2. I don't know much about the elaborate emission controls on later model cars or much about power equipment and extra accessories; 3. All my friends drive either foreign cars or old american cars and this book is written for women like my friends.

The manual is divided into three parts--Tools & Theory; Maintenance & Repair; and Troubleshooting. Part I, Tools & Theory, goes over all the tools you need to work on a car plus some tips on how to use the tools. Also in Part I is an explanation of how a gasoline engine works and identification of the visible parts of the car--both in the engine compartment and underneath the body.

Part II is the repair section of the manual. The emphasis is on routine maintenance services-- oil change, lubrication, repacking front wheel bearings, winterizing, and tune up. There is also an explanation of how to do brake work and tips on doing common general repairs--exhaust system repair, replacing shocks and universal joints, front end and transmission checks.

Part III, Troubleshooting, covers typical car problems--engine won't start or doesn't run right; oil and water leaks; lights, horn, wipers, etc. not working.

The manual is written under the assumption that the reader reads all of Part I before using any of the repair and troubleshooting chapters, because many of the repair explanations are dependent on a basic knowledge of how a car works and where parts are located.

Before you start to use this manual, I'd like to say something about frustration--you have to be prepared to deal with a whole lot of frustration

when you work on cars. The less experience you have
the greater the frustration. However, I have found
ways of dealing with the frustration and not letting
it overcome me. My main tactic is to walk away from
whatever is causing the frustration--give myself
some breathing space so I can calm down and think
the problem out. Or I just go do something else
and forget about the cause of the frustration for
awhile. If you have a job as a mechanic you can't
always do that, but if you're just working on your
own car then you should allow yourself that kind
of space.

A source of frustration and discouragement in
working on cars, at least for me, has been men.
It's real difficult to contend with the machoness
of many men mechanics while trying to get some as-
sistance with or knowledge about your car. One
thing I have found out from experience is though
men may act like they know everything about cars,
a lot of times they don't--and you may know just as
much or more.

One final thing to remember about frustration
is that the more work you do on cars, the more
experience you will have and your frustrating ex-
periences will become fewer in number and less in
intensity.

ABOUT THE GRAPHICS

I've always thought that the most important part of
any skills manual is the illustrations--that they
have to be clear and they have to demonstrate what
the writer is trying to explain. I think Julie's
drawings do both these things and more. They give
the book a liveliness that it otherwise wouldn't
have. She took my ideas for illustrations and used
her ability to recognize what is important in an
illustration along with a great sense of humor to
come up with drawings that are informative, funny,
and unique. My thanks to Julie for working with
me on this manual.

THE PRINTING

The entire book was printed on an old, sometimes
working, sometimes not working, small (Multilith
1250) press. Coupled with the press is an old ca-
mera that produces inconsistent negatives at best
(in offset printing you shoot a picture of what you
want to print thus getting a negative; the image
on the negative is then transferred to a metal

plate and the metal plate put on the press). I
wanted to tell you how The Greasy Thumb was printed,
because I think it's important that women use whatever equipment they have access to to produce what
we need to produce, even though the result may not
be the slick looking books of new york publishing
houses.

The breakdown of the costs involved in printing
2000 copies of this book is as follows:

$1000	paper
600	binders
1000	miscellaneous supplies (plates, nega-tives, chemicals, etc.)
600	building rent and overhead for 3 months
400	illustrator
2400	labor(layout, darkroom, printing, collating, binding; also $1000 of the labor return goes to paying off bind-ing and collating equipment we pur-chased to do the book)

Though the retail price of the book is $5.50, our
costs are based on $2.75 per book, as the book will
be mainly distributed through bookstores and distributors who get a 40%-50% reduction on the retail price.

We had a hard time arriving at a fair price for
the book--one that would pay us for at least some
of the labor involved in putting out the book but
wouldn't be so high that it would make the book un-
affordable for a lot of women. We have tried to make
provisions for women who can't afford the $5.50
price by giving women ordering 5 or more books the
same discount as the bookstores (so you can get together with your friends and order the book together). If there are women who want this book, and
can't afford the discount price, please write us.

THANKS

Though Julie and my name are on the cover of this
book as the author and illustrator, The Greasy Thumb
was actually produced by a whole lot of women who
combined put as much energy or more as we did in
the creation of this book. I want to thank those
women for what they did. Women in Iowa City used
the outlines from the book to work on their cars
and gave me feedback on what was understandable and
what wasn't. One friend typed the entire book,

which took an incredible amount of time and energy--
I can't thank her enough.

One woman did the extensive indexing. Another
woman did the photographs (trying to photograph the
underneath of a dirty greasy car with any clarity
is a real challenge). Two women spent a lot of time
making suggestions on the rough draft and proof-
reading the final copy. And a whole lot of women
helped with the printing, collating, and binding
of the book. I also want to thank the women who
over the last five years have given me the support
and help to learn automechanics and to pass those
skills on to other women through teaching and the
writing of this book.

The Greasy Thumb is dedicated to lesbians everywhere.

FEEDBACK

The worth of this manual is only going to be shown
by the help it gives to a woman working on her car.
If, when using this manual you find any of the explanations and illustrations unclear, or if in your
experience information in the book is inaccurate,
I would really appreciate hearing from you. If
needed and wanted, we will possibly put out a revised edition of the book in the future. Please
send any suggestions, comments, criticism to:

> Barb Wyatt
> c/o Iowa City Women's Press
> 529 S. Gilbert St.
> Iowa City, Iowa 52240

Thank you. BW

PREFACE TO THE 1980 EDITION

Although the cost of this book is now $6.50, and the
cost of its production is different from what was
listed above, we've left all that information in here.
Our desire to make this book as available as possible
to as many women as possible by keeping the price low
is still true, and telling something about the origins
of the book is still an important part of the book to us.

Iowa City Women's Press

TABLE OF CONTENTS

Introduction

Part I   TOOLS & THEORY

    Chapter 1   Tools and Other Needed Information   1

    Chapter 2   How a Car Works   27

Part II   MAINTENANCE & REPAIRS

    Chapter 1   Maintenance Routines   54

    Chapter 2   Lubricant Changes   63

    Chapter 3   A Lube Job   74

    Chapter 4   Repacking Front Wheel Bearings   80

    Chapter 5   Winterizing Your Car   89

    Chapter 6   How To Do a Tune Up   105

    Chapter 7   Brake Repair   129

    Chapter 8   Hints on General Repairs   158

Part III   TROUBLESHOOTING

    Chapter 1   When Your Car Won't Start   170

    Chapter 2   When Your Car Won't Run Right   186

    Chapter 3   When Your Car's Lights, Horn, Wipers Don't Work   198

Glossary   210

Index

PART I

TOOLS
&
THEORY

Chapter 1

TOOLS
and other needed
information

In this chapter I want to go over the basic mechanic tools, some tips on how to use tools, plus talk
a little about the types of hardware you will be
dealing with in working on cars (nuts, bolts, etc.)
and provide some miscellaneous information - like
how to buy parts and things like that.

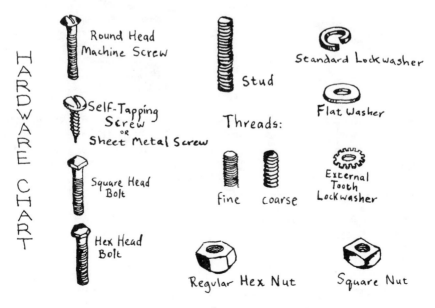

HARDWARE CHART

Round Head
Machine Screw

Self-Tapping
Screw
OR
Sheet Metal Screw

Square Head
Bolt

Hex Head
Bolt

Stud

Threads:

fine   coarse

Regular Hex Nut

Standard Lockwasher

Flat Washer

External
Tooth
Lockwasher

Square Nut

I. BASIC MECHANIC TOOLS

Basic auto mechanic tools are those tools that
would be needed if you plan to do anything more
than oil changes and grease jobs on your car. A
good set of mechanic tools would include all of
these tools in some form or another. Tools that
are for only one kind of job (like an oil filter
wrench or a spark plug gauge) I will talk about
under that job.

A. Wrenches

Wrenches are what you use to remove nuts and bolts.
Basically there are two kinds of wrenches - open
end wrenches or box end wrenches, and a combination
of both, called a combination wrench. (Fig.1) With
combination wrenches, both ends of the wrench are
the same size, whereas in a wrench that is just an
open end or box end wrench, usually the two ends
are different sizes. If you are going to buy a
wrench set, I would recommend getting combination
wrenches as you will probably need both a box end
and an open end wrench of the same size at some
time or other. There are a lot of variations on
the basic wrenches, all made for specialized jobs.
Bleeder wrenches, line wrenches, offset wrenches
are examples. I will be talking about these different kinds of wrenches under the jobs they are
used for.

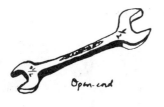
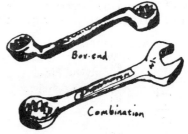

Open-end

Box-end

Combination

Fig. 1

A word about sizes - wrenches and sockets come in
either standard or metric sizes. Standard sizes
start as small as 3/16 of an inch and go all the
way up to 1 inch or more, with a different wrench
or socket size every sixteenth (1/2, 9/16, 5/8 of
an inch, etc.) All american cars made in this
country use standard sizes, and you might find
some foreign cars that use standard sizes also -
Swedish made volvos for example. Metric sizes
start at 6 millimeter (mm) or smaller and go up to
22 mm or more, with a different size every mm (10
mm, 11 mm, 12 mm, etc.) Almost all foreign cars
plus american cars made in foreign countries

(pinto, opel, etc.) use metric sizes. The size of
a wrench or socket refers to the diameter of the
box end or socket or the width between the open
ends on an open end wrench.

In choosing a wrench, use a box end wrench when at
all possible as they grip whatever you are loosening a lot better than open end wrenches do and
prevent a bolt or nut from being rounded off.
Rounding off is what happens when the wrench turns
on the nut or bolt without loosening it and
smashes the corner of the bolt or nut so the wrench
doesn't fit on it properly anymore. (Fig.2)

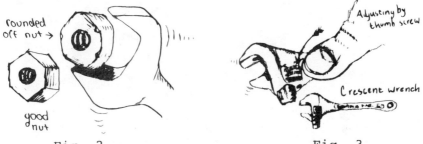

Fig. 2   Fig. 3

There are two other types of wrenches used frequently in working on cars:
1. The crescent or adjustable wrench(Fig.3) is a
very common and useful tool. It is an open ended
wrench that can be adjusted to different sizes.
The wrench itself varies in size from 4 inches all
the way up to 20 inches or more. The standard
crescent wrench is 10 or 12 inches long. Crescent
wrenches can take the place of regular wrenches if
you have no access to regular wrenches, but they do
not have the gripping power of regular wrenches and
thus you have to be careful not to round off the
nut or bolt you are working with. One thing I have
found them particularly useful for is loosening and
tightening square headed bolts because their longer
jaws grip a square headed bolt more securely than
does a regular wrench. In using a crescent wrench,
be sure to adjust the wrench to fit the nut or bolt
as tightly as possible to try and prevent slipping.

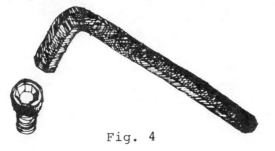

Fig. 4

3

2. Allen wrenches (Fig.4) are made for bolts that have a recessed hexagon hole in them. The wrench is inserted in the hole to turn the bolt. Allen wrenches also are available in both standard and metric sizes and come in a series of sizes up to 7/16 inch, sometimes larger. All Allen wrenches are offset, meaning they look like an L. Use the short end to loosen bolts, as the longer leg of the L gives you some leverage to help loosen a tight bolt.

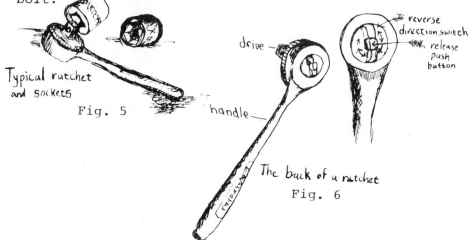

Typical ratchet and sockets

Fig. 5

drive —

handle —

reverse direction switch
release push button

The back of a ratchet
Fig. 6

B. Ratchet and Socket

A ratchet and socket does the same job as a wrench-loosening and tightening a nut or bolt. (Fig.5) It just does it a lot easier and faster because instead of having to take a wrench off and put it on again to loosen the bolt some more (which can be very frustrating when you have difficulty each time getting the wrench back on - something that happens to me a lot - it takes practice), the socket remains on the bolt and you just move the ratchet handle back and you're ready to loosen the bolt some more. All you have to know about a socket and ratchet to use it correctly is that the bolt you are trying to loosen or tighten turns when the ratchet is quiet. When the ratchet makes a noise, just the ratchet itself is moving. You won't have to think about that after using a ratchet for a while, but when you first use one, it is a good thing to keep in mind so you are turning the bolt or nut in the direction you want it to go.

There are many different sizes and shapes of ratchets and sockets , as you might know if you have ever looked through a tool catalog, but there are some basic characteristics of all ratchets and sockets.

4

1. The Ratchet (Fig.6) - A ratchet will always have
three parts - a handle; a switch or button to
change the direction of the ratcheting action, depending on whether you are tightening or loosening
the bolt; and a square hunk of metal attached to
the head of the ratchet. This hunk of metal is
known as the drive and is what holds the socket on
to the ratchet. With some ratchets you just push
the socket on the drive until it snaps into place;
other ratchets have a button you press and then
push the socket on - much easier.

$\frac{3}{8}$ inch drive

$\frac{1}{2}$ inch drive

Socket (12 point)

Fig. 7   Fig. 8

Anyhow, there are different size drives (Fig.7).
The two standard sizes are 1/2 inch and 3/8 inch
drive, as determined by the width of the drive.
There are also 1/4 inch drive ratchets for working
with small bolts and nuts, and 3/4 inch drive ratchets for working with very large bolts and nuts.
The larger the drive, the larger the ratchet will
be, and the more power there will be behind the
turning action. This means that you wouldn't want
to use a 1/2 inch drive ratchet and socket to
loosen a 5/16 inch bolt, as you might break the
bolt off; at the same time, you wouldn't want to
use a 1/4 inch ratchet and socket to loosen a 9/16
inch bolt as you probably wouldn't have enough
turning force to loosen the bolt, and you might
break the ratchet or socket in the attempt.

2. The Socket (Fig.8) - The square hole at the top
of the socket is the drive and is measured the same
way as the ratchet, and of course you would have to
have matching drives in the ratchet and socket in
order for them to fit together, though there are
converters from one drive to another (Fig.9). I
wouldn't use a converter unless it is necessary in
some special situation because the differences in
strengths between different drives may cause a
socket to be ruined. Sometimes a socket will split
or crack if there is too much force behind it.

An important thing to understand about a socket is
the difference between a six point and a 12 point
socket (Fig.10). The most common socket is the 12
point socket, though you can also get 6 point soc-

5

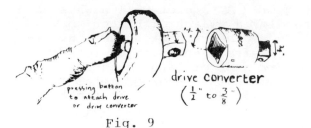

drive converter
$(\frac{1}{2}$" to $\frac{3}{8}$")

pressing button
to attach drive
or drive converter

Socket (6 point)

Fig. 9   Fig. 10

kets fairly easily. The 12 point socket will fit
on to a bolt more easily because there are more
places for the points of the bolt to fit into. For
that reason, they are better to use than the 6
point socket in a tight space. However, they do
not hold the bolt as well and thus there is a
greater possibility of rounding off the points of
the socket or the bolt or both. A 6 point socket
grips the bolt much more securely and because of
that you can apply greater force to turn a bolt
without having to worry about rounding off a bolt.
I personally like 6 point sockets better because it
is so damn frustrating to round off a bolt and then
have to work even harder at getting it loose.
There are too many other frustrations.

6 inches

6 inch socket extension

universal   joint socket

Fig. 11   Fig. 12

Socket sizes are the same as wrench sizes and come
in both metric and standard sizes. Both sockets
and ratchets usually come in sets with a series of
sockets, a ratchet, and a variety of extensions,
depending on the size and expense of the set (Fig.
11). An extension is a piece that is inserted between the socket and ratchet and comes in a variety
of lengths. Another common ratchet attachment is
what is known as a universal joint socket (Fig.12),
which gives the socket greater ability to get into
tight places.

C. Screwdrivers

Screwdrivers are, of course, used to loosen or
tighten screws. There are two different screw
heads and thus two different screwdrivers to use
with them. The two different types are standard
and phillips (Fig.13). There is also a third type
of screw head, the clutch head, which is fairly
uncommon and you probably won't see much of it.

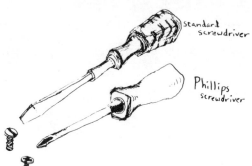

Standard screwdriver

Phillips screwdriver

Fig. 13

Most screws used on automobiles are either standard or phillips. Screwdrivers come in three main sizes and are numbered one, two, and three according to their size. Number one is the smallest size screw driver (I am referring to the point or blade of the screwdriver here), number 2 the medium size, and number 3 the largest. The size of screwdriver you would need would of course vary with the size of screw you are loosening or tightening. It is important to use the right size screwdriver, because it is very easy to ruin the head of a screw by using too large a screwdriver. This is particularly true with phillips screws.

Screwdrivers also come in a whole variety of lengths from about 2 or 3 inches long (known as stubby screwdrivers) to more than a foot long. Usually the longer the screwdriver you are using the better turning force you have to get the screw loose. So if you are having trouble getting a screw loose, try a longer screwdriver; just make sure the <u>size</u> of the screwdriver remains the same and that you don't get a bigger screwdriver with a longer one.

standard offset screwdriver

Fig. 14

One other screwdriver I would like to mention is the offset screwdriver (Fig.14) which comes in both standard and phillips. The offset screwdriver can be very handy in getting to screws that are so close to another engine part that you don't even have the space to use a stubby screwdriver on them.

D. Pliers

Pliers, like wrenches and screwdrivers, are an essential tool in working on cars. There are a vast variety of pliers made for a lot of different jobs, but here I am just going to talk about five basic

7

pliers that can be used in a lot of different jobs.
These are slip joint pliers, channel locks, needle
nose pliers, wire cutters or diagonal pliers, and
vise grips.

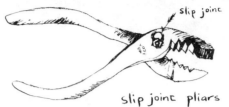

Fig. 15

1. Slip Joint Pliers (Fig.15) - Slip joint pliers
are the conventional pliers that you see everywhere. They adjust to two different sizes by means
of a slot at the joint where the two parts of the
plier are held together. I don't find them as
useful as some of the other types of pliers because
they don't have much gripping power, but they are
good in a situation where you need something held
or turned with a minimum amount of force.

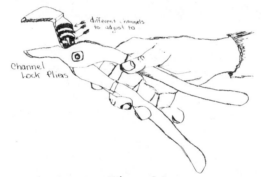

Fig. 16

2. Channel Lock Pliers (Fig.16) - Channel lock
pliers have curved jaws, adjust to at least five
different positions, and have fairly long handles.
I find channel lock pliers really useful, mainly
because of their longer handles, giving you more
leverage in turning something; also the jaws can
be adjusted to hold something an inch or more wide
while the handles of the pliers are still close
enough together to be held in one hand. Channel
lock pliers come in different sizes, from very tiny
ignition pliers about 4 inches long up to very
large channel locks used to loosen things like oil
filters. The standard channel lock pliers size is
about 10 to 12 inches long.

3. Needle Nose Pliers (Fig. 17) - Needle nose pliers
are called that because the two ends of the pliers

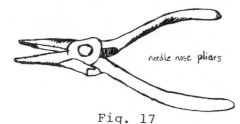

needle nose pliers

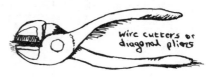

Wire cutters or diagonal pliers

Fig. 17

Fig. 18

come to a sharp point. Needle nose pliers are useful anytime you need to hold something that is too small for your hands to hold easily and also for a variety of other tasks. They don't have much holding power, so usually they aren't good for loosening or tightening anything. You also need to be careful not to break off the tips of the pliers, as that can happen fairly easily and then the pliers are pretty useless.

4. Wire Cutters or Diagonal Pliers (Fig.18) - Wire cutters are pliers that have a sharp edge to them and are able to cut wire and thin metal. They are also very good to use when you need to grip something thin very firmly. For instance, I find them real handy in taking cotter pins out of holes.

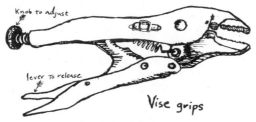

Knob to adjust

lever To release

Vise grips

Fig. 19

5. Vise Grips (Fig.19) - Vise grips are an extremely useful tool, once you learn how to use them. Vise grips are pliers that can be tightened and locked on to whatever you are working on with an extreme amount of force, and thus are good for loosening rounded off bolts or nuts. To use vise grips, adjust them by means of the knob at the bottom of one of the handles so the jaws, when the pliers are closed, are somewhere near the width of the bolt you are attaching them to. Open the pliers (there will be a release lever on one of the handles), put them on the bolt you are working with, tighten them slightly by means of the knob and squeeze them closed. If they aren't tight enough on the bolt, release the pliers by means of the release lever, and continue to adjust the pliers and check their tightness on the bolt until you finally get them so tight on the bolt that you can

just barely squeeze the handles shut. The harder
it is to squeeze the handles shut, the tighter the
grip of the pliers will be. It takes some practice
to learn how to use them correctly, but it is worth
it as they are very useful in a whole lot of situations.

Vise grips commonly come in about three different
sizes ranging from 6 inches long to about 10 or 12
inches long.

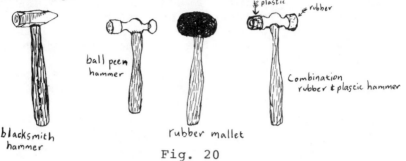

blacksmith
hammer

rubber mallet

Fig. 20

E. Hammers

The final basic mechanic tool is the hammer (Fig.
20). Hammers aren't used as frequently in working
on cars as they are in carpentry or some related
trade, of course, but they are necessary in a variety of auto repair tasks. The basic mechanic hammer is the ball peen hammer. The rounded end of
the hammer is used to get in tighter places and
probably for other things, but I am not sure what.
Ball peen hammers come in a variety of sizes, the
standard size being about 12 to 16 inches long.
Three other mechanics hammers are the rubber mallet,
the plastic hammer, and the blacksmith hammer. The
rubber mallet is a hammer that instead of having a
steel head has a large hard rubber head. The hammer is useful for hitting things that you don't
want to dent or damage in any way. They are especially good for hitting hubcaps on if you have problems getting your hubcaps on without smashing them
up.

The plastic hammer has a plastic head instead of a
steel one, and is also used for hitting things you
don't want to damage in any way. For instance, any
precision-made metal part in which the clearance
between it and another part is just a few thousanths
of an inch could very possibly be dented in such a
way when struck by a metal hammer that it would no
longer fit into the space provided for it. A plastic or rubber hammer, however, can deliver some
force without denting the metal of the part it is
striking. Of course, a rubber or plastic hammer

would be of little value if a lot of force was
needed.

A fourth kind of mechanics hammer is the blacksmith
hammer. Blacksmith hammer is the name for an extra
heavy hammer that is used when a lot of pounding
force is required, and there is little chance of
damaging whatever you are hitting, no matter how
hard you hit it. Pounding on brake drums to try
and get them to come off is one instance that you
might want to use a blacksmith hammer.

chisel   punch

Fig. 21

F. Chisels and Punches

Along with hammers, I should mention chisels and
punches (Fig.21). Chisels and punches are pieces
of metal that are designed to do a variety of
things. Chisels are square, have sharp ends and
are used to cut off bolts, nuts, etc. Punches are
round, have flat ends, and are used to tap things
that you can't get to with a hammer.

G. <u>Basic Mechanic Tool Kit</u>

The tools mentioned above are the basic auto mechanic tools. A fairly reliable mechanic tool kit
would consist of the following:

1. Wrenches
   a. a set of combination wrenches from size 3/8"
      to 7/8"
   b. a 10" crescent wrench

2. Ratchet and sockets
   a. 1/2" drive socket and ratchet set with sockets
      ranging from 1/2" to 1"
   b. 1/2" drive medium length extension (6")
   c. 3/8" drive socket and ratchet set with sockets
      ranging from 3/8" to 11/16"
   d. 3/8" drive short, medium and long extensions

3. Screwdrivers
   a. short, medium and long #2 size screwdrivers
      in both standard and phillips
   b. one #3 and one #1 screwdriver in both stan-
      dard and phillips

4. Pliers
   a. 7" slip joint pliers
   b. 10" or 12" channel locks

c. 6" needle nose pliers
d. 6" diagonal pliers
e. 8" vise grips

5. Hammers
   a. medium size ball peen hammer
   b. medium size combination rubber and plastic hammer

6. Assorted chisels and punches
   (you could get them as you need them, though they do come in sets)

7. Other useful tools for the mechanic tool box:

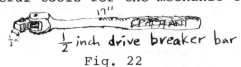
½ inch drive breaker bar
Fig. 22

a. Breaker bar (Fig.22) - a breaker bar is a long (15"-22") bar with a drive attached to one end of it that is used with sockets. Its purpose is to provide greater leverage in breaking a bolt or nut loose. It is just used to first break the bolt loose and then is removed and a ratchet is put in its place to continue turning the bolt. Breaker bars come in 1/2 inch and 3/8 inch drive. Both are real useful, though I think the 1/2 inch drive is more often needed.

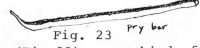
Fig. 23   Pry bar

b. Pry bar (Fig.23) - any kind of long metal bar, preferably with a flat end on one end, that can be used to pry different engine parts. It should be very strong.

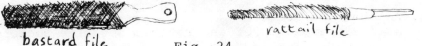
bastard file   Fig. 24   rattail file

c. Files (Fig.24) - various metal files are necessary in working on cars. The two most common files are the bastard file and the rattail file (nice names, huh?). The bastard file is a long file (12 inches or so) that is about an inch wide, is flat, and has filing surfaces on both sides - usually one side has coarser filing threads than the other side. The rattail file is a long thin round file that is used to file inside round openings.

Fig. 25

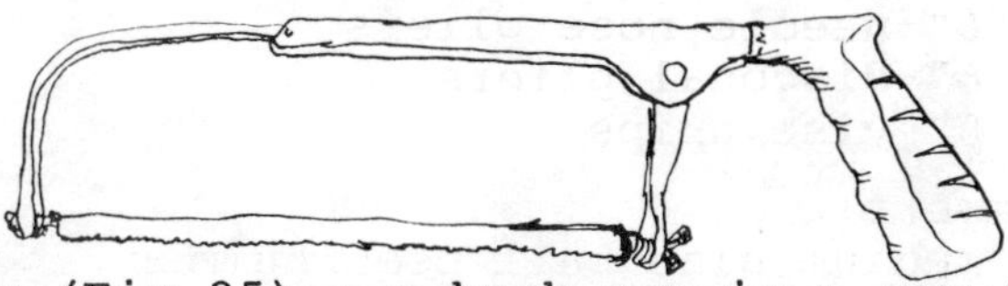

d. Hack saw (Fig.25) - a hack saw is a saw that is designed to saw through metal. Hack saw blades are removable and come in different sizes for sawing different thicknesses of metal. A hack saw comes in handy for those times when you have to resort to sawing a bolt off because you can't get it off any other way (hopefully you won't have too many of those times).

There are literally thousands of other tools for working on cars, some more common than others. You will probably end up acquiring all sorts of odds and ends of tools as you work on your car. It seems like every job requires some sort of special little tool.

H. Other Helpful Items for Working on Cars

I want to talk briefly about three other things you will need to work on cars - cleaning solvent and brushes; trouble light; and creeper.

1. Cleaning Solvent and Brushes - You will frequently need to clean very dirty and greasy car parts. To do this, you need some sort of solvent that cuts through grease and a stiff brush of some sort. For cleaning small parts or tiny areas of a part, an old toothbrush would probably be helpful. Degreasing solvents are made up of different chemicals - gallon containers of solvent can usually be bought at auto parts stores or some service stations. Get a large coffee can with a lid on it or something similar to store the solvent in so it can be used over and over.

2. Trouble Light (Fig.26) - A trouble light is a must in working on cars - if you can't see what you are doing, then the frustration of the job is increased tremendously. Trouble lights come in different qualities and with different lengths of cord. You can get cheap ones at discount stores and better ones with lifetime guarantees at parts stores. Special heavy duty light bulbs can also be purchased to use in trouble lights. Heavy duty light bulbs aren't really necessary, they just don't break as easily when the trouble light gets dropped.

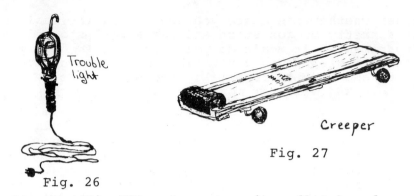

Trouble light

Fig. 26

Creeper

Fig. 27

3. Creeper (Fig.27) - A creeper is a flat board with a head pad on it and small rollers that allows you to roll in and out from under a car easily. If you are planning on doing a lot of work under a car, then I would get a creeper if possible. I think it would also be fairly easy to make one using some caster rollers. Creepers can be bought at discount stores and auto parts stores and come in varying qualities and styles.

II. ABOUT BUYING TOOLS

Tools, any tools, good ones or not, cost money - a whole lot of money, as you know if you have ever priced mechanics tools. Most of us can barely afford to buy a single wrench, much less anything approaching the sort of tool kit I am talking about and the kind you need if you are going to be doing any long time maintenance and repair on your car. The only thing I know to suggest is to collectivize your tool buying - I mean get together with other like-minded friends and buy one set of tools be-tween all of you. Chances are you won't be working on your cars at the same time, so why not one set of tools for 5 people instead of 5 sets? Not exactly the american way I realize, but.... Anyhow, I would suggest that when you do get tools to get good ones that are unconditionally guaranteed for life - in other words, if you break the tool, you can take it back and get a new one no matter how old the tool is. (You do, however, have to be using the tool in a 'proper' manner. For instance, if you use a regular socket on an air wrench and split the socket, chances are they won't replace the socket if you tell them how the socket was split.) Any kind of good tools have that kind of guarantee, so be sure to look for it. Also, con-

sider whether the store you are buying the tool from
is a pretty common store and has a well stocked tool
department. It won't do you much good to have guaranteed tools if you can't take them back to anywhere and have to resort to sending them to a
factory and wait for months to get your exchange
tool.

Used tools are another possibility for lowering the
cost of tool buying. Sometimes you can find good
deals at auctions or secondhand stores, though I
personally haven't had any luck in that area. It
is worth a try because if the tools are a guaranteed brand, you can always have them replaced if
there is something wrong with them.

An alternative to buying tools is to find a
friendly mechanic who would let you do work in his
shop and use his tools (no point in using "his or
hers" because chances are 9 out of 10 that it is
going to be a man). I am sure there aren't too
many of those around, but maybe you will be lucky.
One possibility is to rent space and tools. I have
heard that that is being done on a big business
scale in some cities, but I haven't seen much of it
around here, so I don't know very much about it.
Personally, I think if at all possible it would be
a lot better situation to have your own work space
and tools ("you" being a group of women). The tension, at least for me, of having to do mechanical
work around men who have that arrogant self confidence which is so hard to put down or ignore, is
really awful and makes what could be a fun and
exciting learning situation among women an unbear-
able endurance test. Those are just my feelings,
though. You know what will work best for you and
also what options are available (when it gets to be
0 degrees outside the options are reduced consider-
ably, I realize).

III. ABOUT USING TOOLS

Having access to tools and knowing how to use them
is obviously a necessity in fixing a car. Equally
obvious - at least to us - is how most of us have
grown up never having a tool in our hands except
maybe on a rare occasion and then it was most
likely to be a home repair tool rather than a car
fix-it tool. And so here we are, all ready to fix
something on our car, and becoming more and more
frustrated at our inability to use a tool without

feeling awkward, clumsy, and completely uncoordinated. Well, there are two things I want to say here: one, it takes time - you can't learn in a few hours or days what men have had their whole life to learn. So, it might take you a while longer to do something and you might drop a tool or hit your hand, but you will learn. Just don't forget that it isn't you or your being a woman that makes you 'naturally' clumsy, but rather that society has deprived you from learning what men take for granted. I'm sorry that this sounds so preachy - I guess it sounds that way because it's what I have to tell myself over and over when it takes me so much longer to do a certain job than the guys at work or when I can't figure out how to do something because I don't know enough about using tools.

Two, the "right tool for the right job" is very important, as my carpenter friend always says when she helps build things in the community. I have found that it really makes a difference when you have the correct tool a job needs and also that it is a good tool - that is, a socket isn't going to split on you when you are trying to loosen a nut, etc. Of course, the key to using the right tool is knowing what the right tool is for a certain job. I think once you become familiar with your tools and understand what they can and can't do, that knowledge will gradually come to you. A lot of times it is a matter of just trying different tools, until you find one that works for the job you are doing. Next time you will know what tool to use for that job, and thus the job will become easier to do. Just remember that it takes a lot of time, patience and practice, but eventually the knowledge will come to you.

A. A Few Hints about Getting Things Loose

1. Nuts and Bolts - First, make sure that whatever tool you are using on the bolt fits good and tight. If possible, use either a box end wrench or a socket and ratchet. Never use pliers on a nut or bolt, as the jaws of the pliers will round off the bolt, making it impossible to use a wrench or socket on it. If you have to use an open end wrench because the bolt is too close to something and a box end wrench or socket can't fit all the way around it, be sure to use the open end wrench in the correct position, as that will give you the most turning power (Fig.28). Almost all nuts and bolts tighten clockwise and loosen counterclockwise.

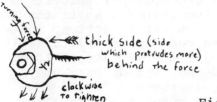
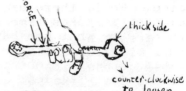

thick side (side which protrudes more) behind the force

turning force

clockwise to tighten

FORCE

thick side

counter-clockwise to loosen

Fig. 28

Be sure when you are trying to loosen a nut or bolt that you are turning it in the right direction. (Sometimes it takes a little thinking to figure out which way is counterclockwise when you are laying underneath a car peering up at some bolt.)

The most important thing to remember in loosening a bolt is leverage - to use your tool and your body in such a way that you exert the most turning force on the bolt. The longer the tool you are using the better, as it provides more turning force. That is why a breaker bar that is 18 inches or more long is such a useful tool. In many cases when you can't get something loose using a wrench or a socket and ratchet, attaching a breaker bar to the socket will give you the needed leverage to break the bolt loose. And if the breaker bar doesn't work, you can put a piece of metal pipe over the end of the breaker bar to extend the bar even further and thus increase your leverage. If you've ever attempted to loosen the axle nuts on a VW's rear wheel, you might have already discovered the usefulness of such a pipe (Fig.29). Also, you should try to position your body in such a way that you are exerting as much of your body strength as possible. For instance, you will be able to exert much more strength if you grasp a wrench with a slightly bent arm than with an arm bent at a 90 degree angle. I also find that if I can pull on a wrench to loosen a bolt versus push on the wrench I can exert a much greater amount of body strength, especially if I

breaker bar

pipe extender

Fig. 29

brace my body against the car so my pulling action doesn't move me rather than the bolt I am trying to loosen. All of this takes a little practice, but if you are lying underneath the car trying to get the oil plug loose, don't give up if you can't get it loose at the first try. Reposition your body until you feel like you are using your maximum body strength: that you are using more than just your arm muscles but are using your shoulder, back and possibly even leg muscles as well. When I first started working on cars, my biggest problem was getting things loose. I always attributed my inability to get things loose to my lack of strength. Men, who were stronger I thought, could therefore get things loose easier than I could. I have since decided I was wrong in thinking that. I hardly ever have any trouble in cracking a bolt or nut loose now, and I don't think I have become all that much stronger than I was a few years ago. Rather I have learned to use as much of my body strength as possible in trying to get something loose, and it almost always works. Of course, knowing what tool is the best to use for a certain job goes along with knowing how to use your whole body. Just keep in mind that you have the strength, it is just a matter of learning how to use it properly.

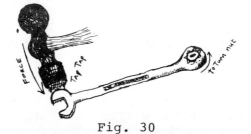

Fig. 30

<u>When you need a little something more</u>, there are certain things you can do to help along the task of trying to loosen a rusted up bolt.

    a. Lubricant - thoroughly soaking the bolt with some sort of penetrating lubricant will help to loosen up the rust on the bolt or nut threads and make it more able to be loosened. Typical penetrants are WD-40, Liquid Wrench, LPS

    b. Impact (Fig.30) - one way to get a bolt loose is to put a box end wrench on the bolt and then tap the end of the wrench with a hammer in the direction you want the bolt to turn. This isn't a good practice to get into, as it puts a lot of stress on your wrench and could damage the end that is being pounded on, but in some instances it can be effective in cracking a bolt loose.

c. Heat - if all else fails, you've beat on the bolt, doused it in penetrating liquid, tried every conceivable tool and body position that you can think of, then you might try heating the bolt. Actually what you would need to heat is what the bolt is screwed into - heat will expand the metal and loosen the thread, thus allowing the bolt to be unscrewed. However, you need to have access to an oxygen-acetylene welding outfit to produce enough heat to affect a cast iron part to the point where it would loosen the bolt. You can try a simple butane torch - it might work in some situations. Using heat isn't much of a viable alternative because most of us don't have access to oxy-acetylene equipment or the knowledge to use it (though it isn't that hard), but I wanted to include this method anyhow, in case you end up taking your car to a garage and having them remove the bolt. Most likely heat is probably what they will use to loosen the bolt.

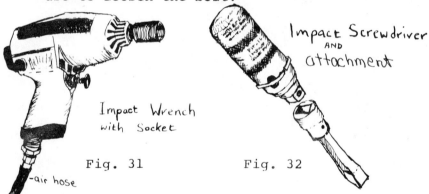

Impact Screwdriver
AND
attachment

Impact Wrench
with Socket

Fig. 31   Fig. 32

-air hose

d. Impact wrenches (Fig.31) - an impact wrench (also known as an air wrench) is essentially a ratchet head driven by compressed air. It exerts a tremendous amount of force and will also remove a bolt or nut very quickly. However, like the use of heat, the use of an impact wrench is not an option available to most of us as things like air compressors and tools driven by air compressors cost a whole lot of money. Of course, if you do happen to have access to such equipment, an impact wrench can be very helpful in removing a hard-to-loosen bolt. I've found, though, that sometimes an air wrench won't loosen a bolt or nut that a breaker bar with a pipe extension will loosen.

2. Screws - Screws are much easier to round out (meaning that the slot where the screwdriver fits gets distorted and thus a screwdriver can't fit tightly into it) and so the most important thing to remember in loosening a screw is to have the right size screwdriver. The screwdriver needs to fit snugly into the slot on the screw head. When attempting to loosen a screw, push as hard as possible into the screw head as you try to turn the screw. This will help prevent the screwdriver from slipping in the slot and rounding it out. If you are having trouble getting the screw to loosen, it will help to use a longer screwdriver. Once I was taking apart a VW engine and having a hard time getting the sheet metal screws loose and someone gave me a screwdriver with about a two foot long blade and that solved all of my problems (or almost all - it's a long story).

Another way to get tight screws loose is to attach a pair of vise grips to the screw head as if it were a bolt or nut and try turning the screw with the vise grips. Sometimes it is difficult to attach a vise grips to a screw head, because of the size of the head or the location of the screw, but if you are able to attach the vise grips securely enough that they won't slip off then usually you will be able to loosen the screw.

For really tight screws, there is a tool known as an impact screwdriver that almost always loosens them (Fig.32). It is pretty expensive I think, but you might be able to rent one. The tool has a screwdriver (or has a drive to attach screwdriver blade sockets) and a thick heavy metal handle. It is spring loaded and you hit the end of the handle with a hammer as you try to turn the screw. The combination of the pounding and the spring tension provide a much greater turning force to loosen the screw.

B. How to Deal with Rounded Off or Broken Off Bolts, Nuts and Screws

If you round off a bolt, nut or screw trying to get it off, then the best tool to use to try and loosen it is a pair of vise grips. If the piece won't come loose just using vise grips, then use either a wrench or a piece of pipe slipped over one of the handles of the vise grips, giving you more leverage. You can also try tapping on the end of the vise grips with a hammer like you would with a wrench and see if that helps. However sometimes all you

will succeed in doing is springing open the jaws of
the vise grips.

If the vise grips don't seem to be working, then
try chiseling a slot in the bolt; insert a chisel
or old screwdriver into the slot and pound the end
(Fig.33). What you want to try to do is to push the
bolt in the direction it needs to go to loosen
(counterclockwise).

Anytime you have to resort to one of these measures,
be sure to replace the damaged bolt, nut or screw
with a new one.

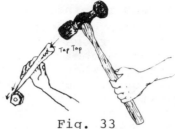

Fig. 33

C. If You Break Something

If you break off a bolt trying to get it loose, the
damage is not irreparable. First, see if there is
any part of the bolt left at all; if so, try to get
a pair of vise grips on the part that is left and
unscrew the remaining section of the bolt. If the
bolt is broken off flush with whatever it is screwed
into, then you will have to drill the rest of the
bolt out, and tap in new threads and get an oversize
bolt for the hole. That isn't much of an explanation, but I don't want to get into explaining in
more detail how to do it, mainly because I haven't
done it enough to be of much help to you. If you
do break off a bolt and will have to drill it out,
then you might want to find someone who has done it
before to give you some advice on what to do. If
you can find a friendly machine shop, they should
be of help. Everyone breaks off a bolt at least
once if not more often (probably a lot more often),
so don't let it bum you out too much.

D. A General Hint About Using All Tools

It helps to wrap a rag around the handle of whatever tool you're using when you try to get something
loose. If you're trying to loosen a bolt with a
wrench and the wrench is hurting your hand, then
you won't be using all your strength to get the
bolt loose. I've gotten so I always use a rag when
I'm trying to loosen a tight bolt or nut. It
really does help.

IV. SAFETY

I want to mention a few things about safety. This
is stuff you probably already know, but it is worth
hearing again. Cars can be very dangerous machines
to work on if you are careless around them. So,
the three things I always tell my auto mechanics
classes are:

1. If you have long hair, be sure and tie it back
   before starting to work on a car. Besides the
   nuisance it becomes, it could be very dangerous
   if you got your hair caught in a part of the
   engine while it was running, etc.

2. If there is more than one person working on one
   car, be sure that everyone knows that you are
   going to start the car before you do, so there
   aren't any hands down where the fan can get to
   them. Also, if you hook up a starter switch to
   the engine (a switch that you hook to the starter
   that enables you to start the car from under the
   hood), be sure you keep your eye on it, so you
   don't lean on it and accidentally turn the engine
   over while your hand is somewhere it shouldn't
   be. (That is one of my tricks - I have had a
   couple of real close calls doing that.)

3. Jacking - if you are going to be doing much
   mechanics work, at some point you are going to
   want to be working on something underneath the
   car, which will necessitate jacking up the car
   and crawling under it (unless you have access to
   a lift - I don't where I work and our women's
   community garage here doesn't either so I'm more
   concerned with jacking). Obviously, if a car
   fell on top of you it is very likely that you
   could get seriously injured or even killed. So
   jacking rules are very important (I have also
   had a close call in this area by not following
   some basic jacking rules.)

   a. First off, if at all possible, try to get
      access to a hydraulic floor jack for jacking
      your car (the kind used in mechanics'
      garages, NOT the little hydraulic jacks sold
      for about $20). (Fig.34) Bumper jacks or
      other jacks designed for changing tires won't
      usually lift your car high enough off the
      ground to get a jack stand underneath it, and
      the cheap hydraulic jacks often won't go low
      enough to be placed under the car, unless you
      are working on a truck or other high-off-the-
      ground vehicle. Besides these drawbacks,
      both jacks are very unsafe, as they do not

22

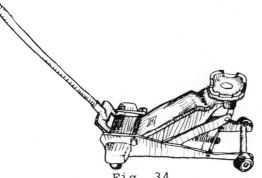

Fig. 34   Fig. 35

provide a wide enough base to balance the
weight of the car. Floor hydraulic jacks are
expensive to buy ($100-200 new) but it might
be possible to find a used one with the cost
split between a group of users. You can also
rent them, or maybe you will be lucky enough
to find a garage that will let you use theirs.
If you do use a hydraulic floor jack, common
jacking places are the engine cross member in
the front of the car (the wide piece of metal
that goes underneath the engine to support it)
and the differential in the rear of the car
(see basic systems of the car if you don't
know what a differential is).

b. With whatever jack you use, be sure and block
the wheels of the car before you start jacking. If you are jacking up the front, put a
piece of wood or concrete block behind the
rear wheels - if you are jacking up the rear,
put the block in front of the front wheels.
Also, be sure you are doing the jacking on a
level section of pavement. Blocking the
wheels prevents the car from rolling off the
jack - a common problem with bumper jacks.
If you are jacking up the front of the car,
it also helps to have the transmission in
gear (any gear) to help prevent the rear
wheels from rolling.

c. Never work underneath a car that is supported
only by a jack. Jacks aren't designed to
hold the weight of the car for any length of
time. Place jack stands (Fig.35) under the
car, and lower the car onto the stands - the
full weight of the car should be resting on
the stands. Where to put the jack stands
varies from car to car. The shop manual and
possibly the owner's manual for your car will
tell you where the jacking points are. If
you don't have access to either of these, try

23

a garage that commonly works on your type of
car - they would be able to tell you where to
put a jack and also jack stands.

d. Before lowering a jacked up car onto jack-
stands, be sure whatever you have blocking the
wheel is up against the wheel. This will as-
sure that the car will lower straight down on
the jack stands. Make sure the legs of the
stands are firmly on the floor and that the
stand doesn't tilt in one direction or another. After lowering the car on to the jack
stands, shake the car to make sure it is
solidly on the stands.

If you are putting both the front and rear of
the car up on jack stands, put the front of
the car on stands first, and then the rear.
Be very careful when jacking the rear of the
car up, that the front part of the car is
remaining securely on the jack stands.

V. BUYING PARTS FOR YOUR CAR

I wanted to put something in this manual about buying parts, because parts stores can be a real hassle
and are places where women are generally treated
like shit (not that this is anything new). Parts
that are used in jobs that people frequently do on
their cars can be bought at discount stores, like
K-Mart. These stores sell things like spark plugs,
oil filters, air filters, fan belts, hoses, etc. at
lower prices than you could buy them for at an
exclusive auto parts store. For doing any work
beyond oil changes and tune ups, however, you pretty
much have to buy your parts at an auto parts store.
When you go to buy parts, you should know certain
things about your car - make, year, model; 4, 6 or
8 cylinder engine; size of engine (cubic inches -
each make has standard engine sizes and usually you
can find this information on a sticker on the valve
cover; if not, your owner's manual should tell you,
or a shop manual for your car); and whether it is
an automatic or standard transmission. It is also
helpful if you can bring the part you are replacing
with you as then you can compare it with the new
part and not have to make another trip back to the
parts store if you got the wrong part (which frequently happens). However, often times you don't
want to take the old part off without having the
new part - just be sure to compare the two parts
and make sure they are exactly the same before you

start trying to install the new one. This can save you a lot of headaches.

Always keep the sales receipt that you get at parts stores. Get rebuilt parts when possible, as they are almost as good as new parts and a whole lot cheaper. Rebuilt parts have what is known as a core charge (brake shoes, water pumps, starter motors, for example) which means that you get charged a certain amount of money (core charge) in addition to the part price, and then the core charge is refunded to you when you give them the old part. To get this refund you usually have to have the sales slip for the new part, so be extra sure to hang on to it when there is a core charge involved.

Car parts, as I am sure you know, are very expensive, especially if you as an individual are buying them, because then you get charged the full price for the part (even though the sales slip might show a discount). Garages get the parts at a true discount because they then resell the parts. If there is any way you can buy parts through a friendly garage, or if a group of you could form a garage and get a retail sales permit (this is what you would need in my state - Iowa - I don't know what other states require), then you would be able to get parts at a discount ranging anywhere from 10% to 40 or 50%. Even with a discount, parts are terribly expensive, but at least you wouldn't be paying the full price for them, which is the same price you would be charged if you took the car to a garage to have the work done. If you do have access to a garage discount then insist that you be given the discount, because I have found that sometimes the parts places automatically assume I am buying parts as an individual even if I tell them it is for the garage I work at. It is like they don't even hear me - all they see is that I am a woman and therefore I must be buying the parts on my own and I couldn't possibly be connected with a mechanics garage. If you can find a parts store where the people are halfway friendly, then frequent it a lot, for as they get to know you they can be of help and will at least be less of a hassle for you.

VI. TECHNICAL MANUALS

There are a variety of technical manuals made for a lot of different cars. Two companies, Chiltons and Motors, put out a manual every year that covers all american-made cars for the last 5 years. Chiltons, at least, also puts out an imported car manual, that covers all of the cars imported into this country. Also, every car manufacturer puts out a shop manual for each model of car manufactured - these aren't commonly sold but can be ordered through the manufacturer. I think it would be helpful to you to have a manual that deals with your car specifically. The trouble with most manuals is that they are written for mechanics and take for granted a whole lot of knowledge - like where things are located. There are books that are written with the car owner in mind, such as the Clymer publication series that covers a lot of different foreign cars. However, I find that these also, being written by men for men, assume a whole lot of knowledge on the part of the reader, though they aren't as bad as the shop manuals. Even with these limitations, I still think it would be helpful to have some sort of manual concerning your car, as it will give you guidelines on how to do various jobs on your car, jobs that I might describe in this manual or that you might have the general knowledge to do, but for which you may not know the little variations your car has. Also, such a manual would be important as a resource for the various specifications for your car (like tune up specifications, fluid capacities, engine rebuilding specs).

Manuals are sort of expensive to buy, but you can try the public library in your town. The one in Iowa City carries quite a few auto repair manuals, including some of the shop manuals for different makes of cars.

Chapter 2

HOW A CAR WORKS

What I want to do in this chapter is to talk about
how a car works. When thinking and talking around
the ideas for this manual with my friends, one of
the response I got most often was to put a chapter
in dealing with what makes cars run - how the
engine of a car works and what all it needs to make
it work. So that's what I will try to do here.
The explanation will be as simple as I can make it,
which of course will leave out a lot of details and
the finer points of engine construction, but I
think it is more important that you grasp the basic
ideas - the other stuff you can pick up later, and
will, while working on your own car. I will talk
about three things in this chapter: how a gasoline
engine works; the basic systems of the car and what
parts make them up; and sort of an introduction to
your car - lifting up the hood and identifying
parts and knowing what system they are a part of.

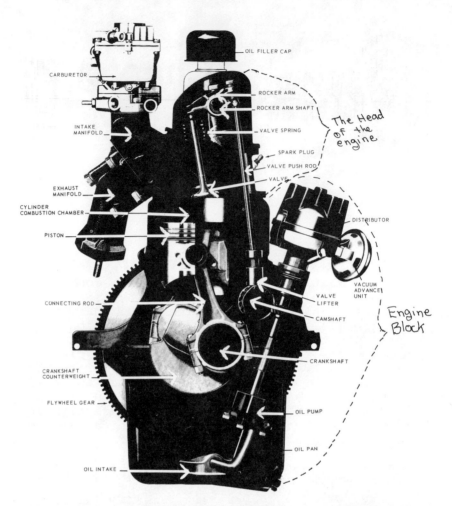

OIL FILLER CAP

CARBURETOR

ROCKER ARM

ROCKER ARM SHAFT

The Head of the engine

INTAKE MANIFOLD

VALVE SPRING

SPARK PLUG

VALVE PUSH ROD

VALVE

EXHAUST MANIFOLD

DISTRIBUTOR

CYLINDER COMBUSTION CHAMBER

PISTON

VACUUM ADVANCE UNIT

Engine Block

CONNECTING ROD

VALVE LIFTER

CAMSHAFT

CRANKSHAFT COUNTERWEIGHT

CRANKSHAFT

FLYWHEEL GEAR

OIL PUMP

OIL PAN

OIL INTAKE

Front section view, Ford Falcon, 144 cu. in., 6-cylinder engine, with principal parts identified.

Fig. 1

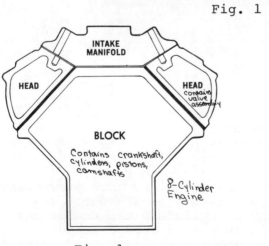

INTAKE MANIFOLD

HEAD

HEAD *contains valve assembly*

BLOCK *Contains crankshaft, cylinders, pistons, camshafts*

8-Cylinder Engine

Fig. 1a

PISTON RINGS

PISTON

CONNECTING ROD

Fig. 3

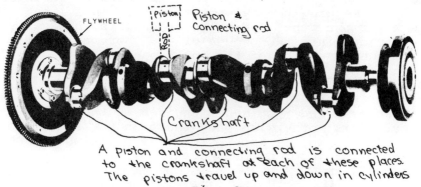

FLYWHEEL

Piston

Piston & Connecting rod

ROD

Crankshaft

A piston and connecting rod is connected to the crankshaft at each of these places. The pistons travel up and down in cylinders

Fig. 2

HOW A GASOLINE ENGINE WORKS

With a very few exceptions, all automobiles are powered by what is known as an internal combustion gasoline engine, meaning a gasoline burning action takes place <u>inside</u> of the engine. There are different types of gasoline internal combustion engines, but the type used in almost all automobiles is the 4 cycle reciprocating engine - 4 cycle meaning that it takes four cycles to complete the combustion (I'll talk about those cycles shortly), and reciprocating meaning that the engine pistons move in a back and forth motion. An exception to this would be Japanese-made Mazdas, which use the Wankel rotary engine.

The main part of the engine is what is known as the <u>crankcase</u> or <u>block</u> (Fig.1). The crankcase contains the <u>crankshaft</u> (Fig.2),to which the <u>pistons</u> are attached and the <u>camshaft</u>, to which the valves are attached. The crankshaft and the camshaft are connected to each other by either a chain or through gears. The lower part of the crankcase houses the crankshaft and the camshaft (the camshaft is above the crankshaft). The upper part of the crankcase is divided into <u>cylinders</u>, round oblong holes in which the pistons (connected via the <u>connecting rods</u> to the crankshaft) travel up and down - one piston for each hole or cylinder. Pistons look like round metal boxes (Fig.3). They have 3 metal rings around the top of them. One ring is the oil ring which prevents the oil on the piston walls from traveling up into the combustion chamber. The other 2 rings are compression rings which help seal tight the cylinder, thus preventing the escape of any fuel mixture or exhaust gases. Of course, the number of cylinders the engine has depends on whether it is a 4, 6 or 8 cylinder engine, the common automobile engine sizes. Most 4

and 6 cylinder engines are what is known as <u>inline</u>
<u>engines</u>, meaning the cylinders are all in a line,
one after the other. 8 cylinder engines, however,
are divided into two groups of 4 - there are 4 cylinders on one side of the engine and 4 on the
other. Both groups of cylinders slant downwards
towards the middle of the engine, forming a V -
thus the name <u>V-8 engine</u>. The only difference
between 4, 6 and 8 cylinder engines is the number
of cylinders; otherwise they function the same,
though they produce more power in proportion to the
increase in number of cylinders.

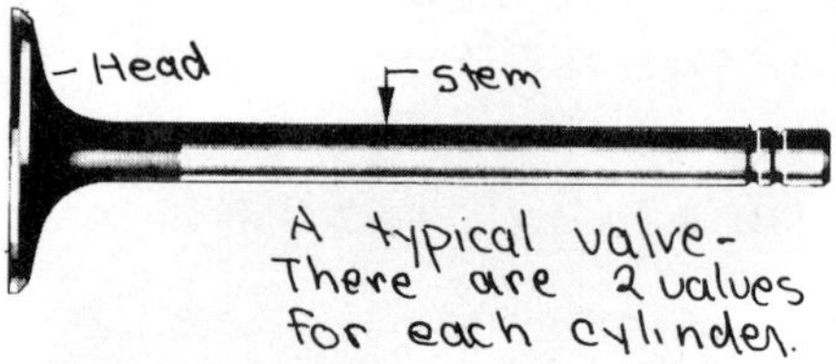

A typical valve-
There are 2 valves
for each cylinder.

Fig. 4

Located at the top of each cylinder are two valves
(Fig.4) - an <u>intake valve</u> and an <u>exhaust valve</u> -
and a <u>spark plug.</u> The area where they are located
is known as the <u>combustion chamber</u>. The part of
the valve that goes into the combustion chamber is
round and somewhat flat. It looks about like a
thick half dollar, and is called the head of the
valve. The head is attached to a piece of metal
about the size of a pencil called the stem. When
both valves are closed, meaning the heads are flat
against the surface of the chamber, and the piston
is at the top of the cylinder, the chamber is
sealed and all fuel and air are trapped in a small
area. When the valves are open, meaning the head
of the valve moves a little ways away from the surface into the chamber, then the chamber is no
longer sealed and either fuel can come into the
chamber through the intake valve, or exhaust gas
can escape the chamber through the exhaust valve.

Now I want to talk about what happens in each of the
cylinders - the 4 cycles of the engine (Fig.5).
Another term for cycle would be stroke. A stroke
is the movement of the piston the length of the
cylinder, either up or down. There are 4 strokes
or cycles - Intake, Combustion, Power and Exhaust.
Remember that the piston is attached to the crankshaft and as the crankshaft turns the piston moves
up and down in the cylinder. The Intake is the
first stroke - the piston starts at the top of the
cylinder and moves down, creating a suction that
draws in the fuel mixture through the intake valve
which is open. The exhaust valve is closed. When
the piston gets to the bottom of the cylinder, the

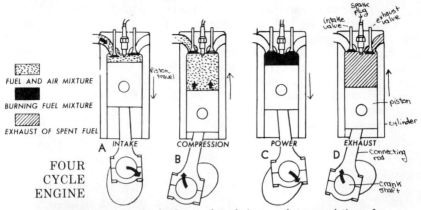

FUEL AND AIR MIXTURE

BURNING FUEL MIXTURE

EXHAUST OF SPENT FUEL

FOUR
CYCLE
ENGINE

Provides one power impulse for four strokes of piston; each two revolutions of crankshaft.
A. On Intake Stroke, inlet valve opens; piston draws fuel and air mixture into cylinder.
B. On Compression Stroke, both valves are closed. Rising piston compresses mixture.
C. At upper limit of piston movement; both valves closed, mixture is ignited. Explosion forces piston downward on Power Stroke.
D. On Exhaust Stroke, exhaust valve opens, rising piston pushes spent gas from cylinder.

Fig. 5

intake valve closes. The combustion chamber is now sealed with both valves closed. The piston starts back up the cylinder, squeezing or compressing the fuel mixture (which at this point is a vapor, not a liquid) into the combustion chamber at the top of the cylinder. This stroke is called the Compression stroke because it is compressing the fuel mixture, thus making it highly volatile. When the piston reaches the top of the cylinder, the spark plug fires, igniting the compressed fuel mixture and creating an explosion. The explosion drives the piston back down the cylinder. This is called the Power stroke. When the piston reaches the bottom of the cylinder, the exhaust valve opens and the piston travels up the cylinder, pushing all the gases left over from the combustion out through the exhaust valve. This is the Exhaust stroke. When the piston reaches the top of the cylinder, the exhaust valve closes, and the intake valve opens and the piston is ready to start over again with the Intake stroke. These then are the 4 strokes or cycles of the engine - Intake, Compression, Power and Exhaust. The purpose of the 4 cycles is to produce the power that turns the crankshaft and thus ultimately moves the car (the crankshaft is connected to the drive shaft which delivers the turning power of the crankshaft to the rear wheels- I will explain that more under basic systems of the car). When the explosion is produced in the combustion chamber the piston is forced down with a great deal of power and thus the crankshaft is turned (Power stroke). These strokes are happening

31

at different times in different cylinders, and thus a power impulse is delivered to the crankshaft all the time. The crankshaft initially starts turning because the starter motor manually turns it - just like cranking the old Model T's by hand. But once the combustion starts happening in the cylinders (almost immediately after the crankshaft starts turning) then the crankshaft is turned by the power strokes of the pistons.

It is obvious from this explanation (or I hope it is) that the valves have to open and close at exactly the right time and that the spark plug has to fire at just the right time. The spark plug firing is the purpose of the ignition system - I will talk about that more in a little bit.

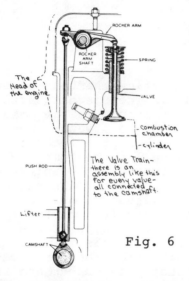

Fig. 6

The Head of the engine

ROCKER ARM

ROCKER ARM SHAFT

SPRING

VALVE

Combustion chamber

cylinder

The Valve Train- there is an assembly like this for every valve- all connected to the camshaft.

PUSH ROD

Lifter

CAMSHAFT

Timing gears that connects the crankshaft to the Camshaft. located at front of engine. the bottom gear is the crankshaft, the top is the camshaft.

Fig. 6a

The valves are a part of what is known as the <u>valve train</u> (Fig.6) which eventually connects the valves to the camshaft. The valve train consists of the valves, rocker arms, rocker arm shaft, push rods, lifters, and the camshaft. The camshaft, as I said before, is connected to the crankshaft by either a chain or gears. These are called the <u>timing chain</u> or <u>timing gears</u> because the engine is built in such a way that the right valves will be open or closed (determined by the camshaft) at the same time that the piston is in the proper stroke (determined by the crankshaft) - this is called the mechanical timing of the engine and is different than the timing that you do when you do a tune up. (Fig. 6a)

How does the camshaft cause the valves to open? The camshaft (Fig.6,Fig.7) is a long thick rod type shaft with lobes down the whole length of it. There

Timing gear — A lobe

An 8-cylinder engine camshaft. The valve
train assembly in Fig. 6 connects to each one
of the lobes.

Fig. 7

is one lobe for each valve, so in a 6 cylinder
engine having 12 valves (2 valves per cylinder)
there would be 12 lobes on the crankshaft. The
camshaft, being powered by the crankshaft via the
chain or gear, is constantly turning, though it
turns at half the speed of the crankshaft - once
for every two revolutions of the crankshaft. Riding
on each part of the camshaft where there is a lobe
is a <u>lifter</u> - a small cylinder of metal (about 2"
long). Setting on the lifter is a <u>push rod</u>, which
is a long thin rod that reaches up to where the
valves are at the top of the cylinder. The valves,
rocker arms and rocker arm shaft and the hunk of
metal that they are attached to make up what is
known as the <u>head</u> of the engine.(Fig. la) The head
is a separate part of the engine from the crankcase
(though it doesn't look like it when you look at an
engine) and can be removed to do work on the valves.
The valves are sitting in the head with their stems
sticking upward and their heads or faces downwards
into the combustion chambers. (The head of the
engine combined with the top of the crankcase actually make up the combustion chambers.) On the
other side of the head, in line with the valves,
are the push rods coming up from the camshaft. In
between each valve stem and each push rod, there is
a <u>rocker arm</u> which rocks on a shaft (the <u>rocker arm</u>
<u>shaft</u>). As the camshaft turns, the lifters, riding
on the camshaft, get pushed up when the lobes come
around on the shaft (Fig.8). The pushing up of the
lifter in turn pushes up the push rod. The push
rod pushes up on one end of the rocker arm causing
the other end of the rocker arm to go down (on to
the valve stem), thus pushing open the valve. When
the lobe on the camshaft turns away from the lifter,
the lifter comes back down and a spring on the valve
pulls it closed, thus pushing the rocker arm back up
on the valve end, and back down on the push rod end.
The camshaft is built so that the lobes are located
at different intervals around the shaft, thus constantly opening and closing the valves. Remember
that a valve opens every time one of the high spots
comes around on the camshaft, and that there could
be (and in fact is) more than one valve opening at
the same time in different cylinders.

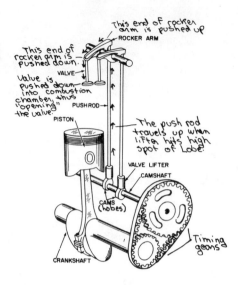

Fig. 8

An exception to this method of valve operation is
what is known as an overhead cam engine. An overhead cam engine refers to the location of the camshaft. Instead of being located in the crankcase
near the crankshaft, the camshaft is located in the
head of the engine right above the valve stems. As
a result, the valves are operated directly off the
camshaft and the rest of the valve train (lifters,
push rods, rocker arms & shaft) is eliminated. As
with any engine, anytime you reduce the distance
that the power is transferred, greater efficiency
is obtained. A lot of 4 cylinder foreign cars have
overhead cam engines - Datsuns and Toyotas for
example.

This, then, is how an engine works. The pistons
are traveling up and down in the cylinders going
through the Intake, Compression, Power and Exhaust
strokes, powering the turning of the crankshaft.
The crankshaft in turn powers the camshaft, which
is opening and closing the valves in conjunction
with the different strokes of the piston. Of
course, all of this is happening tremendously fast.
The RPM's you always hear about stand for revolutions per minute, and refer to the number of revolutions the crankshaft makes in one minute. The
average idling speed is about 800 rpms, and as the
speed of the car increases the rpms increase,
meaning the crankshaft will turn 2000-4000 times a
minute when you are driving at highway speeds.

ENGINE NEEDS SYSTEMS

In order to produce power at such a rate, the
engine needs several things to keep it going. It
needs fuel to provide the combustible mixture for
the explosion; it needs spark to ignite the explosion; it needs lubricant to keep it running
smoothly; it needs to be cooled as it runs; and it
needs to allow the exhaust gases it produces some
means for escape. The deliverance of these five
engine needs - fuel, spark, lubrication, cooling
and exhaust - make up the five main systems of the
car.

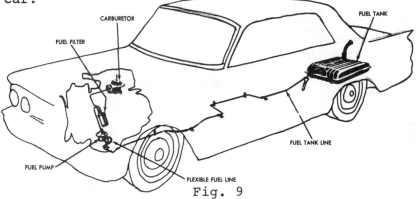

Fig. 9

1. FUEL SYSTEM

The purpose of the fuel system (Fig.9) is to deliver
the proper mixture of fuel and air to the engine for
it to burn. The main part of the fuel system is the
carburetor, which mixes gasoline with air producing
a fine vapor (about 12 parts air to 1 part gasoline)
This mixture is then transferred to the intake
valves through the intake manifold, which is a large
piece of cast iron coming out from the bottom of the
carburetor that has a passageway going to each cylinder. The other parts of the fuel system are the
gas tank (usually located in the rear of the car),
the fuel pump (located down low on one side of the
engine) which pumps the fuel from the tank to the
carburetor, and the fuel lines connecting the tank
to the pump and then to the carburetor. Oftentimes
there is a fuel filter located on the line between
the pump and the carburetor, which filters out dirt
and other foreign particles from the gasoline before
it gets to the carburetor. The fuel filter, like
an oil and air filter, needs to be changed regularly (more on that under maintenance).

An exception to this type of fuel system is what is
known as a fuel injected system. In fuel injected
engines, the carburetor is eliminated, and a meas-

ured amount of gasoline is squirted directly into
the air entering the combustion chamber, producing
the same end effect as the carburetor system - a
measured mixture of fuel and air. It is thought
that this system produces a more responsive engine.
Fuel injected systems are being used more and more,
especially on the more expensive foreign cars -
Volvos and Saabs, for example.

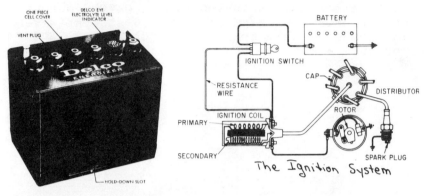

Fig. 10   Fig. 11

2. ELECTRICAL SYSTEM (SPARK)

The basis of all of the electrical system is the
battery (Fig.10), which produces the electricity
needed to support the different operations of the
electrical system. The electrical system has 4
main components - the ignition system, the charging
system, the starter motor, and the electrical accessories.

   a. Ignition System - The purpose of the ignition
      system (Fig.11) is to deliver an electrical
      spark to the right combustion chamber at
      exactly the right time to ignite the fuel
      mixture. I will explain more on how the ig-
      nition system does this in the section on
      tune ups. The parts of the ignition system
      are the ignition switch (where the key goes),
      coil, distributor (with points, condensor,
      rotor & distributor cap), spark plugs (one for
      each cylinder), and the electrical wires
      connecting all of the ignition parts.

   b. Charging System - The purpose of the charging
      system (Fig.12) is to keep the battery charged
      up and to produce electricity to run the ac-
      cessories (lights, radios, etc.). The main
      component of the charging system is the
      generator or alternator. Older cars have
      generators - the main functioning differences
      between generators and alternators are that

36

an alternator will charge at idle speed,
whereas a generator won't; and that the alternator will produce more charge needed to run
all the accessories on modern cars. The
generator or alternator is run by means of a
fan belt that is connected to the crankshaft
pulley (a pulley on the end of the crankshaft)
Other parts of the charging system are the
voltage regulator which regulates the output
of the generator or alternator, and the wires
connecting the parts.

Voltage
regulator

Generator

Fig. 12

Alternator

c. Starter Motor - The sole purpose of the
starter motor (Fig.13), which is also known as
the cranking motor, is to start the crankshaft
turning. The starter motor is a simple electrical motor with a gear on it that meshes
with the flywheel on the crankshaft (the
flywheel is a large round metal disc with
teeth on it that is located on the end of the
crankshaft at the back of the engine). When
the starter motor is operated, the gear
(called starter drive or Bendix) moves forward
and meshes with the teeth on the flywheel and
turns it. Once the crankshaft starts turning
on its own, the starter drive moves back into
the starter motor. The starter motor is located in the back of the engine down low on
one side.

Starter
drive
activator

Solenoid

Starter Motor without
Solenoid - Ford

Fig. 13

Starter Motor with
Solenoid - GM

d. Accessories - Virtually all of the accessories
on the car are run by the electrical system.
Standard accessories include lights, windshield washer and wipers, heater, defroster
and horn. Of course there is an endless
variety of other junk that is put on cars,
like air conditioning, tape decks, etc.
(Sorry for my prejudices - it is just that the
more stuff that is added to a car, the harder
it becomes to work on it. Air conditioning
particularly makes it difficult to get to the
engine, even to do a tune up.)

Oil sending unit

Fig. 14

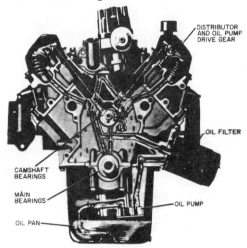

DISTRIBUTOR
AND OIL PUMP
DRIVE GEAR

OIL FILTER

CAMSHAFT
BEARINGS

MAIN
BEARINGS

OIL PUMP

OIL PAN

3. LUBRICATION SYSTEM

The purpose of the lubricating system (Fig.14) is
to constantly lubricate the moving engine parts and
also to help cool the engine. With the engine parts
moving at the rate of speed that they do and with
constant touching of metal on metal, there has to
be a continuous lubrication of all parts or the
metals would wear extremely rapidly and also probably heat to such a point that they would fuse
together and destroy the engine. Almost all automobile engines have what is known as a full pressure
oil system in which the oil is delivered under
pressure to all moving parts of the engine. This is
done by means of an oil pump which is located inside
the oil pan underneath the crankshaft. The oil pan
is the large metal pan piece that you see when you
crawl underneath your engine that has a bolt (the
oil plug) in it somewhere that you take out to
drain the engine oil. The oil is pumped from the
oil pan by passageways to all moving parts of the
engine - crankshaft, connecting rods, pistons, cylinder walls (although not a moving part), timing
gears or chain, camshaft and valve train. A third

part of the lubricating system is the <u>oil sending</u>
<u>unit</u> which registers the amount of oil pressure
there is either by means of an instrument panel
light or gauge. The oil sending unit is usually
located on the side of the engine and is a small
plug-looking object with a wire leading to it.

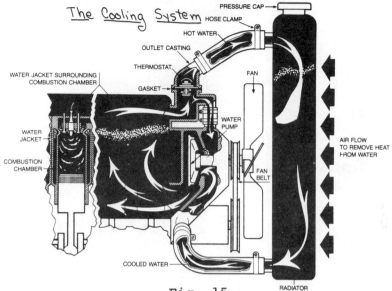

The Cooling System

Fig. 15

4. COOLING SYSTEM

The purpose of the cooling system (Fig.15) is to
cool the engine and keep it from overheating. The
combustion that occurs in the cylinders produces a
great amount of heat - up to several thousand
degrees Fahrenheit. Obviously there needs to be
some system to cool down the cylinders. The lubricating system helps to cool the engine, but the
main excess of heat is reduced through the cooling
system. The cooling system does this by pumping
cooled water through the engine and circulating the
water through water jackets - spaces around the
cylinder walls. Water is pumped by means of a
<u>water pump</u> (located behind the fan in front of the
engine) that is powered from the crankshaft pulley
via the fan belt (the same belt that is hooked to
the generator or alternator). Hot water comes out
of the top of the engine through the top radiator
hose into the <u>radiator</u>. The radiator cools the
water by means of veins that the water trickles
down through. The <u>fan</u> blows air through the radiator helping the water to cool. The cooled water
then comes out the bottom hose of the radiator,
circulates through the engine absorbing the heat of
the cylinders, and then comes back out of the

engine through the top radiator hose and is then cooled again. A thermostat is located where the water comes out of the engine into the top radiator hose. The purpose of the thermostat is to restrict the water flow when the engine is cold, thus allowing the engine to heat up faster. Once the engine reaches normal operating temperature, then the thermostat opens up and allows the water to flow unrestricted.

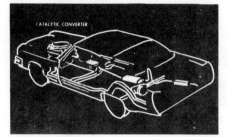

Exhaust system showing muffler, resonator (rear), and exhaust pipes

Exhaust manifold not shown

Fig. 16

5. EXHAUST SYSTEM

The purpose of the exhaust system (Fig.16) is to take the gases left from the combustion in the engine and direct them to the outside air through a muffling system so as to reduce the noise of the explosion in the combustion chambers. The gases leave the combustion chamber through the exhaust valve and are then directed into the exhaust manifold. The exhaust manifold looks much like the intake manifold - it has a passageway leading from each cylinder, with the passageways coming together at the exhaust pipe. The exhaust pipe runs underneath the car to where it hooks up with the muffler (sometimes there will be two mufflers). The muffler quiets the noise of the exhaust, and then directs the exhaust gases out to the rear of the car through the tail pipe. Different exhaust systems have different numbers of pipes and occasionally mufflers, but they all have these three components - the exhaust pipe that leaves the exhaust manifold, a muffler, and a tail pipe.

OTHER SYSTEMS

The ignition, fuel, lubricating, cooling and exhaust systems are the systems of the car that are essential for the engine to function. There are other systems of the car that are not related to the engine, but are important in making the car a

40

drivable vehicle. These systems are the transmission and drive train, the suspension and steering, and the braking system.

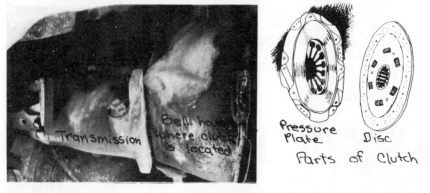

Fig. 17

1. TRANSMISSION AND DRIVE TRAIN

The purpose of this system is to take the power that is produced by the engine in the form of the turning crankshaft and transmit it to the rear wheels to turn them and move the car down the road.

   a. Clutch - The first part of the drive train is the <u>clutch</u>, located immediately behind the engine next to the flywheel (Fig.17). The purpose of the clutch is to connect and disconnect the engine to the transmission - the engine is disconnected when changing gears (when you press on the clutch pedal) and connected when in gear (when you let up on the pedal). In automatic transmissions what is known as the torque converter, or the fluid coupling, takes the place of the clutch, doing the same job.

   b. Transmission - Right after the clutch is the <u>transmission</u>. The purpose of the transmission is to transmit the power of the engine to the drive shaft. The transmission does this through a series of gears. With the low gears and reverse gear, the transmission lessens the turning speed of the engine, so the drive shaft turns at a slower speed than the engine does, but with a greater amount of power. With the transmission in high gear, the turning speed of the engine is transferred directly to the drive shaft, so both the engine and drive shaft are turning at the same rate of speed and with the same amount of power. If a car is equipped with overdrive, this means that the transmission has

41

an additional gear which allows the drive
shaft to turn at a faster rate of speed than
the engine. This could only be used in
fairly high speed driving - the purpose of it
is to increase gas mileage. Manual and automatic transmissions serve the same purpose;
it is just that in an automatic transmission
the changing of gears is accomplished automatically through the movement of fluid,
whereas in a manual transmission the gear
changing is done manually (womanually) by you.

Universal joint   drive shaft

Fig. 18

c. Drive Shaft - Connected to the transmission
   is the drive shaft, a long narrow hollow tube
   that goes from underneath the middle of the
   car to the differential, located between the
   rear wheels (Fig.18). The drive shaft is
   connected to the transmission and differential
   by universal joints (known as u-joints), one
   where the drive shaft goes into the transmission and one where it goes into the differential. Some cars have a third universal joint
   located in the middle of the drive shaft.
   The universal joints allow the drive shaft to
   turn at different angles, thus compensating
   for irregularities in road surfaces, and for
   the up & down movement of the car frame.

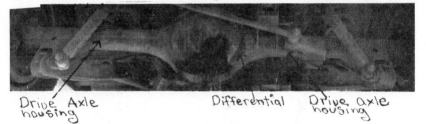

Drive Axle   Differential   Drive axle
housing   housing

Fig. 19

d. Differential - The fourth main section of the
   drive train is the differential (commonly
   known as the rear end) and the drive axles
   (Fig.19). The differential is a gear box
   located at the rear of the car (the big ball-
   looking object you see when you look underneath your car from the back end of it). The

42

purpose of the differential is to take the turning power of the drive shaft and deliver it to the axles to which the rear wheels are connected. This transmitting of power is done through a series of gears inside the differential.

The power of the engine moves from the engine to the transmission via the clutch, from the transmission to the differential via the drive shaft, and from the differential to the rear wheels via the rear axles (Fig.20).

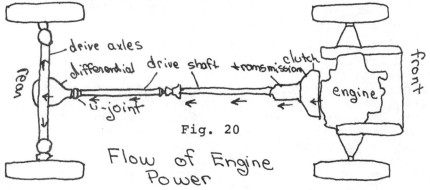

Fig. 20

Flow of Engine Power

There are two exceptions to this flow of engine power. One is when the engine is located in the rear, as it is on the VW bugs. In this situation, the power of the engine is directed straight to the rear wheels by what is known as a transaxle, a sort of combination transmission and rear axles. The other exception is cars that have front wheel drive. This is the same situation as the bug, the only difference being that the engine is in the front so the power of the engine is transmitted directly to the front wheels. A lot of new small cars, especially foreign cars, have front wheel drive. They are very good for driving in snow as the weight of the engine is over the wheels that have the turning power, thus providing a greater amount of traction.

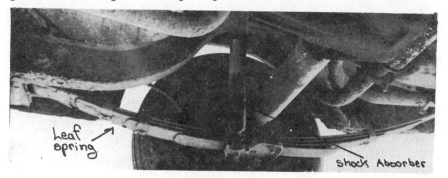

Fig. 21

shock absorber————

coil spring————

Fig. 22

2. SUSPENSION AND STEERING

Suspension is the system that suspends the car
(body, frame, engine, transmission and drive train)
above the wheels of the car. To do this, springs,
either leaf or coil, are used one at each wheel
(Fig.21). The weight of the car rests on these
springs. Another part of the suspension system is
the shock absorbers (Fig.22). Shock absorbers
don't support the weight of the car, but rather
absorb the up & down motion of the wheels as they
hit bumps, holes, etc. so that the whole car
doesn't go up & down with the wheels. A shock
absorber is located at each wheel.

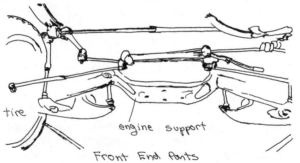

tire

engine support

Front End Parts

Fig. 23

The steering system is what keeps the car going
down the road in a straight line, and what turns it
when you turn the wheel (Fig.23). The steering
system is commonly known as the 'front end' and its
components, the front end parts. Ball joints, an
upper and a lower one located at each front wheel,
allow the front wheels to turn at sharp angles.
There is a steering gear box located on the shaft
connected to the steering wheel that contains the
gears that transmit the turning action of the
steering wheel to both front wheels. The rest of
the front end parts consist of various linkage that
hook the steering column and gear box to the wheels.

Some of these parts are the tie rods (one at each wheel), steering idler arm, and the drag link. I don't know a whole lot about front end parts and they vary quite a bit (or so it seems to me) from car to car, so I probably won't be discussing the front end in much detail in this manual.

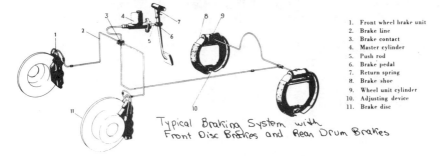

1. Front wheel brake unit
2. Brake line
3. Brake contact
4. Master cylinder
5. Push rod
6. Brake pedal
7. Return spring
8. Brake shoe
9. Wheel unit cylinder
10. Adjusting device
11. Brake disc

Typical Braking System with Front Disc Brakes and Rear Drum Brakes

Fig. 24

3. BRAKE SYSTEM

The braking system (Fig.24) is, of course, what stops your car. All cars have what is known as hydraulic brakes, meaning braking pressure is applied through the movement of fluid. I will be talking in more detail about how brakes work in the section on brake repair. Parts of the braking system are the <u>master cylinder</u>, <u>brake lines</u> to each wheel, and a <u>wheel cylinder</u> and <u>brake shoes</u> (for drum brakes) or <u>pads</u> (for disc brakes) at each wheel.

* *

The engine, with its necessary systems, the transmission and drive train, the suspension and steering systems, and the braking system are all the mechanical parts that make up your car. Any work you will be doing on your car will be work on one of these systems, even if it is something as simple as an oil change (not that oil changes are always simple, I know). I have just gone over each system briefly and will talk in more detail about them when we get into repairs. In the final part of this chapter, I want to try to relate all this talk about systems to what you see when you open the hood of your car or crawl underneath it. I think it is important before you start working on your car that you get some sense of what things are when you are looking at your engine, and have at least some knowledge of what they do. Also, I remember when I first started learning about cars that I had a lot

of trouble with repair manuals because they never
tell you where a certain part - like the brake
master cylinder, for instance - is located because
they just assume you know ('you' being a man, of
course). I'm trying not to make any assumptions
like that in this manual, so I want to be sure that
you have at least some idea where different parts
of the car are located. Actually even if you never
work on your car, it still would be helpful to have
an understanding of how your car works and what
things are, so you will be less likely to be ripped
off by some smooth talking mechanic who sees you and
his eyes light up, "Ah, a woman - I'll be able to
sell her anything."

WHAT YOU SEE WHEN YOU OPEN THE HOOD OF YOUR CAR

Of course, what you see is going to vary from car
to car - what cylinder engine you have, how new the
car is (therefore how much more emission control
stuff there is; anytime I can't identify something
on the engine of a car I assume it is emission control stuff as it varies so widely from car to car
and there is a whole lot of it on newer cars), and
whether or not your car has things like power
brakes, power steering or airconditioning. However,
no matter what kind of car you have, they will all
have the systems parts described previously, and
they will all look pretty much alike and most of
them will be located in approximately the same
places. The photographs are of a 1966 Ford Mustang
with a 6 cylinder engine. (Fig. 25)

The most obvious thing when you open the hood of
your car is the engine. You can't see the working
parts of the engine - crankshaft, camshaft, pistons,
valves, etc., but what you are seeing is the crankcase and head, together known as the engine block,
which looks like one big hunk of metal. You can see
where the head is bolted to the crankcase by looking
for a seam along the length of the engine just below
the spark plugs (the spark plugs are located in a
row about a third of the way down the engine on the
side and have thick insulated wires leading to
them). This seam is where the head gasket is located, the gasket that seals the passageways from
the crankcase to the head. On the top of the engine
is the valve cover (1, if you have a 4 or 6 cylinder
engine; 2, if you have a V-8 engine). The valve
cover covers the valve train. Also on top of the
engine is the air filter, the large round pan-look-

Fig. 25

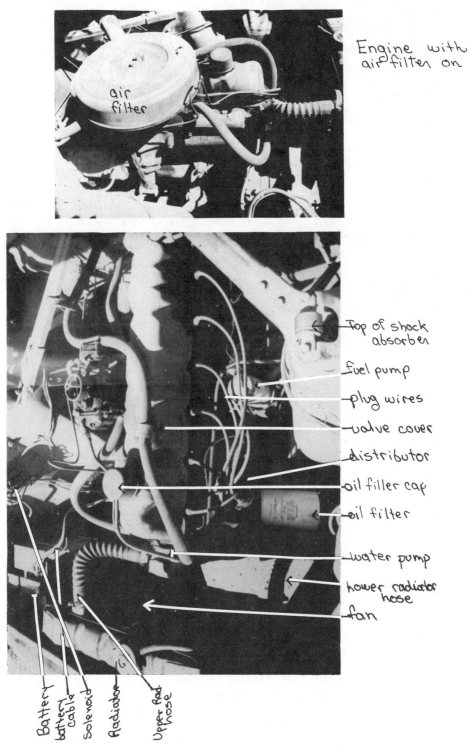

Engine with air filter on

air filter

Top of shock absorber

fuel pump

plug wires

valve cover

distributor

oil filler cap

oil filter

water pump

lower radiator hose

fan

Battery

battery cable

Solenoid

Radiator

Upper Rad. hose

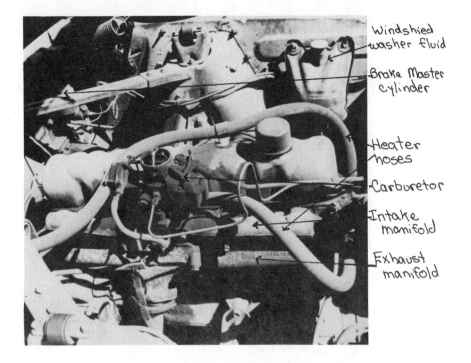

Windshied
washer fluid

Brake Master
cylinder

Heater
hoses

Carburetor

Intake
manifold

Exhaust
manifold

ing object. Below the air filter is the carburetor
(you have to remove the air filter to see it), and
below the carburetor is the intake manifold (difficult to see on some cars and may not be distinguish-
able to you from the rest of the engine). You might
also find the distributor and/or the coil located
somewhere near the top of the engine - otherwise
they are down along the side somewhere. The distributor has a lot of thick wires coming out of the top
of it - the wires that go to the spark plugs. On
General Motors cars the distributor is located near
the back of the engine; on Ford and other make cars,
the distributor is located near the front of the
engine. To find the coil, follow the wire coming
out of the middle of the distributor cap - it will
connect to the coil.

Directly in front of the engine is the fan. Right
behind the fan, what the fan is hooked to actually,
is the water pump. The water pump is another part
that is hard to see as separate from the engine.
Also in front of the engine is the crankshaft pulley
(located below the fan and water pump) and the alternator or generator (to one side of the fan). The
fan belt hooks the fan, crankshaft pulley, and alternator or generator together. If you have power
steering or airconditioning you would also have a
belt going to these parts from the crankshaft
pulley. A third part that you might have connected

48

to a belt would be an air pump - an emission control device.

On the side of the engine (one side or the other - it varies with different makes of car) is located the exhaust manifold. On V-8's you have 2 exhaust manifolds, one located on each side of the engine. The exhaust manifold is the part that comes out of the engine to hook up with the exhaust pipe going back to the muffler. Down low on the side of the engine, usually near the front, is the fuel pump - if you can't find it, trace the metal or rubber hose that goes to the top of the carburetor (the fuel line) - it will hook up with the fuel pump. Also located on the side of the engine, down low and way in the back (very hard to see) is the starter motor, which looks like an oatmeal-box-size metal cylinder laying next to the engine (in some cases with a smaller cylinder on top).

Separated from the engine are the radiator (in front of the engine with a large hose going out of the top and bottom hooking up with the engine), the battery (with cables leading to the two posts on it), and the voltage regulator (a small rectangular box that is sometimes very difficult to locate - a lot of times it is sort of buried under the fender). Located on the <u>fire wall</u>, the sheet of metal that separates the engine compartment from the passenger compartment, is the brake master cylinder (near the driver's side of the car), the motor that operates the windshield wipers, usually looking like a small cylinder, and the motor that operates the heater blower, usually a large round object.

All of this is pretty much what you will see under the hood of your car. You will also probably see a whole lot of wires leading every which way, hoses connecting all kinds of things, and a lot of strange looking objects that you have no idea what they are. I wouldn't worry about it a whole lot - if you are able to identify the parts that I went over, then you should have a pretty good sense of what your car is all about. So much of the other stuff you see is connected with the electrical accessories system and emission controls, which you would rarely be doing any repairs on.

Fig. 26

UNDERNEATH ENGINE

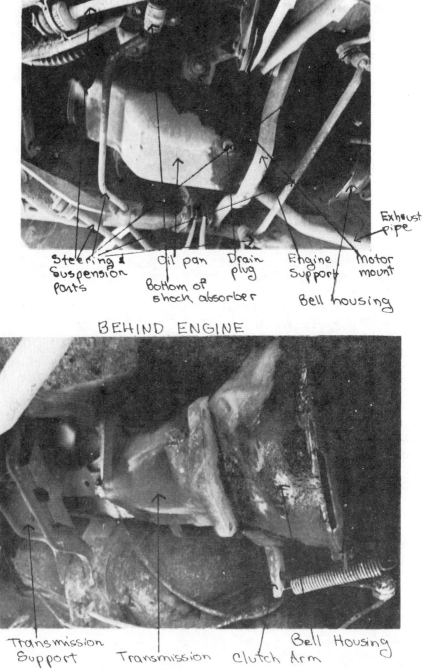

Steering & Suspension Parts
Oil pan
Bottom of shock absorber
Drain plug
Engine Support
Bell housing
Motor mount
Exhaust pipe

BEHIND ENGINE

Transmission Support
Transmission
Clutch Arm
Bell Housing

50

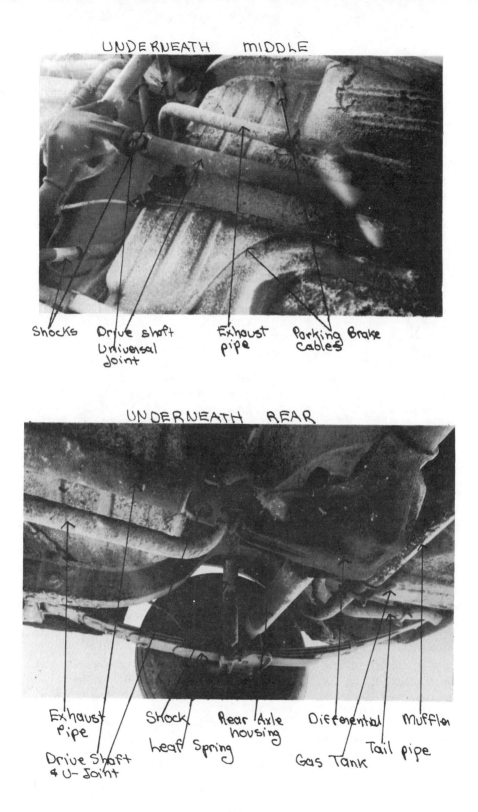

UNDERNEATH MIDDLE

Shocks   Drive shaft   Exhaust   Parking Brake
           Universal   pipe   cables
           Joint

UNDERNEATH REAR

Exhaust   Shock   Rear Axle   Differential   Muffler
Pipe   housing
    Drive Shaft   Leaf Spring   Tail pipe
    & U-Joint   Gas Tank

WHAT YOU SEE WHEN YOU CRAWL UNDERNEATH YOUR CAR

Well, first off, before attempting to identify what
is underneath your car (Fig.26), I would put it up
on jack stands or use a hoist somewhere. It is
pretty hard to see anything very clearly when it is
two inches from your nose. By the way, if you don't
have access to a jack or hoist, you could drive
your car up on a curb, so that the wheels on one
side of the car are up on the curb and the other
two are at street level. This should raise your
car up enough that you can get underneath it without
getting too claustrophobic. Be sure to block the
wheels - you don't want the car to start rolling
with you underneath it. A word about being underneath cars - when I first started working on cars
it bothered me a lot to have to crawl underneath
them. I have since gotten over that and I think
that is due to two things - getting the car high
enough off the ground using jack stands or the curb
method so that you have some space to move around
in; and knowing that the car is safe, that the
wheels are blocked and that it is firmly on the
jack stands, so you know that it isn't going to
start moving with you under it. If you can do those
two things, I think it will help under-the-car
paranoia if you suffer from that.

Lying underneath the front of the car you will first
see the steering linkage - the series of rods in
front of the engine that hook from one wheel to the
other. There will also be springs (leaf or coil)
and shock absorbers located near each wheel. Directly underneath the engine is the oil pan - the
large pan-looking object (probably covered with
dirt and oil) with a bolt on it somewhere (the oil
drain plug).

Right behind the engine and connected to it is the
bell housing, the large metal shell that houses the
clutch. Directly behind the bell housing is the
transmission. If you have an automatic transmission, there won't be a separate bell housing. The
transmission sort of looks like the underneath of
the engine, though not as large. It might also
have a drain plug located on it somewhere (particularly automatics, which have a small pan and a

plug). Behind the transmission is the drive shaft, the long metal tube that goes to the back of the car. Look for the universal joints at the beginning and the end of the drive shaft. Also in this middle area of the car, you should be able to see the exhaust pipe and muffler.

Underneath the back of the car is the differential, the bulbous mass in between the rear wheels; the rear axle housing which juts out from the differential to the rear wheels and houses the axles; the springs and shock absorbers located near each wheel; the exhaust system tail pipe; and the gas tank (usually located directly under the trunk of the car - you might mistake it for the bottom of the trunk).

If you can try locating all these parts under the hood and underneath the car, and keep in mind what system they are a part of and something about their function, then you should end up, hopefully, with a pretty good sense of what makes up your car.

PART II

MAINTENANCE
&
REPAIRS

In this section of the manual I am going to deal
with: 1) the maintenance routines for your car -
          how often to check and change fluids,
          belts, hoses, etc;
       2) go through the basic service routines -
          oil change, lubrication, wheel bearings,
          winterizing, tune ups; and
       3) explain in varying amounts of detail some
          larger repair jobs you can do on your
          car - replacing shocks, exhaust, univer-
          sal joints and brake work.

Chapter 1

MAINTENANCE ROUTINES

One of the first things you should do in learning
to maintain your car is to read through the owners'
manual for your car. If you don't have one, you
can usually get one from the dealer in town that
sells your make car, even if you have an older car.
A lot of the knowledge in the owners' manual is
superfluous bullshit, but there is some knowledge
there that you need to know. It will tell you how
often the various fluids in your car should be
changed, and what fluids and how much of them should
be used. The owners' manual should also tell you
the location of the jack, its component parts and
how to use them; the location of the fuse box and
what each fuse is for and what amperage (size) it
is; tire pressure when your car is loaded or
unloaded; how often the service routines should be
performed; and assorted other bits of information
that you might need to know in maintaining your car.
What I want to do in this chapter is to present sort
of a general maintenance check list that can be
used in conjunction with the information in your
owners' manual. If you don't have an owners' manual, then this list could serve as maintenance
schedule for your car, although you will need to
know the weight and quantity of the various fluids
used in your car. If you don't have that information, you can call the dealer for your car and ask

the service department there, or you could find the information in a Chiltons or some other repair manual that covers your year and make of car.

The following chapters tell how to perform the maintenance routines on the systems that will be checked out in this chapter (how to change the engine oil, for example).

MAINTENANCE SCHEDULE							
Fluid	Check	Change	Mileage when change				
Engine oil	monthy	3000 m. Filter-6000m					
Automatic Trans	monthly	24,000 m.					
Standard Trans	3 months	24,000 m.					
Differential	3 months	24,000 m					
Brake fluid	3 months	not necessary					
Radiator water level	monthy	Flush out 2-3 years					
Battery water	monthly	not necessary					
Windshield Washer Solvent	monthly	not necessary					
Service Routines:	Every	mileage When Performed					
Tune up	12,000 m or 12 mo.						
Lubrication	3,000 m. or 3 mo.						
Repacking front wheel bearings	6,000 m.						
Tire Rotation	6,000 m.						
Winterizing	yearly						
General Check	6 mo.- yr.						

MAINTENANCE SCHEDULE

Fluids

A note about fluids - any rapid drop in fluid level (for example using 2 or more quarts of engine oil per month) would probably indicate a leak in that system somewhere. (See Part III, Chapter 2, Fluid Leaks.)

55

1. ENGINE OIL

Check: Engine oil should be checked at least once a month, more if you burn a lot of oil or have leaks. Average consumption of oil is about 1 quart per month or every 1000 miles - older engines will tend to use more oil. To check the oil level, the engine should be warmed up. It should not be checked when the engine is cold (when it is started up after sitting for a long time). However, it shouldn't be checked when the engine is real hot, either (like after driving for an extended period of time on the highway). The reason for this is that oil thins out when hot and thickens when cold, and thus you will get an inaccurate reading if the engine is real hot or cold. Check the oil with the engine not running. Pull out the engine oil dipstick, wipe it off, put it back into the dipstick hole and make sure that it goes all the way down into the hole; pull the dipstick back out again and see where the oil comes to on the stick. Most dipsticks (though they vary from car to car) will have two main marks with a space between them. The last mark - furthest up the stick towards the top - indicates the level the oil should be (Fig.1). The second mark usually indicates one quart low on oil, depending how far it is down the dipstick.

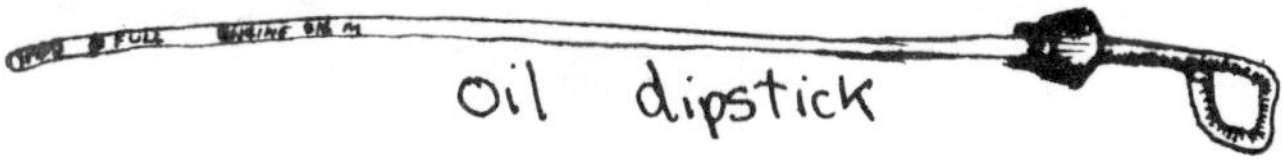

Oil dipstick

Fig. 1

Change: Engine oil should be changed every 3000 miles or 3 months. Small car manufacturers sometimes recommend that the oil be changed every 2000 miles or 2 months. The oil filter is changed every other oil change, though your manual might recommend changing the filter with each oil change. It certainly won't hurt to change it every time you change the oil and probably would be beneficial to your engine, but filters are kind of expensive and it is not really all that necessary to change it that often. Do whatever you think.

2. AUTOMATIC TRANSMISSION FLUID

Check: I would check automatic transmission fluid once a month though there should be no drop in the fluid level unless you have a leak somewhere. Check it with the engine running. The dipstick is located in the back of the engine. Sometimes it is difficult to see, but keep looking for it - if you have an automatic transmission, then you have to have a

dipstick somewhere. The procedure is the same as
with checking engine oil - pull the stick out, wipe
it off, put it back in, and take it out again and
see what it reads. On most automatic transmission
fluid dipsticks there will be a reading for when the
engine is warm and when it is cold, although some
you can only read when the engine is warm. The
marks on the stick usually indicate full and one
quart low. Add automatic transmission fluid with
the engine running - pour it down the dipstick hole.
The easiest way to do this is to use a funnel with
a flexible metal hose attached to it (Fig.2) though
you might be able to rig up something else. Most
automatic transmissions use what is known as Type B
automatic transmission fluid. Fords, however, use
a special type of transmission fluid, Type F, also
known as Ford Automatic Transmission Fluid.

Fig. 2

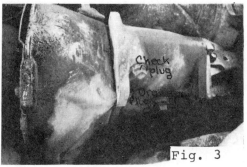

Fig. 3

Change: How often to change automatic transmission
fluid varies from car to car. Some manufacturers
recommend that the fluid is never changed, unless
there is some sort of difficulty; many manufacturers
however, recommend that the fluid be changed every
24,000 miles. Regardless of the mileage, if the
fluid is dark looking or burnt smelling and hasn't
been changed recently, be sure to change it.
Another indication that the fluid might need changing is if your transmission is slow to shift
(although this could also indicate other transmission problems).

3.   STANDARD TRANSMISSION FLUID

Check: Standard transmission fluid should be checked
every time you do a lubrication job on your car
(every 3000 miles or 3 months), although there
should be no appreciable drop in the fluid unless
there is a transmission leak. To check the fluid
level, you have to crawl underneath the car to
where the transmission is (you might have to jack
up the front of the car). There should be a plug

with a square head, or an indented square plug, somewhere on the side of the transmission about halfway between the top and bottom of the transmission.(Fig. 3) If you have an older car, the transmission will probably be covered with dirt and grease, so the plug might be hard to locate, but it will be there somewhere. Loosen the plug and take it out (I find that an adjustable wrench - crescent wrench usually works pretty well with a square headed plug, but be sure to get the jaws as tight as possible on the plug. If it has an indented square head, then the drive part of a ratchet might fit it). After removing the plug, if the hole is large enough, stick your finger in the hole and see if you feel any oil. The fluid should be about level with the hole, so you should be able to feel oil somewhere between the tip and first joint of your finger. If the hole isn't large enough for a finger to fit into, then the way you know there is enough fluid in the transmission is that a small stream of fluid should run out of the hole when the plug is removed. More fluid is added through the same hole where you check the level (see Part II, Chapter 2, changing standard transmission fluid).

Change: This will also depend on what the manufacturer recommends for your car, but standard transmission fluid is commonly changed around every 24,000 miles.

4. DIFFERENTIAL FLUID

Check: Differential fluid should be checked every time you check the standard transmission fluid or about every 3000 miles or 3 months. The fluid shouldn't be low every time you check it unless the differential is leaking. Checking the differential fluid is the same procedure as checking the standard transmission fluid. There will be a check plug located somewhere on the side of the differential or in the middle of the back of the differential (if you are looking at it from the back of the car). (Fig. 4). The check plug is generally larger than the check plug on the transmission. You check the level of the fluid in the same manner - stick your finger in the hole and see if the fluid registers somewhere between the tip of your finger and the first joint. Fluid is added through the same hole (see Part II, Chapter 2, changing differential fluid).

Change: As with the standard transmission, different manufacturers vary on how often to change differential fluid, but usually the fluid is changed about every 24,000 miles.

check
plug   Differential

Fig. 4

5.   BRAKE FLUID

<u>Check</u>: Check the brake fluid about every 3 months.
There should be no drop in the fluid, though eventually small amounts will evaporate. If the fluid
is down every time you check it, then you are
leaking brake fluid somewhere. Such a leak could
be potentially dangerous in terms of the braking
ability of your car, so you should determine the
cause of the leak as soon as possible (see. Part II,
Chapter 7). Check the fluid at the master cylinder
reservoir, located on top of the master cylinder
(on many master cylinders, the reservoir is part of
the body of the master cylinder, not a separate
piece). Some cylinders will have a rod that goes
across the top to keep the cap on. Put a long
screwdriver through the space between the rod and
the cap, and pry up on the screwdriver, pushing the
rod off of the cap (Fig. 5). You can then remove
the cap and see the brake fluid. The brake fluid
should be close to the top of the reservoir. Other
master cylinders will have a large screw-on cap.
Sometimes this cap is rusted and you can't unscrew
it with your hand. In that situation, the best
tool I have found to remove it is a pair of large
channel lock pliers, adjusted so that the jaws can
grasp the cap with the handles of the pliers close
together. That should give you enough leverage to
loosen the cap.

If the brake fluid is low, add enough fluid to the
reservoir to fill it close to the top. Brake fluid
comes in pint and quart cans. If you have disc
brakes, be sure to get fluid that is for disc

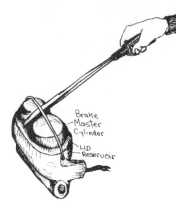

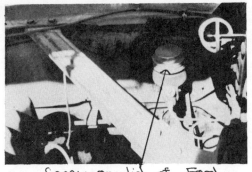

Screw-on lid of Ford master Cylinder

Fig. 5

brakes. After filling up the reservoir, close up
the fluid can tightly, as air will contaminate the
fluid and make it unusable in the future. Brake
fluid is very expensive, so it is a shame to waste
it that way. Another thing about brake fluid - if
you get it on the paint of your car, it will eat it
right off, even if you just have some on your hands
and put your hands on the car (I left my finger-
prints permanently on a friend's car that way).

Change: Brake fluid isn't normally changed. At
some point your car will be needing brake work, and
then new brake fluid is introduced into the system
by bleeding the brakes (see Part II, Chapter 7,
bleeding the brakes).

6. RADIATOR

Check: Check the water level in the radiator about
once a month, or more often if you have a water
leak. To check the water level, remove the radiator cap and look down into the radiator. The water
should be up to about 1 or 2 inches below the top
of the radiator; the veins of the radiator should
not be showing. It is best to check the water
level when the engine is cold. Don't remove the
radiator cap when the engine is hot, because the
water is under pressure and might come spurting
out. Also, turn the radiator cap slowly to allow
the pressure a chance to lessen gradually, rather
than all at once. When you add water to the radiator (in the winter add antifreeze instead of water)
do not put cold water into a hot engine, as you
could possibly end up with a cracked engine block
that way (like when you put an ice cold glass into
hot dishwater).

Change: I would change the water in the radiator
and engine about every two or three years or when

the water gets real dirty and rusty looking. Usually this is done when you are putting antifreeze
in your car for the winter (see Part II, Chapter 5,
winterizing your car).

7. BATTERY

Che__: Check the water level in the battery about
once a month. You should lose about one ounce of
water per cell (each hole where you put water is
one cell) per month. To check, remove the cell
covers and look down into each hole. The water
should come up to the bottom of the hole (called
the split ring). (Fig. 6) Add water to each cell
that is low. You are supposed to use distilled
water, but probably not many service stations or
garages do. It is a good idea, however, because
the minerals in non-distilled water will work on
the battery acid and reduce the life of the battery.

Change: You don't change the fluid in batteries.

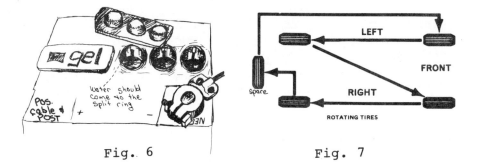

Fig. 6   Fig. 7

8. WINDSHIELD WASHER FLUID

Check: How often you need to check the washer fluid
depends on how often you use your washers - in
sloppy winter weather you will, of course, be using
them more often, so you should check the washer
container periodically. Some cars have plastic
bottles in various sizes, others have a plastic bag.
Washer fluid containers are usually located on the
inside of the fender in the engine compartment.

Service Routines

1. TUNE UP

This includes checking and replacing, if necessary:
points, spark plugs, air filter, fuel filter, pcv
valve, plug wires, distributor cap, and rotor. A
tune up should be done every 12 months or 12,000
miles on 6 and 8 cylinder engine cars. On 4 cylinder engine cars, it is often recommended that a
tune up be performed every 6000 miles or 6 months.

2. LUBRICATION

This includes checking all fluid levels and greasing
the front end parts. A lube job, as it is known,
should be performed every 3 months or 3000 miles.

3. REPACK FRONT WHEEL BEARINGS

In general, this should be done every 6000 miles
(but some manufacturers specify repacking front
wheel bearings much less often).

4. TIRE ROTATION

To maintain even tire wear, the tires should be
rotated every 6000 miles. Standard tread tires
(versus radial tires) should be rotated according
to the diagram (Fig. 7). Radial tires are just
switched from front to back, and back to front.
Radial tires should remain on the same side of the
car throughout their use on the car.

5. WINTERIZING YOUR CAR

This includes: checking antifreeze and possibly
flushing the cooling system; checking and replacing,
if necessary, radiator and heater hoses, fan belt,
windshield wipers; checking condition of battery;
adding antifreeze to washer solvent. If you live
in a climate with cold winters,then winterizing your
car should be done before the cold season starts.
If you live in a climate that you don't have a
winter or at least not a very cold one, then sometime during the year you should go through these
checks on your car.

6. GENERAL CHECK

A general check of the condition of your car, including shocks, brakes, u-joints, oil and water
leaks, safety check (lights, horn, wipers, etc.),
front end parts and exhaust system, should be done
every 6 months to a year. Sometimes if you can
catch a part when it is going bad and replace it,
you will save yourself doing a lot more expensive
and involved repair later.

Chapter 2

LUBRICANT CHANGES

ENGINE OIL

A. Tools Needed

1. Oil Filter Wrench for replaceable filters (Fig.1)

Older model cars - usually pre 1964, although it
varies with the make of car - do not have replaceable oil filters, but rather have a cannister that is
removed by loosening the bolt at the bottom of it.
The filter inside the cannister is replaced. If
you have this type of filter you won't need an oil
filter wrench, but just a box end or crescent wrench
to fit the bolt on the bottom of the cannister.

2. Something to open cans of oil with

A church key will work fine; also there are special
openers made for oil cans that have a pour spout
connected to them (Fig.2).

3. A Crescent Wrench or Box End Wrench to fit the
   oil drain plug on your car.

B. Supplies/Parts Needed

1. Cans of Oil

2. Oil Filter (Fig.3)

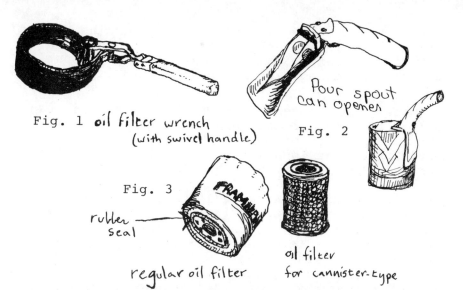

Fig. 1 oil filter wrench
(with swivel handle)

Fig. 2

Pour spout
can opener

Fig. 3

rubber
seal

regular oil filter

oil filter
for cannister-type

Places where you buy oil filters have charts that
tell you what filter is for your car. Cannister
filters look much different than regular oil filters - they are made out of thin metal and have a
lot of holes in them for the oil to filter through.

3. Pan to drain the old oil into (an old dishpan
   works fine)

4. Plenty of Rags

C. Information Needed

1. How many quarts of oil your car holds with a
   filter

2. The weight of oil recommended for your car according to the season

Generally, lighter weight oil (10 or 20 weight) is
recommended for use in the winter. Heavier oil (30
or 40 weight) is recommended for use in summer
months. There are also all-season oils: 10-30,
10-40, etc. The reason for different weight oils
in different seasons is that in the winter you need
a lighter weight oil because the cold weather
causes your oil to thicken. In the summer, the
heat causes the oil to thin and thus you need a
heavier oil. There are also detergent and non-
detergent oils. Detergent oils have a cleaning
agent in them. As with all of this information,
your owners' manual should tell you which type of
oil to use.

D. Steps

1. It is best to do an oil change when the engine

is hot, because the oil thins out and drains a lot better, carrying out the dirt in the engine with it. If your car is cold, let it run at idle until the heat gauge shows normal or the cold light goes off.

2. Loosen and remove the drain plug on the oil pan. To find the plug, crawl underneath the front of your car (you may or may not have to jack it up depending on the location of the oil plug and how close to the ground your car sits). Right below the engine is the oil pan - the engine oil pan is quite large as distinguished from the smaller oil pan on an automatic transmission (standard transmissions don't have oil pans). Somewhere on the engine oil pan - it could be in the front or in the back or on the side - there will be a large bolt with its head flat against the pan. That is the oil drain plug. The best tool to use to loosen the plug is a box end wrench the size of the plug. If you don't have the correct size wrench, a crescent wrench will work fairly well, as long as the plug isn't too difficult to get loose. Sometimes oil drain plugs can be hard to get loose, though once they first loosen, usually they will unscrew the rest of the way by hand. If you are having trouble getting the plug loose, here are some things to try:

   a. If you are using a crescent wrench, get a box end wrench the right size. It will provide you with a lot better holding power on the plug.

   b. Position your body so you use your maximum strength. I usually put the wrench on the plug so the other end of the wrench points somewhere in between the engine area and the rear wheels (this is if the plug is on the bottom of the pan). Then I stretch out and grab the end of the wrench with my arm slightly bent and my other arm holding on to the left front tire to brace myself. Then I pull with all my might on the wrench, and USUALLY the plug comes loose.

   c. Tapping on the end of the wrench with a hammer also helps sometimes to loosen the plug.

   d. Using a breaker bar and socket will also help to loosen the plug.

3. Once the plug is loose, unscrew it the rest of the way and let the dirty oil drain out. You should have your pan to catch the dirty oil underneath the plug as you are taking it out, as oil will start draining out before you get the plug all the way

out. Many plugs have a copper washer on them -
watch for it so you don't lose it in the oil. Let
the oil drain about 10 minutes.

4. While the oil is draining out, you can be removing the oil filter. Like the plug, once you
first loosen the filter, you should be able to
unscrew it the rest of the way by hand. The oil
filter looks like a can and is usually located on
one side of the engine down low. On some cars they
stick straight out from the engine, on other cars
they stick straight down. Another way to recognize
the filter is that it is usually a bright color -
like white, green, orange or yellow. Of course, if
the filter hasn't been changed in a long time and
if you have a lot of oil leaks, then it might be
covered with grease and dirt and look like the rest
of the engine. If you have a cannister type of
filter, it will almost always be located pointing
straight down from the side of the engine.

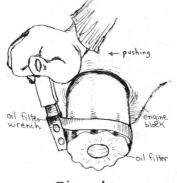

Fig. 4

a. To loosen a regular type filter, put the oil
   filter wrench on the filter so that when you
   push the handle in the direction you want the
   filter to turn (counterclockwise), the wrench
   tightens on the filter and turns it (Fig.4).
   Depending on the location of the filter, you
   may have to loosen it from underneath the car
   or you may have to stand up and lean over the
   engine. You should have a pan under the filter, because as you loosen it, oil will start
   to drip out. After removing the filter, turn
   it upside down in the drain pan to empty out
   the old oil. The filter will be filled with
   oil when you take it off the engine, so watch
   that you don't dump it out on the floor or on
   yourself. Another method of removing an oil
   filter is to use a large pair of channel lock
   pliers. The long handles provide greater
   leverage to turn the filter than does an oil

filter wrench, though sometimes the filter is located in such a position that it is hard to get channel locks on it. A third method of getting a stubborn filter loose is to push a long screwdriver through the filter (punching holes in it) and use the screwdriver as a lever to turn the filter with.

b. To remove the cannister type of filter, loosen the bolt at the bottom of the can with a wrench or socket and ratchet. When the bolt is all the way unscrewed, both the bolt and cannister will come off at the same time. The replaceable filter is inside the cannister. Clean the inside of the cannister in solvent before putting the new filter in it.

c. When you remove the old filter, regular or cannister, make sure that the rubber seal on the filter came off with it. On regular filters there is a round rubber ring on the end of the filter that screws into the engine. On cannister type filters, there will be a rubber ring where the can fits into the engine - these seals commonly stay on the engine, so be sure to check for it. You will get a new seal with the new filter.

5. After all the oil is drained out, replace the oil drain plug and tighten it good and tight (don't put all your weight to bear on it, just as tight as you can get using your arm). If the plug doesn't have a copper washer, it might be a good idea to get one, as it helps prevent oil from leaking out the drain hole. You should be able to get one at a parts store.

6. Installing the new filter

a. Regular filter - Rub a little fresh oil on the rubber seal on the new filter and then screw it on to the engine by hand. It should screw on fairly easy, though sometimes they are hard to get started. Once the filter contacts the engine, tighten it 3/4 of a turn more (these directions are usually on the filter or on the box it came in). The rubber seal will tighten the filter on to the engine- if you tighten the filter too much yourself, then you'll have a hard time getting it off the next time you change the filter.

b. Cannister type filter - Fit the new seal up into the groove where the cannister fits into. On some Chevy's there's a plate you have to take off to get to the rubber seal. Place the new filter into the cannister, put the bolt up through the bottom of the cannister, and put it up into place on the engine. Start screwing the bolt into the engine by hand and tighten it securely with a wrench or socket and ratchet.

7. Remove the oil filter cap (usually located somewhere on the valve cover, though some cars have a separate filler tube. The cap will be large and will either screw on or pull on and off). Add the right amount of oil to the engine, pouring it slowly to make sure the oil has a chance to drain down into the engine. Replace the filler cap.

8. Start the engine and let it run until the oil light goes off or until the oil pressure gauge is reading the right amount of pressure. Shut the engine off and then check the oil level at the dipstick. Add more oil if it reads low. Check around the oil plug and oil filter for leaks.

If the oil light doesn't go off in a matter of 30 seconds or so, shut the engine off and see if you have any bad leaks. Sometimes, for instance, if the old filter seal is left on the engine and you don't know it and put the new filter on, you will have a terrific leak - like the oil will probably pour out all over the floor. Very embarrassing. However, it happens to everyone at least once (men included), so don't let it bother you too much.

You should be careful not to put oil into your engine beyond the amount specified, as excessive oil causes a strain on the oil seals in the engine and will make them wear faster.

Transmission Fluid Gun
Fig. 5

STANDARD TRANSMISSION AND DIFFERENTIAL

I am going to describe how to do a fluid change for just the standard transmission, as the steps involved in doing a fluid change for either the standard transmission or the differential are basically the same.

68

A. Tools Needed

1. Wrench to remove drain and filler plugs

This will probably be either a square-headed plug, in which case use a crescent wrench, (there are also 8-point sockets which are made for square-headed bolts. They come in different sizes and in 1/2" and 3/8" drive); or an indented square plug, in which case use a 1/2" drive ratchet, fitting the drive part into the plug.

2. Transmission Fluid Gun (Fig.5)

3. Can Opener - to remove top of oil cans

B. Supplies/Parts Needed

1. Cans of lubricant

2. Pan to drain fluid into

3. Plenty of rags for messes

C. Information Needed

Type, weight and amount of lubricant needed (most transmissions and differentials use 90 wt. gear lube, but you should check what is specified for your car).

D. Steps

1. Engine should be warm. Locate both the filler plug (the same plug that you check the fluid level at) and the drain plug. The drain plug will be located somewhere on the bottom of the transmission case and will probably be the same type of plug that the filler-check plug is. Remove both the filler and drain plugs using the tools listed in <u>Tools Needed</u> and the methods listed under removing the engine oil drain plug.

2. Allow the lubricant to drain out for about 10 minutes and then replace the drain plug, tightening it securely.

3. To fill the transmission, you will need a filler gun. (You can usually get one at discount department stores in the auto section.) Make sure the handle of the gun is pushed all the way in. Insert the hose of the gun into the can of lubricant; pull out on the handle until it is all the way out - this will suck the lubricant up into the gun. Remove the hose from the lubricant (leaving the handle of the gun pulled all the way out) and insert the hose

into the filler hole on the transmission. Push on
the handle until it is all the way into the gun -
this will force the fluid out of the gun and into
the transmission. Repeat this process until fluid
starts to run out of the filler hole. The gun will
hold only about 1/2 pint or so of lubricant at a
time, so it might take quite a few loads to fill the
transmission.

4. Allow all the excess fluid to drain out of the
filler hole and then replace the plug and tighten
it securely.

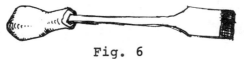

Fig. 6

AUTOMATIC TRANSMISSION FLUID

A. Tools Needed

1. Wrench or Socket & Ratchet to remove drain plug

2. Can Opener

3. Metal Funnel with flexible hose attached to it
   (See Fig. 2, Part II, Chapter 1)

For removing pan:

4. Socket, Ratchet and Extension (3/8" drive will
   work best) to remove pan bolts

5. Gasket scraper (Fig. 6)

A gasket scraper is a tool that looks like a putty
knife (actually a putty knife will work pretty well
for a gasket scraper) that is used to scrape off
pieces of gasket that stick to engine or parts
surfaces.

B. Supplies/Parts Needed

1. Cans of automatic transmission fluid

2. Pan gasket and gasket sealer, and possibly
   screens if you remove the pan - get at parts
   store

3. Pan to drain fluid into

4. Plenty of rags

C. Information Needed

Type and amount of automatic transmission fluid

D. Steps

Some automatic transmissions will have a drain plug located in the pan and some won't. Whether the transmission has a drain plug or not, you probably should remove the pan at least one of the times you change the transmission fluid, in order to clean or replace, if needed, the filter screens. If there is no plug on the pan, then the pan would have to be removed every time the fluid is changed. Drain the fluid with the engine warm, though transmission fluid gets extremely hot, so be careful not to scald your hand.

1. Jack up the front of the car and put it on jack stands.

2. Remove the drain plug if there is one and allow the fluid to drain out. The plug will be located in the pan (the pan usually looks something like a cake pan and is located behind the engine pan under the transmission). If there is no drain plug, then loosen all of the pan bolts (small headed bolts around perimeter of pan) and allow the fluid to leak out. Once most of the fluid has leaked out, remove the rest of the pan bolts, and take down the pan. Sometimes the pan is stuck on to the engine because of the gasket - knocking the pan on its side, or wherever you can get to it, with a rubber mallet should help to loosen the gasket and allow the pan to be removed. If that doesn't work, you can pry a little on the pan by inserting a thin blade screwdriver between the edge of the pan and the transmission. Be careful when you do this, however, not to bend the edge of the pan.

engine← →transmission

Torque Converter
of automatic transmission

located between
engine and transmission

Fig. 7

3. If you can find the drain plug for it, then the torque converter (the large round doughnut-looking object in front of the transmission next to the engine--Fig. 7) should also be drained. A manual for your car should help you locate the drain plug. If not, remove the screens underneath the torque converter, put the car in neutral, and turn the converter with a long pry bar or whatever will work. Somewhere on the converter there should be a small squarehead drain plug. If you don't find it I wouldn't worry about it too much - draining the converter makes the transmission fluid change more thorough, but it isn't absolutely necessary.

4. After removing the pan, look up into the transmission (what you are looking at is known as the valve body). There should be one or more screens - small or large. Remove these screens (they are usually attached by small screws or bolts). They can be cleaned with solvent and blowing compressed air through them. However, if they are ripped or very dirty and clogged up, then they should be replaced. Transmission repair shops sometimes have old screens in good condition that they'll probably sell pretty cheap.

5. Using a gasket scraper or putty knife, scrape off any remaining bits of pan gasket from the transmission surface. This surface has to be very clean or the new gasket will leak. Be very careful not to get any dirt or gasket bits into the valve body, as an automatic transmission will not work with even the slightest amount of dirt in it.

6. Scrape off the remaining gasket from the pan. Clean the pan thoroughly in solvent.

7. Put the new gasket on the pan. First make sure that the gasket fits the pan, and that all the holes line up. If the gasket is a little bit too small, soak it in water for a few minutes and it will expand enough to fit the pan. Put gasket sealer (directions for its use are on the sealer can) on one side of the gasket, and on the pan. Wait a few minutes until the sealer becomes tacky, and then stick the gasket on to the pan, lining up the bolt holes.

8. Put the screens back in the valve body, making sure the screws holding them are tight.

9. Put the pan up into place on the transmission and start all of the pan bolts - don't tighten any of them down until they are all started because you might need to shift the position of the pan slightly to get them all started.

10. Tighten all the pan bolts down, switching from one side of the pan to the other every other bolt. Don't put too much weight on tightening the bolts, as they will strip out if turned too tightly.

11. Replace the drain plug if there is one and tighten securely.

12. Filling the transmission:

The automatic transmission is filled through the hole where the automatic transmission dipstick is (near the back of the engine). Remove the dipstick. Put about three quarts of fluid down the hole. To do this, you will need to use a funnel with a hose that you can put in the hole (Fig. 2, Chapt. 1) unless dipstick is located in such a position that you can pour fluid into the hole directly from the fluid can.

Start the engine and pour the remaining number of required quarts down the dipstick hole. Warning: The number of quarts of fluid specified for your transmission might include filling the torque converter, so if you didn't drain the converter, put 2 or 3 quarts less than the number specified and then check the fluid level before adding any more.

13. Let the engine warm up and check the fluid level on the dipstick. Add more if needed.

14. Check for leaks around the transmission pan or drain plug.

Chapter 3

A   LUBE   JOB

Basically, what a lube job at a service station
refers to is checking all of the fluid levels
(engine, transmission, rear end, radiator, battery,
brake master cylinder) and topping them up if necessary; greasing the front end parts; and if you're
lucky you might get a few extras thrown in like
oiling the door hinges. I already went over
checking fluid levels in Chapter 1 of this section,
and it is up to you if you want to oil the door
hinges on your car (not a bad idea), so in this
chapter I am going to just explain how to grease
the front end of your car. Greasing the car refers
to pushing grease into the grease fittings - located
mainly on the front end parts, but possibly in other
locations.

A. Tools Needed

Grease gun, preferably with a rubber nozzle on it
instead of a metal one so you can twist the nozzle
around to get into tight places (Fig.1).

B. Supplies/Parts Needed

1. Grease for the grease gun - it comes in tubes
   designed for the guns (Fig.1).

2. Rags

Tube of Grease

Grease Gun

Fig. 1

C. Information Needed

Though not absolutely necessary, it would be very
helpful to you if you can find a diagram showing
the greasing points on your car. Service and tune
up manuals sometimes have this information. If you
can't find it, however, don't worry about it, because you should be able to find the greasing points
just by looking at the front end parts (more on
that under Steps).

D. Steps

1. Loading the grease gun - When you buy a grease
gun there should be directions on how to load it.
It isn't very hard once you get the hang of it.
Grease guns differ, but basically here is how you
load one:

    a. Pull back the oval handle at the end of the
       gun until it is all the way out, notching it
       in the hole where the handle comes out. This
       will hold the handle in place.

    b. Unscrew the end of the gun with the nozzle on
       it.

    c. Remove the empty cardboard grease cartridge.

    d. Remove the end marked on the new cartridge,
       and put the cartridge in the tube with the
       open end towards the nozzle.

    e. Screw the end of the gun back on.

    f. Release the handle by moving it out of the
       notch and push it all the way in (or as far
       as it will go). This will compress the
       grease.

    g. Pump the lever on the side of the gun until
       grease starts coming out of the nozzle. Some-
       times it is recommended that you loosen the
       end of the gun slightly and pump the lever a

bit to push the excess air out. Then tighten
the end back up and continue pumping until
grease comes out of the nozzle.

2. Locate all the grease fittings (also called
grease zerks) on your car (Fig.2). To locate the
fittings, crawl underneath the front of the car (it

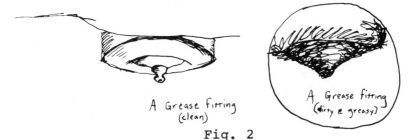

A Grease Fitting
(clean)

A Grease fitting
(dirty & greasy)

Fig. 2

will probably be helpful to have the front of the
car jacked up, although it may not be absolutely
necessary - depends on how high your car is off the
ground). The first place to look for grease fittings would be on the inside of each wheel - there
should be an <u>upper</u> and <u>lower ball joint</u>, which sort
of look like squished rubber balls. There will be
a grease fitting at each of these ball joints (Fig.
3). A second place to look for grease fittings is
the steering linkage that connects the two front
wheels - this is a series of rods underneath and to
the front of the engine. Some of the joints·where
these rods connect will have grease fittings (Fig. 3).

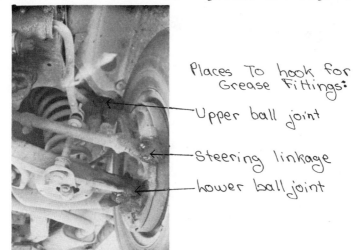

Places To hook for
Grease Fittings:

Upper ball joint

Steering linkage

Lower ball joint

Fig. 3
One of the best ways to find grease fittings - both
on ball joints and on steering linkage - is to look
for places on the linkage and around the wheels
that are covered with old dirt and grease. You will

almost always find a grease fitting there. Usually you will have to wipe away all the old grease and dirt to see the fitting. One word of caution - don't mistake the brake bleeder screw (located next to the brake line which will be going into the back of the wheel) for a grease fitting. Many of them are about the same size as a grease fitting and sort of look the same. However, it shouldn't have any grease around it whatsoever.

If you can't find any grease fittings on the front end parts on your car (there should be anywhere from 4 to 12, though 6 to 8 fittings is probably the most common amount) you might have what are known as sealed fittings, meaning the fittings are permanently filled with grease and you don't add grease to them. If this is the case, then the joints of the linkage should be clean and lacking in any old grease or dirt deposits.

Some cars have grease fittings at other locations. The most common place to have grease fittings besides the front end would be the universal joints along the drive shaft (possibly only the front or the rear will have fittings or they may both have fittings) (Fig. 4), and, if your car has leaf springs, where the springs are attached to the body of the car. (See Fig. 21, Part I, Chapter 2)

Grease Fitting on universal joint

Fig. 4

3. Once you've located all of the grease fittings, wipe them clean with a rag. Put the end of the grease gun nozzle on the fitting. You will have to have the nozzle in a straight line from the fitting. If it is at an angle, the nozzle won't go on the fitting. Apply a little pressure to push the nozzle on the fitting, and usually it will make a "click" sound when the nozzle is in place. Once the nozzle is in place, you don't usually have to hold it on the fitting; it will stay there by itself until you pull it off. Some grease guns are made so you have to hold the nozzle on to the fitting. When getting

a grease gun, avoid getting that kind as it is hard to hold the nozzle and pump at the same time.

4. Move the lever away from the gun and then push it towards the gun - this will pump grease into the fitting (Fig. 5). Look to see that the grease is not coming out around the fitting, but rather is going into the joint - the rubber cup will start to bulge. If the grease isn't going into the joint, try and wiggle the nozzle around to get a better fit. Sometimes you will be able to get some grease into the joint, while the rest of it goes out around the fitting. If you can't get <u>any</u> grease into the joint no matter what you do, then you probably should replace the fitting (see Step 5).

Pump grease into the joint until it starts oozing out around the top of the joint. Usually about three pumps will be enough. If you are greasing a u-joint that has grease fittings, about one pump should be enough. Wipe off the excess grease.

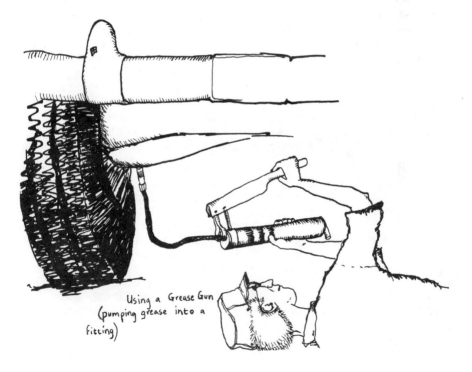

Using a Grease Gun
(pumping grease into a fitting)

Fig. 5

5. TO REMOVE A FITTING

The base of the fitting will be hexagon shaped so you can fit a small size open end wrench on it. A box end wrench would be better, but it may not go over the top of the fitting. The fittings unscrew out of the joint, and then a replacement fitting can be screwed into the joint. Sometimes the old fittings are just clogged, and if you have access to compressed air then you can blow air through the fitting once it is out and that will unclog it. However, if the fitting still won't accept grease, then it should be replaced. Take the old fitting with you to the parts store when you go to get the new one, as there are a lot of different fittings and they aren't always categorized by the type of car.

Sometimes the fittings are sort of rusted and very hard to get off, and being so small, they break off quite easily. If the fitting won't turn with a normal amount of force, I wouldn't put your whole weight behind it, because it will probably break off for sure. Once it has broken off, you won't be able to grease the joint, and about the only thing you can do to replace the fitting is to replace the joint it is in, a job you don't want to tackle until the joint is worn enough that it becomes necessary (see Part II, Chapter 8, checking the front end). Of course, you are in the same place if the fitting doesn't accept grease, but at least as long as the fitting is there, there is hope that you might get it to accept grease.

Not getting grease into the joints on a regular basis will make them wear faster, but it isn't the immediate necessity that it is, say, if there is no oil getting to the engine. There will be grease in the joint - the grease it was originally packed in and the grease added to the joint until the fitting quit working. Over a period of time, however, the grease will break down and not lubricate the joint as well. If the grease isn't replenished, then the joint will begin to wear. Eventually front end joints will have to be replaced even if greased regularly.

Chapter 4

REPACKING FRONT
WHEEL BEARINGS

GENERAL EXPLANATION: The wheels of a car turn on
spindles. The wheel bearings allow the wheels to
spin freely on the spindles. The rear bearings are
part of the drive axles and are sealed bearings,
meaning they do not require any lubrication or repacking. The front wheel bearings should be cleaned
periodically and packed with special wheel bearing
grease. The center of each wheel is the hub - the
part that goes over the spindle (Fig.1). The
bearings are located inside the hub. There are two
sets of bearings for each hub: an inner bearing,
the larger of the two bearings; and an outer bearing. There is also an oil seal on the end of the
hub next to the inner bearing that keeps the bearing grease sealed in the hub, not allowing it to
leak out into the brake shoes. What you do when you
repack the bearings is to remove the wheels, take
the bearings out of the hub, clean them, repack
them with grease, and put the bearings back in the
hub with a new oil seal. The bearings are called
roller bearings, because they are made up of a
whole lot of tiny metal rollers held together by
two rings. Older (pre 60's) cars have ball bearings - these bearings are made up of small metal
balls instead of rollers.

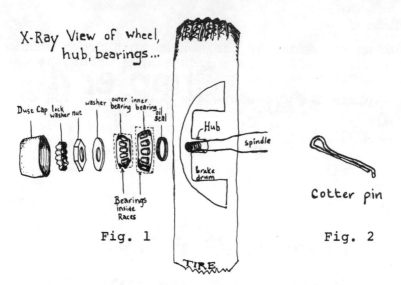

X-Ray View of wheel, hub, bearings...

Dust Cap · lock washer · nut · washer · outer bearing · inner bearing · oil seal · Hub · spindle · brake drum · Bearings inside Races

Fig. 1

Cotter pin

Fig. 2

TIRE

A. Tools Needed

1. 10" or 12" crescent wrench
2. Diagonal pliers
3. Channel lock pliers
4. Ball peen hammer
5. Short piece of broom handle (about 8" long)
6. Stiff wire brush
7. Jack and jack stands

B. Supplies/Parts Needed

1. Wheel bearing grease

Get grease made especially for wheel bearings as it has a high melting point, necessary because of the heat generated by the brake drums.

2. Cleaning solvent
3. Plenty of clean rags
4. 2 cotter pins (size large enough for wheel bearing nuts); you can usually get these at most hardware stores (Fig.2)
5. 2 front wheel oil seals - get at auto parts store

C. Information Needed

Specifications - none.

D. Steps

1. Jack up the front of the car so both front wheels are off the ground. Place jack stands under the car and let the car down on to the stands.

(I'll explain the procedure for one wheel. You do the same thing for both wheels. You can do the procedure for both wheels at the same time or do the complete procedure on one wheel and then do the same procedure for the other wheel, in which case you would only have to jack one wheel up at a time. It doesn't matter which way you do it. The only thing to remember is that if you do both wheels at the same time, be sure and keep the bearings straight so you know which bearings came from which wheel.)

2. The tire is attached to the brake drum by the lug nuts. The brake drum and tire together make up the wheel. The center of the drum is the hub of the wheel. The wheel is held on to the spindle by means of a spindle nut, located under the dust cap. Remove the hub cap (as if you were changing a flat tire). In the center of the wheel there is a round cup - this is called the dust cap. Occasionally, some cars are missing the dust cap - you should replace it if your car doesn't have one because they prevent dirt and dust from getting into the bearings.

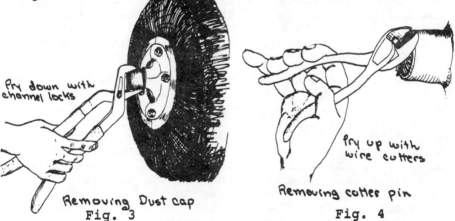

Pry down with channel locks

Removing Dust cap
Fig. 3

Pry up with wire cutters

Removing cotter pin
Fig. 4

Remove the dust cap. The best way I have found to do this is to use a pair of channel lock pliers, adjusted to their widest notch, and grab the top and bottom of the cap with the pliers and pry up or down, whichever seems to work best (Fig.3). If you can't get the cap to come all the way off by using the pliers, you should be able to move it enough to get a screwdriver in where the cap comes out and use

the screwdriver to pry it out. If these methods
don't work, there is a tool known as a dust cap
puller which will almost always remove a dust cap.
Maybe you could borrow one from a gas station or
friendly garage.

3. After taking off the dust cap, there will be a
large nut - the spindle nut - with a cotter pin
going through it. Remove the cotter pin by using
a pair of wire cutters: straighten out the ends of
the pin that are bent, grab the other end of the
cotter pin as close to the nut as possible, and
then pry with the wire cutters up against the nut,
bending the cotter pin as you pull it out (Fig.4).
If you end up breaking off both ends of the pin so
you can't grab hold of it with the wire cutters,
then use a thin punch and a hammer and tap the
remainder of the pin out through the hole.

4.Some spindle nuts have a large metal piece that
fits over them - remove it (it will come right off).
Then remove the nut using a crescent wrench. The
nut shouldn't be hard to loosen.

5. Grab hold of either side of the tire and pull
the wheel toward you a bit or rock it back and
forth (don't take the wheel all the way off). This
movement should push out the flat washer and the
outer bearings that are back in the hub on the
spindle. If the wheel won't move at all, it means
that the brake shoes are out against the drum
holding the wheel on and the adjustment on the
shoes will have to be backed off to allow them to
come away from the drum. (See Part II, Chapter 7,
adjusting brakes.)

6. Take the flat washer and outer bearing off the
spindle. Put the spindle nut back on and turn it
a few times. Grab the wheel again and jerk it
hard towards you, pulling the wheel all the way off
the spindle (if it won't come off, then it's the
brake shoe problem - see brake adjustment). If you
are lucky, the inner bearing (a bearing just like
the outer bearing though larger) and the oil seal
(a flat rubber and metal ring combination) will
come out of the hub and be left hanging on the
spindle. Remove the nut and take them off.

7. A lot of times just the bearing will come out of
the hub, or sometimes neither the bearing or seal
will come out. If this happens, you will need to
remove the seal from the hub. I have found two
methods for doing this:

    a. Place the wheel flat on the floor so you are
       looking at the outer side of the wheel (the

side where the lug nuts go). Stick a short
piece of broom handle down through the hub
until it catches the edge of the seal (you
might want to turn the wheel over and look at
the seal - it is the round ring flush with
the end of the hub - so you know where the
edge is). Tap on the end of the broom stick
with a hammer pushing the seal out of the
hub (Fig.5). Be careful not to hammer on the
bearing, because you might damage it. Also,
don't use a metal punch instead of the wood
stick, because you might accidentally pound
on the bearing and that will probably ruin it
for sure. Once the seal is out the bearing
will probably fall out, or else can easily be
lifted out of the hub.

b. If the broom stick method fails, another way
to get the seal out is to turn the wheel over
so you are looking at the seal. Wedge an old
screwdriver in between the edge of the seal
and the hub. Tap on the screwdriver until
you dent the seal in (Fig.6). You can then
usually pry the seal out with a screwdriver.
Just be careful not to hammer on the bearing.
You are going to replace the seal, so it
doesn't matter how much you damage it getting
it out; the only thing to worry about is the
bearing, as you don't want to replace the
bearing unless absolutely necessary - they
are pretty expensive.

Note: Now that you have the wheel off, it would be
a good time to check the brake shoes and
wheel cylinder (see Part II, Chapter 7,
checking brakes).

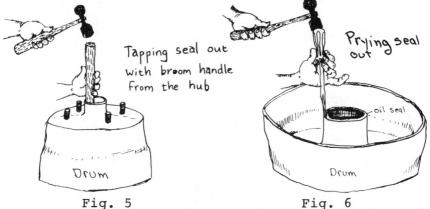

Tapping seal out
with broom handle
from the hub

Prying seal
out

oil seal

Drum

Drum

Fig. 5   Fig. 6

8. Clean both bearings and the flat washer in clean
solvent. Get them as clean as you possibly can,
removing all the old grease. Soaking them helps;

also using a stiff wire brush to clean them. Dry them thoroughly. Compressed air is the best thing to use, but if you don't have access to an air compressor (not many of us do, I know) then dry the bearings as best you can with clean lint-free rags or paper towels. It is very important not to get any dirt, dust, lint, etc. into the bearings, because it will make them wear extremely fast.

9. Carefully examine both of the bearings, looking for pits (tiny pin holes), scores (deep scratches), and the like (Fig.7). Spin them and make sure that they spin freely in both directions. If for some reason you think the bearing is bad (you might want to take it to an auto machine shop to have checked), then replace it. They don't need to be replaced with normal wear but if they get dirt in them, or have been running with a very small amount of grease, then they might have been damaged.

10. Wipe out the inside of the hub with clean rags. Inspect the place in the hub where the bearings sit (known as the bearing race - it will be a shiny band of metal near both ends of the hub). Look for the same sort of damage as the bearings - pits, scores, etc. (Fig.8). The bearings and race come as a unit, so if either one is damaged then you have to replace both of them. You do not have to replace both bearings in the hub, however, if only one of them is damaged. If you are going to replace one of the bearings, then the race should be removed - I'm not real sure how to get them out and I know they can be a pain to do, so you might want to take the wheel to an auto machine shop and have them remove it.

Rollers
are pitted & scratched
Worn Roller
Bearing
Fig. 7

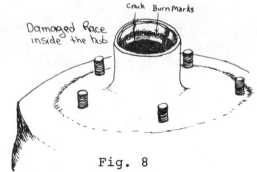

Damaged Race
inside the hub

Crack Burn Marks

Fig. 8

11. Repack the wheel bearings with fresh grease. To do this, place a glob of grease (about a tablespoon) on the center of your palm. Holding the bearing in your other hand, press the rollers hard into the grease making the grease ooze out the top and bottom of the bearing in between the rings that

hold the rollers together. Do this all the way
around the bearing until it is filled with grease
(Fig.9). Check the top and bottom to make sure
there aren't any little spaces between the rings
with no grease and that the grease is spread
throughout the bearing. Smear a coat of grease
around the outside of the bearing. Repack each
bearing and then place them on a clean rag and
cover them to keep dirt out.

Packing a
Bearing with
grease.

Bearing Packed
with grease

Fig. 9

12. Wipe off the spindle and smear some grease on
it. Coat the inside of the hub with grease and
smear grease on the races.

13. Lay the wheel flat on the floor, so the inner
side of the wheel is facing you. Put the large
inner bearing in its race. The bearing goes in
with the smaller end pointing towards the middle of
the hub. Place the new oil seal in the hub so that
the flat part of the seal is facing out towards
you. Gently tap the seal all around with a
rubber hammer. The seal needs to be started
straight or it won't go in. If one side gets
cocked (tilted sideways) pop the seal out with a
screwdriver (be careful not to damage the rubber
part) and try again. Another method to install the
seal is to place the seal in the hub and then put a
block of wood over it and tap on the block with a
hammer. This helps to exert an even pressure all
around the seal and keep it from getting cocked
while going in. Tap the seal in until it is flush
with the edge of the hub.

14. Turn the wheel over and check and see where the
race is for the outer bearing, so you have an idea
how far back in the hub the bearing will need to
go. Put the wheel back on the spindle. Sometimes
this is sort of a hassle to do, because you need to
see the spindle to line the hub up with it. If you
can get a friend to look and see where the wheel
goes while you hold the wheel, that should help.

Push the wheel back as far as it will go on the spindle.

15. Place the outer bearing on the spindle with the smaller end of the bearing pointing towards the middle of the hub. Push the bearing back into the hub until it goes into the race and the wheel spins freely on it.

16. Setting the bearing - When you have the bearing in the hub, put the flat washer on the spindle and then the spindle nut. Tighten the nut as tight as you can get it using the crescent wrench, turning the wheel as you tighten the nut. Then loosen the nut with the wrench and then tighten it <u>by hand</u> (this is so not to have too much pressure against the bearings which keep them from spinning freely). Spin the wheel to make sure it turns freely. There may be a slight drag or scraping noise from the brake shoes - that's okay.

17. Put a new cotter pin in the hole through the spindle and nut, and bend the ends of the cotter pin around the nut (Fig.10). You can loosen the nut slightly to line up with the cotter pin hole, though it should be fairly close if you set the bearings correctly.

<u>Don't forget the cotter pin</u> - it is essentially all that is keeping the wheel on the spindle, and having the wheel fall off while the car is zooming down the road could cause you problems.

18. Tap the dust cap back over the hub with a hammer. Try to start the cap straight and not cock it, and then it should go on fairly easily.

19. Replace the hub cap.

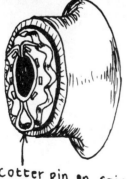

Cotter pin on spindle bent both ways

Fig. 10

Fig. 11

DISC BRAKES - If you have disc brakes on the front
wheels of your car instead of drum brakes, then the
procedure is somewhat different. You can take off
the tire and then get to the dust cap and the outer
bearings. To get to the inner bearings, however,
you have to remove the brake calipers and then the
discs, a fairly large job. Instead of doing that,
you can get an attachment for a grease gun that
allows you to squirt grease under pressure back
into the hub to the inner bearings (Fig.11). I
would do that instead of going through the hassle
of taking the brake caliper and disc off. The
outer bearings can be repacked using the method
described in this chapter. The parts will be pretty
much the same - dust cap, spindle nut, cotter pin,
washer and outer bearing.

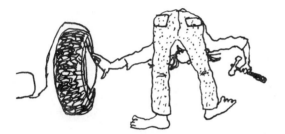

Chapter 5

WINTERIZING YOUR CAR

This chapter is called winterizing your car, but the jobs I am going to go over would be done on a car in any climate - it is just that if you live in a climate where there is a cold winter, then you should check all these things on your car sometime in the fall before it starts getting cold. You don't want to have a frozen engine or be caught somewhere in subzero weather replacing a broken fan belt. The jobs I am going to discuss are: 1)checking and replacing antifreeze in the radiator, including how to flush the cooling system; 2)cleaning the battery to get it ready for the winter; 3)replacing fan belts; 4)checking and replacing heater and radiator hoses; 5)replacing the thermostat; 6)replacing wiper blades.

ANTIFREEZE AND THE COOLING SYSTEM

Antifreeze is put into the water of the cooling system to prevent it from freezing in the winter and from boiling in the summer. So even if you live in a climate that doesn't have below freezing temperatures, you will still need to put antifreeze in your car to keep the water from boiling in hot

weather. Keeping the water from boiling or freezing
is extremely important - if the water in the engine
freezes it will probably cause the engine block to
crack, as water expands when frozen. This would,
of course, ruin your engine. If the water boils,
besides losing most of the water, it can cause the
engine to overheat and possibly damage the internal
parts.

Unless you have water leaks, you should only need
to check the amount of antifreeze in the water about
once a year - before winter in cold climates and
before summer in hot climates. You can buy cheap
antifreeze testers at discount stores that work
fairly well (Fig.1). Usually they only will work
when the coolant is either hot or cold, so be sure
to follow the instructions on them. Squeeze the
rubber ball on one end and insert the other end into
the coolant in the radiator. Slowly let out on the
rubber ball, sucking fluid up into the tester.
Inside the tester there are 4 or 5 little balls -
the number of balls that float tell you how much
antifreeze there is in the coolant. There should
be enough antifreeze to register at least 10 degrees
below the coldest it normally gets in your area -
if it gets down to 20 degrees or more below zero,
then the antifreeze should test to at least 30
degrees below zero. I don't think there are testers
to measure high temperatures, or at what point the
coolant will boil. If you live in that hot of a
climate, then I would suggest going by the instructions on the back of the antifreeze containers as
to how much antifreeze is necessary for your car.

If you have just added either antifreeze or water
to the radiator, then run the engine a while before
testing the coolant so the freshly added liquid
will have a chance to mix in with the rest of the
coolant - otherwise, you will be testing either
straight antifreeze or straight water.

If the coolant doesn't test to the level that it
should, then antifreeze should be added to the
radiator. If the coolant is dirty and rusty looking, then you might want to flush out the cooling
system and add fresh water and antifreeze - this
would not need to be done every year.

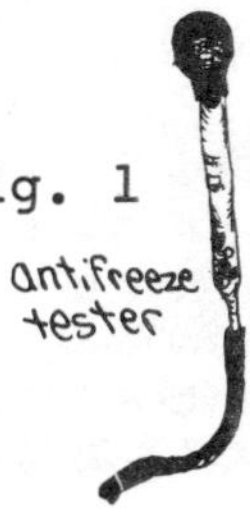

Fig. 1

antifreeze
tester

A. Tools Needed

1. Channel lock pliers

2. Medium standard screwdriver

B. Supplies/Parts Needed

1. Enough antifreeze to lower coolant level to correct reading

2. Water and hose (if flushing cooling system)

3. Flushing compound

4. Clean pan to drain coolant into

C. Information Needed

Number of gallons of water your cooling system holds.

D. Steps

ADDING ANTIFREEZE

1. If you just want to add enough antifreeze to lower the coolant freezing point to the right level, then you won't need to drain the whole radiator and cooling system. First determine how much antifreeze you will need to add. There are charts on the back of antifreeze containers that have this information according to the size of your cooling system. These charts, however, are usually based on filling the entire cooling system instead of just adding enough antifreeze to keep your car from freezing in the winter - the anti- freeze makers, of course, would like you to drain all your coolant out every year. So if you can't figure out from what the chart says about how much antifreeze you need, you could add 1 quart for every 10 degrees that you want the antifreeze level to drop. Try that and then check the coolant to see if you are putting enough antifreeze in. It certainly won't hurt to put in too much antifreeze, except in your pocketbook, but it will really hurt if you don't have enough.

2. Drain the radiator of about the amount of anti- freeze that you are going to add. (If you are planning to flush out the cooling system, then drain the entire radiator.) To drain the radiator, there should be a 'petcock' located at the bottom of the radiator or on the side near the bottom (Fig.2). The petcock (don't ask me where the name comes from) works just like a little water faucet. You turn it counterclockwise and it lets out water, you turn it clockwise and it shuts off the water. Remove the radiator cap before turning the petcock; this will allow the water to run out of the petcock

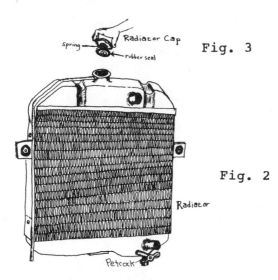

Fig. 3

Fig. 2

with more pressure. If the petcock won't turn by hand, then a pair of channel lock pliers will usually help to loosen it. Be careful, however, not to twist it off. Once the petcock is loosened, you don't have to take it all the way out, just turn it until there is a steady stream of water coming out. Drain what looks like the amount of coolant you need to get out of the radiator (better to drain too much than not enough) into a clean pan, and then close the petcock.

3. If you can't get the petcock loose, or if your radiator doesn't appear to have one (some don't), then the radiator can be drained by removing the bottom radiator hose at the radiator. The disadvantage of doing this is that you have no choice but to drain the entire radiator, as the coolant will come out in a woosh. This method drains the coolant a lot faster than the petcock, however. To remove the bottom hose, unscrew the hose clamp until the clamp is loose on the hose. Pull on the hose, twisting it back and forth, until you work it off the radiator flange (the part of the radiator that the hose fits on to). Sometimes hoses can be a real hassle to get off. If it's stuck, you can start the hose moving by prying on the edge of it with a screwdriver. Be careful when removing it not to twist it back and forth too much, as you can crack the radiator flange.

4. Now would be a good time to check out the radiator hoses - see hose section. Also, check the radiator cap. There should be some sort of rubber seal on the inside of it (Fig.3). If the seal is cracked or swollen looking, then the cap should be

92

replaced, as water will leak out around the seal unless it is in good shape. When you replace the radiator cap, make sure you get one that is the right pressure - it is usually marked on the old cap. If not, a parts store, or the charts at the auto department in discount stores, can tell you what pressure cap your car needs. All coolant systems operate under a certain amount of pressure as determined by the radiator cap, so it is important to get the right cap.

5. After closing the petcock or putting the bottom radiator hose back on, add the correct amount of antifreeze to the top of the radiator. If after adding antifreeze the coolant level doesn't come up above the radiator veins, then add the drained off coolant until it does. Replace the radiator cap, and then start the engine. Look for leaks around the bottom hose or petcock. If none, then drive the car around a bit, and check the antifreeze level again.

FLUSHING THE COOLING SYSTEM

1. Drain the radiator and leave the petcock open (see above). You don't have to drain the old coolant into a clean pan as you won't be reusing it.

2. Drain the engine block. There is a petcock located on the engine block like the one on the radiator. Six cylinder engines have one that is usually located on the side of the engine opposite the carburetor. V-8 engines have two petcocks, one located on each side of the engine near the back. Sometimes these are hard to find, so you might have to hunt around for them. The petcocks can be very difficult to get loose, mainly because you can't get to them because of where they are located. If you can't get the petcocks on the engine loose, then an alternative is to get a special dummy radiator cap that allows you to attach a hose to it (sold in auto parts stores).

3. With the petcocks open, stick a hose into the top of the radiator. Run water through the cooling system until it starts coming out clear (don't run cold water through a hot engine - best to do this when the engine is cold). If you are unable to get the petcocks open, then use the dummy radiator cap. Attach a hose to it, remove the top radiator hose at the radiator, and run water through the engine until it comes out clear at the radiator hose. If you were unable to get the petcock open on the radiator and had to drain it through the lower

radiator hose, first flush out the radiator by running water into the top of the radiator and out
through the bottom hose. When the water starts
coming clear out of the bottom hose, then hook it
back up to the radiator and run water through the
entire system.

4. There are special coolant flushing compounds
made that help get rid of the rust in the cooling
system. Instructions for their use come with the
compounds.

5. Allow all the water to drain out and then tighten
the petcocks and/or reinstall hoses.

6. Add the right amount of antifreeze (this is where
the chart on the back of the container is helpful)
and then fill the radiator with water (so it is
above the veins).

7. Leave the radiator cap off. Start the engine
and slowly add water to the radiator as the level
drops (there will be air pockets in the engine and
as they disappear the engine will take in more
water). Fill the radiator until the water is 1 inch
from the top. Replace the cap and check the antifreeze after driving for a while.

HOSES AND THERMOSTAT

A. Hoses

There are two sets of hoses that need to be checked
before winter - the radiator hoses and the heater
hoses. (You might also have a lot of other hoses
on your car, especially if you have air conditioning. Emission control apparatus also contributes
a lot of hoses.) The radiator hoses are the two
large hoses connected to the radiator, one at the
top and one at the bottom. The heater hoses are
smaller hoses (usually about 1 inch outside diá-
meter) that circulate water to heat the passenger
compartment of your car (Fig.4). They are long
hoses that go into the firewall at some point.
Check all these hoses for cracks (especially around
the clamps), brittleness, and general signs of wear.
Replace any hoses that look to you like they might
start leaking in the course of the winter. Hoses
are fairly easy to replace - Just unscrew the clamps
and pull them off. Sometimes they are difficult to
get to, especially the heater hoses, which can make
them more of a hassle to replace. You don't need to

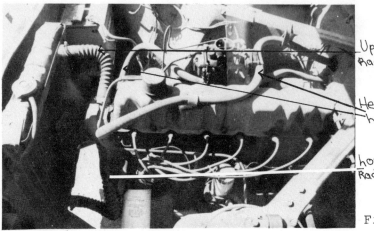

Upper Radiator Hose

Heater hoses

Lower Radiator hose

Fig. 4

drain the cooling system to replace any of the hoses except the bottom radiator hose. Some water will come out of the hoses, but I wouldn't worry about it. Just make sure to check the water level in the radiator when you are done replacing the hoses.

You might also have trouble getting the new hoses on. A can of silicone spray will help a whole lot - spray the inside of the hose and the part that it is supposed to fit over. This will help the hose to slide on easier. Actually any sort of lubricant should help, but silicone is especially good because it is made for lubricating rubber.

Replacement hoses can be bought at discount stores, some auto parts stores (though many of them only carry it in large quantities) and gas stations. To know what size you need, bring the old hose for comparison, matching the length and inside diameter of the hose. If the hose clamps are rusted and worn, they should also be replaced.

B. Thermostat

The purpose of the thermostat(Fig.5) is to restrict flow of water through the engine when the engine is cold, thus causing the engine to heat up faster. If your engine heats up very slowly (as determined by the heat guage or when the cold light goes off), or if the engine overheats, then you might have a faulty thermostat. There are also separate thermostats for summer and for winter, and some car manufacturers recommend that the thermo-stat be changed every summer and winter - you should check your owners or shop manual for your car about

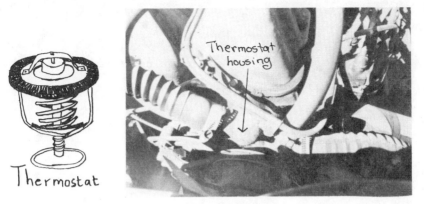

Thermostat

Fig. 5   Fig. 6

that. The thermostat is very easy to get to, especially if you are replacing hoses, draining the
radiator, etc.

The thermostat is located where the top radiator
hose goes into the engine (Fig.6). Remove the top
hose from where it goes into the engine, and then
remove the screws holding the thermostat housing
(the housing is what the radiator hose hooks on to).
Remove the thermostat. You can test a thermostat
to see if it is working by putting it in a pan of
cold water and heating the water up and seeing if
the thermostat opens up. If nothing happens with
the thermostat when the water is heated up to
boiling point, then you have a faulty thermostat.
You can get a new thermostat at a parts store - it
comes with a rubber gasket or seal of some sort.

Install the new rubber gasket around the thermostat
edge. Put the thermostat in its place in the
engine with the spring part down, and the arrow, if
it has one, facing the radiator (unless the thermostat comes with directions otherwise). Replace the
thermostat housing and tighten down the bolts.
Replace the upper radiator hose.

BATTERY CARE

To start a car in cold weather, you need maximum
power out of the battery. That's why it is a good
idea to clean the battery posts and cables and
replace frayed cables before winter comes. Also,
over a period of time corrosion will build up
around the battery posts and that should be cleaned
to prevent the stopping of electrical connection at
the battery.

A. CLEANING BATTERY.

1. Tools Needed

a. Wrench or pliers to loosen battery cable clamps

b. Battery clamp puller (Fig.7) or old screwdriver

c. Pocket knife

d. Wire cutters if need to replace clamps

2. Supplies/Parts Needed

a. Baking soda

b. Cup of water with brush

c. A lot of water to rinse battery

d. Grease (any kind - grease gun stuff, wheel bearing, etc.)

3. Information Needed

None

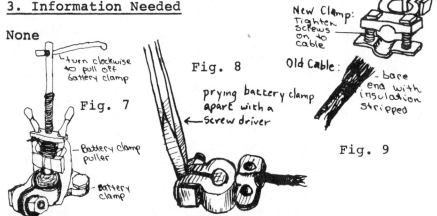

turn clockwise to pull off battery clamp

Fig. 7

Battery clamp puller

Battery clamp

Fig. 8

prying battery clamp apart with a
Screw driver

New Clamp:
Tighten Screws on to cable

Old Cable:
bare end with insulation stripped

Fig. 9

4. Steps

a. Disconnect battery cables, disconnecting the
negative cable first. To do this, loosen the clamp
with a wrench. Wiggle the clamp and see if it will
come off. If not, try prying the clamp apart with
an old screwdriver. If the ends of the clamp are
smashed close together you can try wedging the
screwdriver into where the ends come together by
hitting on the end of the screwdriver with a hammer
(Fig.8). If all that fails to remove the clamp,
you can get a battery clamp puller fairly cheap at
discount stores and use it to remove the clamps
(Fig.7). Directions on how to use the pullers
usually come with them. Actually, I haven't had
much success using clamp pullers, especially the

cheap ones, so I would try the screwdriver method or anything else you can think of first. The posts on a battery will break off, so keep that in mind when removing the clamps.

b. Check the condition of the cables and clamps. If the cable is frayed and worn, then it should be replaced. New cables (get at discount stores - bring your old cable to compare length) have clamps already on them. Just the clamp can also be re-placed. The main reason to replace a clamp is if you can't get it to tighten on the post - the clamp comes all the way together but still isn't tight. Clamps can be bought at any parts or auto depart-ment of discount stores. To replace a clamp, cut the old clamp off the cable right behind the clamp. Strip about one half inch of insulation off the cable. Insert the bare cable between the two metal pieces provided for it on the new clamp (Fig.9). Tighten the screws holding the two metal pieces together and the cable is all ready to go.

c. Clean the posts and clamps. Spread a little baking soda diluted in water over the top of the battery, around the posts and on the clamps. The baking soda neutralizes the battery acid and gets rid of the acid deposits on the battery and clamps. Let the soda fizzle for a little bit and then rinse clean the top of the battery and the clamps.

d. With a pocket knife, scrape all around the posts and inside the clamps, removing a thin layer of metal until the surfaces are shiny. Be careful not to touch the knife from one post on the battery to the other, as it will spark and ruin your knife blade (I ruined my favorite pocket knife doing that).

e. Put the cables back on the battery posts. Put the positive cable on first and then the ground or negative cable. If the negative cable is put on first, then the engine and car is grounded and if you accidentally make a metal to metal connection from the positive cable to the car somewhere, you will get a sparking action (more explanation about that under troubleshooting the electrical system). Make sure you get the right cable on the right post, as reversing the cables will probably burn out your alternator (very expensive to replace). If you get the cables confused, the ground or negative (-) battery cable is bolted somewhere to the engine or the body of the car. The positive (+) cable goes either to the starter motor or (if a Ford) to a little box on the fender. Tighten the clamps good and tight and smear the posts and clamps with grease. The grease will help prevent the buildup of acid deposits.

You can test the charge in the cells in your battery
with a tester similar to the antifreeze testers and
it can probably be purchased in the same place.
First, make sure that the water level of each cell
is correct. If you have to add more water, wait to
test the cells, as the water will need to mix with
the other fluid in the battery (drive the car
around for awhile). There is a battery cell for
each one of the holes in the top of the battery.
Test each cell with the tester(Fig. 10)--it works
in the same manner as the antifreeze tester. All
the cells should read charged. If they are all
down about the same amount (reading half charge,
for instance), then the battery needs recharging
and you should look for the reason for the discharge (see Part III, Chapter 1). If only one or
two cells read discharged, however, then you might
have a bad cell in the battery. The only thing you
can do about that is to replace the battery. However, before doing that (batteries are very expensive), I would see if you could borrow a hydrometer
(Fig.11), which is a much more accurate battery
tester, or go to a garage that you trust (if there
is such a place) and have them test the battery.
Getting an accurate reading with a hydrometer can
only be done with the battery fully charged, so if
you think your battery is bad and it is also run
down, then have it charged up first before testing
it.

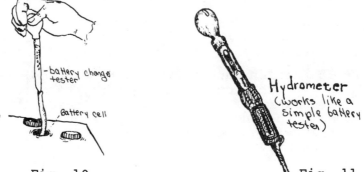

Fig. 10　　　　　　　　　　　　　　　Fig. 11

FAN BELTS

This section will deal with how to replace the
basic fan belt of the engine - the belt connecting
the crankshaft pulley, the fan, and the alternator/
generator. If your car has air conditioning, power
steering or an emission control air pump, then

there will be a belt for each of these devices, all
hooking up with the crankshaft pulley. I think if
you know how to replace the main fan belt, then you
probably will be able to figure out how to replace
the other belts, as they are all hooked up pretty
much the same way.

If your fan belt has cracks in it, or is all the
way to the end of the adjustment and still loose,
then it should be replaced. I will go over how to
replace it, which will also include how to adjust
the belt, if you aren't going to be replacing it.

A. Tools Needed

1. Wrench to fit nut or bolt on adjusting bracket,
   and also to fit the bolt or nuts where the generator or alternator is attached to the engine

2. Long pry bar of some sort

B. Supplies/Parts Needed

New fan belt - can be bought at discount stores or
auto parts store. It would help to take your old
belt along to compare length, though the new belt
should be a little bit smaller as the old belt will
have stretched some.

C. Information Needed

None

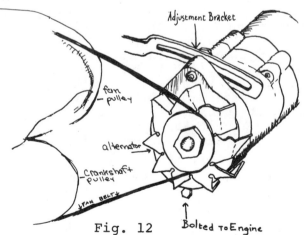

Fig. 12

D. Steps

1. The fan belt is replaced (or tightened) by moving
the alternator/generator back and forth along a
bracket (Fig.12). (From now on in this section I'll

just use the word alternator, though all of the steps will apply to both an alternator or generator) To loosen the fan belt and remove it, loosen the bolt where the alternator is attached to the bracket and push the alternator forward. The alternator is supposed to pivot on the bottom bolt(s) that attaches it to the engine, but sometimes (a lot of times) it doesn't. If you can't get the alternator to move after loosening the bolt at the bracket, then loosen the bolts at the bottom of the alternator that attach it to the engine. They don't have to be real loose, just loosening them a small amount should allow the alternator to pivot forward.

2. Push the alternator as far forward as the bracket will allow. If the alternator won't go all the way to the end of the slot in the bracket, then loosen the bolt that holds the bracket to the engine. This will allow the bracket to change position in relation to the alternator, which will usually allow the alternator to move all the way forward. Slide the fan belt off the alternator and crankshaft pulley and out around the fan.

3. Put the new fan belt on in the same way that you took the old one off. Since it is not all stretched out like the old fan belt, you may not be able to easily slip it over all three pulleys (alternator, crankshaft, fan). The easiest way I have found to get the belt on all three pulleys is to first put the belt on the crankshaft pulley and the alternator pulley and then try to work it onto the fan pulley. Turning the fan pulley by hand as you work the belt on to the pulley seems to help. If no matter what you do you can't get the belt on the fan pulley, then slip it onto the fan pulley as far as it will go on the side of the pulley in the direction the pulley turns when the engine is running. Tap the ignition key - the turning over of the engine will usually pull the belt on to the fan pulley (don't <u>start</u> the engine, just turn the key a little bit so the engine will turn over briefly).

4. Once the belt is on all three pulleys, then you need to adjust the belt tension and tighten down the alternator. A rule of thumb as to how tight the belt should be is that when you press down on the belt halfway between two of the pulleys, you should be able to depress it about 1/2 inch (Fig.13). It is important not to get the belt too tight, as it can cause the bearings in the alternator to wear very rapidly. It is also important not to get the belt too loose, as then the alternator pulley won't

turn continually, and thus won't be charging the electrical system. A symptom of a too loose belt is a run down battery.

The best way I know to tighten the fan belt is to insert a long metal pry bar of some sort between the alternator and the engine block. Wedge the bottom of the pry bar against the engine (make sure it isn't against any part that might bend or break) and pry the top of the bar out against the alternator, moving the alternator along the adjustment slot until the belt is at the right tension (Fig.14). It is real handy to have a friend around at this point to tighten up the bolt in the adjusting slot while you are holding the alternator in position with the pry bar. If you aren't so lucky, then you will have to hold the pry bar with one hand and tighten the bolt with the other hand. Once the bolt is tight, remove the pry bar and check the tension of the belt. If it's okay, then tighten the bottom bolt(s) of the alternator if you had to loosen them to move the alternator. After driving the car a few hundred miles, check the belt tension again. The belt might loosen up somewhat as its new-belt stiffness is worn out of it.

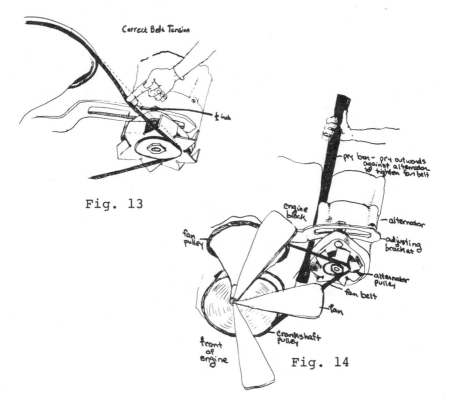

Correct Belt Tension

½ inch

Fig. 13

pry bar - pry outwards against alternator to tighten fan belt

engine block

alternator

fan pulley

adjusting bracket

alternator pulley

fan belt

fan

crankshaft pulley

front of engine

Fig. 14

WINDSHIELD WASHER AND WIPERS

If you live in a snowy winter place like Iowa, then
it is important to have windshield wipers and
washers that work (though none of the cars I've had
for the last 6 years have had washers that work)
and are in good condition. If one or the other
doesn't work, see Part III, Chapter 3 to find out
what is wrong.

About the only thing you need to do for the washers
for winter is to add antifreeze solvent to the water
in the washer tank so it doesn't freeze. Washer
solvent can be bought at discount stores and comes
either in concentrated form in which you have to
mix it with water or in already mixed, ready-to-use
form. If the water in the washer container does
freeze up before you have a chance to add solvent,
then remove the container and stick it in a bucket
of hot water to unthaw it. If the container has
an electrical motor attached to it, don't put the
motor in the water.

Replacing Wiper Blades (Fig. 15)

Different cars have different methods of replacing
wiper blades, but once you understand how to do it,
it isn't very difficult. I will explain briefly
how to replace Anco wiper blades as they are very
commonly used. Wiper blades should be replaced
anytime the rubber of the wiper is slit or torn.
Check the edges of the wiper especially for wear.

To replace the blades, first remove the whole wiper
from the arm on the car. Most wipers have a tab
where the blade connects to the arm. Push up on
this tab with a small screwdriver and pull the wiper
blade assembly off the arm. Sometimes the wiper
assembly might be difficult to get off and you may
have to twist the blade some back and forth to get
it off. Once the wiper assembly is off the car,
you can replace the wiper blade much easier (though
it can be done while the wiper is still on the car).

To remove the old blade, pull one end of the blade
out of the notches holding in at the end of the
wiper. Press the red button on one side or other
of the blade and remove that half of the metal part
from the rest of the wiper assembly. Now you should
be able to slide the rubber wiper blade all the way
out of the assembly. Installing a new blade is the
reverse of these steps.

Fig. 15

Steps to Remove a Wiper Blade
(Reverse Steps to Install new blade)

Step 1: Remove wiper blade assembly from wiper arm on car

Step 2: Press red button to release 1 of the metal brackets

Step 3: Pull metal bracket away from assembly and slide off wiper blade

Step 4: Slide wiper blade out of remaining bracket.

Chapter 6

HOW TO DO A TUNE UP

In this chapter I first want to explain what the ignition system is all about and what you are doing when you do a tune up. The rest of the chapter will be devoted to explaining how to do a tune up. For me, it really helps to have some sense about how things work, so when problems come up (as they frequently seem to do) I have some idea in what direction to go in solving the problem.

THEORY

The purpose of the car's ignition system is to deliver electrical current to the spark plugs, causing them to "fire". The firing of the plugs provides the spark to ignite the combustible fuel mixture in the combustion chamber. The purpose of the tune up is to make sure that the electrical current gets to the right spark plug at the right time and with the right amount of intensity. A spark plug "fires" because electrical current travels down through the plug, coming out on the electrode end, at which point there is a gap in the conductor of the electricity (the metal). The electrical current jumps across the gap causing an arcing or spark (Fig.1). This spark ignites the compressed fuel mixture in the combustion chamber.

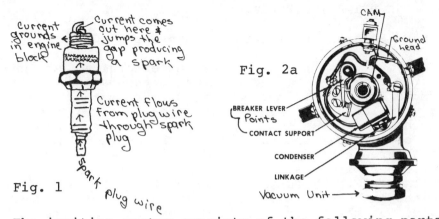

Fig. 2a

Fig. 1

The ignition system consists of the following parts: coil, distributor, spark plugs, primary and secondary wires. The parts of the distributor (the ones you need to be concerned with in doing a tune up) are: rotor, points, condensor, distributor cap and the vacuum advance unit (Fig.2).

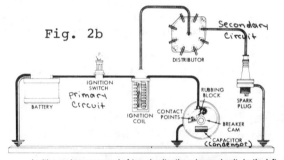

Fig. 2b

Ignition system composed of two circuits: the primary circuit, to the left, consists of battery, resistance wire, ignition switch, primary winding in ignition coil, distributor contact points, capacitor, and low voltage wiring connections; the secondary circuit, at the right, includes secondary winding in coil, distributor, spark plugs, and cables.

The ignition system is composed of two separate electrical circuits - the primary circuit and the secondary circuit. Primary circuit wires are small as they carry a relatively low voltage (about 100 volts). Secondary circuit wires are thick and heavily insulated as they carry up to 20,000 volts. In explaining how the ignition system works I am going to trace the flow of electrical current through these two circuits. I have included a diagram to show the flow, but it might also be helpful for you to trace the circuits on the ignition system on your own car. Remove the cap and rotor from the distributor (see how to under the How To Do A Tune Up section) and then you will be able to see all of the ignition parts.

A. THE PRIMARY CIRCUIT

Parts: Points, Condensor, Primary Wires, Coil

When you turn the ignition key on, electrical current starts flowing from the battery to the positive side of the coil (the sides of the coil are marked negative (-) and positive (+) like the battery; you may have to clean some of the grit off the top of the coil to see the markings). The current then goes through the primary windings of the coil (coils of copper wire inside the coil), causing a buildup voltage of the electrical current from the 12 volts of the battery to about 100 volts. The current then comes out the negative side of the coil and flows to the distributor. At the distributor the current flows to the points by means of a small wire that hooks up with the wire from the coil coming into the distributor. If the points are <u>closed</u>, then the current goes through the points and is grounded in the engine through the distributor (thus the current returns to the battery). This completes the primary circuit. If the points are <u>open</u>, the circuit is broken and the Secondary circuit takes over.

Set of Contact Points

Points Close   Points Open

Fig. 3

B. What Makes Points Open and Close

Contact points are the name for two pieces of metal that come apart and then come into contact with each other at a very rapid rate (Fig.3). The points sit inside the distributor next to the shaft in the middle of the distributor. When the engine is running, the distributor remains stationery. However, the shaft in the middle of the distributor is turning (it runs off the camshaft). The points assembly has a small block (called the rubbing block) which rides on the shaft. The shaft is not round, but rather has lobes or high spots on it - one for each cylinder of the engine (if you have a 6 cylinder engine, the shaft would have 6 high spots on it). When the rubbing block of the points hits one of these lobes, it causes the points to open. The primary circuit electrical current is flowing through the points - when they are closed, the circuit is completed and the current flows through them. When the points are open, the cir-

cuit is broken and the Secondary circuit takes
over. This action happens every time the rubbing
block of the points hits one of the high spots on
the shaft. In one complete turn of the shaft, the
points will open however many high spots there are
on the shaft.

C. THE SECONDARY CIRCUIT

Parts: Distributor Cap and Rotor, Secondary Wires
       (plug wires), Spark Plugs, Coil

The secondary circuit takes over when the points
open and break the current flow through the primary
circuit. In very simplified terms, the opening of
the points and breaking of the primary circuit
causes a collapse of the magnetic field in the coil,
and the electrical current starts flowing through
the secondary windings in the coil (thousands of
coils of copper wire). The combination of these
two events - collapse of magnetic field and flow
through the windings - causes a high voltage to be
built up, anywhere from 10,000 - 20,000 volts. The
high voltage current then flows out the top of the
coil, called the coil tower, to the center of the
distributor cap. The current flows through the top
of the distributor cap to the rotor which is turning
on the distributor shaft. All of the spark plug
wires are attached to the distributor cap and have
metal terminals that the rotor touches as it turns
on the shaft. These terminals can be seen on the
inside of the cap. The electrical current is sent
to the middle of the rotor and flows to the tip of
the rotor and from there to one of the spark plug
wire terminals. The current then travels along the
spark plug wire to the spark plug and fires it, and
then the current is grounded through the engine
block (thus returning to the battery). The secondary circuit takes over every time the points open;
so, essentially, a spark plug fires every time the
points open. The opening and closing of the points
and the distribution of the secondary circuit to
the plug wires is dependent on the turning of the
distributor shaft. In one complete revolution of
the shaft, the points open and a plug fires for
every cylinder of the engine.

D. What Effect Does a Tune Up Have on the Ignition
   System?

When you do a tune up, you are doing essentially
three things:

1. Making sure the plugs are in good condition so

they will fire properly and that the gap on the plugs is set correctly so they will fire with the right amount of intensity;

2. Making sure the points are in good condition and that the gap (when the points are open) is the correct width, as the point gap width affects the timing of the plug firing;

3. Making sure the rotor is delivering the current to the right spark plug wire at exactly the right time so that the plugs fire according to the engine specifications (this is called "timing").

HOW TO DO A TUNE UP

The essentials of a tune up are replacing the points and the spark plugs and setting the dwell, timing, and idle speed. Many mechanic shops also replace the condensor, but this isn't really necessary unless your points are burning out a lot (like every 1000 miles). Normally a tune up is done about every 12,000 miles on 6 and 8 cylinder cars, and about every 6,000 miles on 4 cylinder cars. I am going to go over the essentials of doing a tune up and then talk about other jobs that might be included in a tune up as needed (compression test, replacing air and fuel filter, etc.).

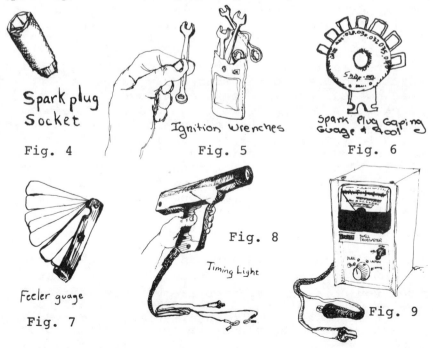

Spark plug
Socket

Fig. 4

Ignition Wrenches

Fig. 5

Spark Plug Gaping
Guage & tool

Fig. 6

Feeler guage

Fig. 7

Timing Light

Fig. 8

Fig. 9

A. Tools Needed

1. Spark plug socket (Fig. 4) and ratchet and also possibly a short extension

Most spark plugs - foreign and american - require a 13/16 inch spark plug socket. However, a few cars have a smaller plug which uses a 5/8 inch socket.

2. Medium size standard screwdriver

3. Ignition wrenches (Fig.5) or small crescent wrench

4. Spark plug gaping gauge (Fig.6)

5. Flat feeler gauges of different thicknesses (Fig.7)

6. Timing light (Fig.8)

7. Dwell-tachometer (Fig.9)

8. Assorted wrenches

B. Supplies/Parts Needed

1. Spark plugs - 1 for each cylinder

These can be bought at discount stores. They have charts to tell you what kind you need. Also check the tune up specifications for your car to see if a certain type of plug is recommended (especially if you have a foreign car).

2. Set of contact points

These can also be bought at discount stores, but I wouldn't recommend getting them there, as a lot of times they aren't very good. Get points at an auto parts store.

3. Cam lubricant for the distributor shaft

Sometimes you will get a small capsule of lubricant with the set of points. You can also buy a tube of lubricant, though the size they come in will last you for the rest of your lifetime, probably. Also, wheel bearing grease will work okay.

4. Piece of white chalk

C. Information Needed

Most of the information needed can be obtained from the tune up specification chart for your make of car (Fig.10). Such charts can be found in any auto repair book. Also, the owners'/shop manual for your car would have the information. Sometimes I

have just called up the local dealer for the make
of car and asked them for the tune up specs.

1. Spark plug gap (in thousandths, like .035)

2. Point gap (also in thousandths)

3. Degrees of dwell or dwell angle

4. Timing (will be something like 6BTDC)

5. Idle speed rpm (will be different specs for
   automatic and standard transmission)

6. Valve clearance if the valves are to be adjusted
   (mostly 4 cylinder foreign cars)

Information not found in a tune up chart, but which
you need to know (usually can find it in the introduction section of your make of car in a Chilton's
manual, etc.):

1. Location of #1 spark plug

2. Location of timing marks (not absolutely necessary)

TUNE UP SPECIFICATIONS

OLD CAR SPECIFICATIONS: For 1946-65 Tune Up Specifications see back of book.

★When using a timing light, disconnect vacuum tube or hose at distributer and plug opening in hose or tube so idle speed will not be affected.

Year	Engine	Spark Plug Type AC	Spark Plug Gap Inch	Distributor Point Gap Inch	Distributor Dwell Angle Deg.	Firing Order	Ignition Timing BTDC (1)	Ignition Timing Mark	Hot Idle Speed Std. Trans.	Hot Idle Speed Auto. Trans. (1)	Comp. Press. Lbs. (1)	Fuel Pump Press. Lbs.
1966	V6-225	44S	.035	.016(1)	30	Fig. Q	5°	Fig. B	550(1)	550D(1)	165	4¼ 5
	V8-300, 340 2 B.C.	45S	.035	.016(1)	30	Fig. C	2½°	Fig. B	550(1)	550D(1)	165	4¼ 5
	V8-340 4 Bar. Carb.	44S	.035	.016(1)	30	Fig. C	2½°	Fig. B	550(1)	550D(1)	180	5½ 7
	V8-401, 425	44S	.035	.016(1)	30	Fig. D	2½°(1)	Fig. A	500(1)	500D(1)	180	5½ 7
1967	6-225 Except Cal.	44S	.035	.016(1)	30	Fig. Q	5°	Fig. B	550(1)	550D(1)	165	4¼ 5
	6-225 California	44S	.035	.016(1)	30	Fig. Q	5°	Fig. B	650(1)	600D(1)	165	4¼ 5
	8-300 Except Cal.	0®	.035	.016(1)	30	Fig. B	2½°	Fig. B	650(1)	550D(1)	165	4¼ 5
	8-300 California	0®	.035	.016(1)	30	Fig. B	2½°	Fig. B	650(1)	600D(1)	165	4¼ 5
	8-340 Except Cal.	0®	.035	.016(1)	30	Fig. B	2½°	Fig. B	550(1)	550D(1)	165	4¼ 5
	8-340 California	0®	.035	.016(1)	30	Fig. B	2½°	Fig. B	650(1)	600D(1)	165	4¼ 5
	8-400 Except Cal.	44TS	.035	.016(1)	30	Fig. B	2½°	Fig. B	500(1)	500D(1)	180	5½ 7
	8-400 California	44TS	.035	.016(1)	30	Fig. B	2½°	Fig. B	550(1)	550D(1)	140	5½ 7
	8-430 Except Cal.	44TS	.035	.016(1)	30	Fig. B	2½°	Fig. B	550(1)	550D(1)	180	5½ 7
	8-430 California	44TS	.035	.016(1)	30	Fig. B	2½°	Fig. B	600(1)	550D(1)	140	5½ 7
1968	6-250(1) Std. Tr.	46N	.030	.019	32	153624	TDC	Damper	700(1)	—	130	4 5
	6-250(1) Auto. Tr.	46N	.030	.019	32	153624	4°	Damper	—	600D(1)	130	4 5

First find your year
can and
engine size

Fig. 10   Example of a Tune Up Chart

D. Steps

1. REPLACE SPARK PLUGS

    a. Remove the plug wires from the plugs by grab-
       bing the wire where it fits on to the plug,
       twisting and then pulling. Be sure you know
       which wire goes to which plug as they have to
       be put back on in exactly the same place.

    b. Remove the old plugs using a socket and rat-
       chet. Fit the socket snugly on the plug and
       then push the handle counterclockwise. It
       helps to hold the socket straight on the plug
       with one hand and then to push down or pull

up on the ratchet handle with the other hand. Sometimes plugs are very tight and hard to get out. Try using a breaker bar if you can't get the plugs loose with a ratchet.

c. When you take the old plugs out, examine the electrode area to see what kind of condition the plugs are in. Different things to look for are: (Fig.11)

1) Covered with black powder - that is carbon and usually means there is too rich of a fuel mixture going to the combustion chamber (by too rich I mean too much gasoline in proportion to air). That indicates a need for carburetor adjustment. Carboned-up plugs could also result from a lot of in-city driving, especially in the winter when the choke is on a lot.

2) Real white looking with a hard glaze and shiny spots on them - that usually means the opposite of the carboned-up plugs, a too lean fuel mixture (not enough gasoline in proportion to air) and also indicates a need for carburetor adjustment.

3) Covered with oil - that usually indicates that there is oil leaking into the combustion chamber. Don't confuse oil on the threads of the plug, which could have dribbled down from a leaking valve cover gasket, with oil on the electrode. Two reasons for oil on the electrode would be bad oil rings on the pistons, and/or bad oil seals on the valve stems. If you have this kind of condition, be sure and do a compression test on the engine.

#1 Covered with Black powder   #2 White looking and worn   #3 Covered with oil

Fig. 11

d. Compression test - With all the spark plugs out, now would be a good time to do a compression test if needed (see Compression Test at the end of this section).

e. Gapping the plugs - This refers to setting the width of the gap on the new plugs to an exact amount (see Information Needed). To do this use a spark plug gapping tool. Different numbers are marked on the gauge like 28, 35, 40, etc. These refer to thousandths of an inch and correspond to the gap width in the tune ups specifications (.035 would be 35 on the gauge). Use the wire that is the closest width to what the gap for your plugs is supposed to be. Insert the correct wire into the gap on the spark plug. You should be able to pull it out with just a little tug. If the gap isn't correct, widen or narrow it by using the slots on the end of the spark plug gauge to pry the curved piece of metal of the plug one way or the other until you get the correct gap (Fig.12).

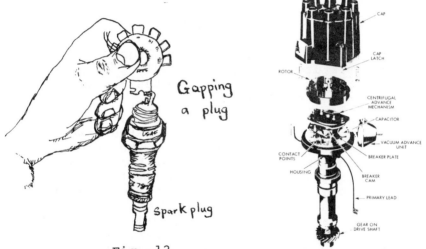

Gapping
a plug

Spark plug

Fig. 12

CAP

CAP
LATCH

ROTOR

CENTRIFUGAL
ADVANCE
MECHANISM

CAPACITOR

VACUUM ADVANCE
UNIT

CONTACT
POINTS

BREAKER PLATE

HOUSING

BREAKER
CAM

PRIMARY LEAD

GEAR ON
DRIVE SHAFT

Fig. 13

f. Put the new plugs in the engine. Start each plug by hand and then tighten them with the socket and ratchet. Be sure to start the plugs by hand because you don't want to cross thread the threads in the spark plug holes (this is what happens when the plugs aren't started in the holes correctly). Make sure the plugs are tight. Plugs too loose will cause compression to leak out around them.

g. Replace the wires on the plugs - be sure they go on all the way. Usually they make a sort of snapping sound when they go on and you shouldn't be able to pull them off very easily.

2. REPLACE THE POINTS

   a. Remove the distributor cap. Some caps are
      held on by two clips that you pop off with a
      screwdriver. Others, especially on GM cars,
      are held on by screws. On Delco distributors,
      the kind that is on most General Motors cars,
      the screw is actually a spring loaded clip.
      You push down on the screw and turn it about
      half a turn and this releases the cap.

   b. Remove the rotor. Many rotors just pull
      straight off. On Delco distributors you
      remove the rotor by unscrewing the two screws
      on top of the rotor. This will still leave
      the centrifugal weights up above the points -
      don't try to remove them (Fig.13). You will
      be able to get to the points without removing
      them. When you take the rotor off a Delco
      distributor, look at the underneath of it and
      notice there is a square peg and a round peg,
      so it can go back on only one way.

   c. Inspect the inside of the cap. Look for thin
      hairline cracks between plug wire terminals
      on the cap (Fig.14). Also check to see that
      the small piece of carbon in the center of
      the cap is springy to touch (some cars are
      made with hard ones - that's okay). Look for
      any cracks on the rotor. This would also be
      a good time to check the coil for cracks.

      Pull off the coil wire - the large wire from
      the center of the distributor cap to the
      center of the coil - and look around the coil
      tower for cracks (Fig.15). If you find any
      cracks on the coil, distributor cap or rotor,
      replace that part.

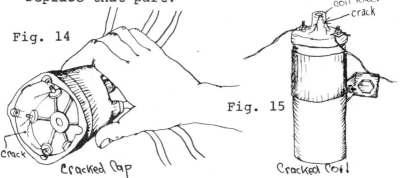

Fig. 14

Fig. 15

Cracked Cap

Cracked Coil

   d. Disconnect the small short wire leading from
      the condensor to the points and any other
      wires connected to the points. Be sure you
      know where these wires go on the points.

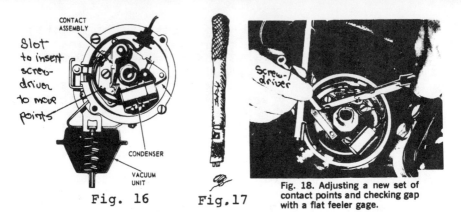

CONTACT
ASSEMBLY

Slot
to insert
screw-
driver
to move
points

CONDENSER

VACUUM
UNIT

Fig. 16   Fig.17

Fig. 18. Adjusting a new set of
contact points and checking gap
with a flat feeler gage.

e. Remove the screw(s) holding the points to the
   distributor plate and remove the points (Fig.
   16). Be careful not to drop the screws down
   into the distributor.

f. Place a small dab of cam lubricant on the
   shaft where the points touch and smear it
   around the shaft.

g. Install the new points - be sure the nob on
   the bottom of the points is inserted into the
   hole for it on the distributor plate. Replace
   the screws. If you have a hard time getting
   the screw started, a tool known as a screw
   starter would help - it holds the screw until
   it is started in the hole (Fig. 17).

h. Reconnect the wires leading to the points.

3. SETTING THE POINT GAP

There are two ways to set the point gap - one is by
using a feeler gauge of the right thickness and the
other is to use a dwell meter. By far, the dwell
meter is a more accurate method. If you have a
Delco distributor (General Motors cars) then you
have to use a dwell meter to set the point gap.
Cheap dwell meters that work well enough can usually
be bought at discount stores. However, even the
cheap ones are $15.00 or more. You can also probab-
ly rent both a dwell meter and a timing light from
a rental place.

   a. Using a feeler gauge (you can't do this on a
      Delco distributor because you can't get to
      the points well enough):

      1) Crank the engine either by tapping the
         ignition key until the engine just barely
         turns, or by turning the crankshaft pulley
         (bottom wheel the fan belt is connected to)

by hand until the rubbing block of the points
rests on any high spot on the distributor
shaft. (The car has to be in neutral to turn
the crankshaft pulley.) The distributor
shaft will turn as the engine turns.

2) When the rubbing block of the points is on
the shaft, the points should be open. Insert
a feeler gauge of the correct thickness (see
Information Needed) into the gap between the
points. If the gap is correct, you should
feel a slight tug on the gauge as you pull it
out. If the gap isn't correct, loosen the
screw holding the points very slightly. Insert a screwdriver in the slot on the points
provided for it and move the points (Fig.16,18).
To open or close the gap, you are moving that
part of the points with the rubbing block
towards or away from the shaft. If you move
it towards the shaft, that applies greater
pressure to the spring tension of the points
and thus they will open further when the
rubbing block hits the high spot on the shaft.
The reverse works when you move the points
away from the shaft. Set the gap to the
correct amount and tighten down the screws.
To check your gap setting, hook up a dwell
meter, turn the engine on and see what
reading you get.

b. Using a dwell meter

1) Hook up the dwell meter - the red end goes
to the negative side of the coil; if the negative isn't shown on the coil, then it is the
side that has the small wire (primary circuit)
leading from the coil to the distributor.
The black lead goes to any ground on the
engine (any metal part of the engine, like a
bolt, etc. Avoid attaching to the carburetor
because of the danger of sparking near gasoline). Set the meter for dwell reading for
4, 6 or 8 cylinders. If the meter only has
6 and 8 cylinder readings, and if you have a
4 cylinder car, use the 8 cylinder reading
and multiply it times 2. For instance, if
the correct dwell reading for your car is
supposed to be 50 degrees, then the meter
should read 25 degrees on the 8 cylinder
scale.

2) on non GM cars

a) Install the points and tighten them
down. Leave the rotor and distributor cap

off. Have a friend get inside the car and try to start the car. The car won't start because the distributor cap is off, but you will be able to read the dwell reading on the meter while the engine is turning over (see Information Needed for correct dwell reading). The dwell measures the number of degrees the distributor shaft turns in a circle between when the points open. If the dwell reading is too high, it means the point gap is too narrow and if the dwell reading is too low, it means the point gap is too wide. With the engine off, correct the gap by moving the points back and forth with a screwdriver (see how to in the feeler gauge section), and then crank the engine again to check it. Keep doing that until you get the correct dwell reading. When you are changing the point gap, remember to loosen the screw(s) only slightly so you can just barely move the points, and also to only move them very small amounts.

b) If you aren't getting any dwell reading when you crank the engine, it might mean that you don't have a good ground connection for your meter. Try moving the connection around. Another reason for no reading is that you have the points set either so far out or so far in that they are never opening or never closing. Look at the points while someone cranks the engine to make sure they are opening and closing. (They will make a small electrical spark when opening and closing.)

c) Replace the rotor and distributor cap.

d) Start the engine, and check the dwell reading again. It might possibly change with the engine running. If so, reset the points and check again with the engine running.

3) If you have a General Motors car with a Delco distributor (which is what almost all GM cars have) then the dwell is set in a slightly different way:

a) Install the points and tighten the screws.

b) Put the rotor back on (making sure the round and square pegs fit in their proper places). Put the distributor cap back on.

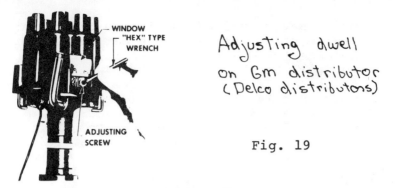

WINDOW
"HEX" TYPE
WRENCH

ADJUSTING
SCREW

Adjusting dwell
on Gm distributor
(Delco distributors)

Fig. 19

The front of the cap has a little piece of
metal that can be raised up and down. The
dwell is adjusted by raising this window
and inserting an allen wrench into the
fitting for it on the points (look at it
on the old points so you know what size
allen wrench to use)(Fig.19).

c) Start the car. While the engine is
running, turn the allen wrench inserted in
the points one way or the other. This
will change the dwell reading on the meter.
Adjust the points until you get the correct
reading on the meter.

4. TIMING

What you are doing when you time an engine is
putting a light in the electrical circuit of the
number 1 spark plug (the secondary circuit). Every
time the plug fires, your timing light will flash.
Your engine is constructed so that when you shine
the flashing timing light on the timing marks on
the crankshaft pulley and the engine block, the
two marks should line up. If they don't, it means
the #1 plug isn't firing at the right time and you
have to make adjustments so that it does (explained
in the procedure).

   a. The first thing to do when you time the car
      is to locate the timing marks. They will be
      in 2 places - on the crankshaft pulley (bot-
      tom wheel the fan belt is hooked to) and on
      the engine block next to the pulley (Fig.20).
      One will be a series of marks (20, 10, 0, 10,
      20, etc.) and the other mark will be just one
      mark - sometimes this is a pointer on the
      engine block that juts out over the pulley.
      Cars vary as to whether the series of marks
      is located on the pulley or on the block.
      You might have to turn the crankshaft pulley

118

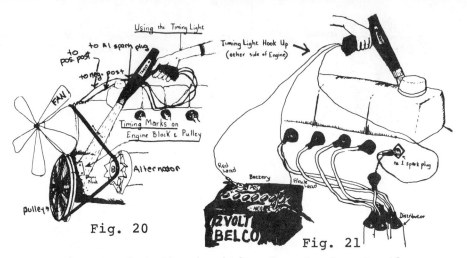

Fig. 20

Fig. 21

by turning the ignition key to locate the marks on it.

Clean off the marks and mark the correct one (Information Needed) with white chalk. Also mark the single mark with white chalk. The timing marks sometimes read BTDC or ATDC. TDC stands for Top Dead Center and is 0 degrees in the series. This means that the piston is at the very top of the cylinder. BTDC means Before Top Dead Center, meaning the piston hasn't quite reached the top of the cylinder, and ATDC means After Top Dead Center, meaning the piston has reached the top of the cylinder and is starting to travel down the cylinder. Most cars are tuned at some degree of BTDC, meaning that the plugs fire a little bit before the piston reaches the top of the cylinder in the compression stroke.

b. There are two kinds of timing lights - battery powered and not battery powered. The battery powered kind, which are quite a bit more expensive, produce a strobe light that can be seen in daylight. The non battery kind just produce a regular light that is very difficult to see in daylight.

With the engine off, connect the timing light to the #1 spark plug (see Information Needed for location: the #1 plug doesn't refer to the physical location of the plug in the engine, but rather to its location in the firing order; therefore it is necessary to know where the #1 plug is located in the engine). Usually there is a connector with the timing light which you put on the plug and then the

119

plug wire goes on the connector. Timing
lights have different methods for doing this,
but just remember you are inserting the timing
light in the current going to #1 plug, so
somehow you have to hook up the spark plug
wire going to the #1 plug to the timing light,
and then a wire coming out of the timing
light has to go back to the wire leading to
the plug or to the plug itself (Fig.21). If
the timing light is battery powered, connect
the red lead to the positive side of the battery, and the black lead to the negative side.

c. Unless it says not to in the tune up specifications, disconnect the vacuum line(s) leading
to the distributor. The vacuum unit on the
distributor is the round disc on the outside
(some distributors, however, don't have a
vacuum unit). There will be either a rubber
hose or a metal tube leading to it (Fig.22).
The hose can just be pulled off; the tube will
have a small nut where it goes into the vacuum
unit. Unscrew the nut and pull the line out
of the vacuum unit. Turn the engine on and
let it warm up until it is running at idle
speed (should be about 800 rpms or less, as
measured by a tachometer - the dwell meter is
most likely a combination dwell-tachometer,
so you will be able to read the engine rpms).

d. Shine the flashing timing light on the timing
marks. The light works like a strobe light
and will make the marks appear stationery.
If the two timing marks line up the timing is
correct. If they don't, it means the #1 plug
is not firing at the right time. Remember
that the rotor, revolving on the distributor
shaft, carries the current to each plug wire
terminal in the distributor cap. To change
when the #1 plug fires, turn the distributor
so that the current is delivered from the
rotor to the plug terminal at the right time
(remember you are changing the location of the
plug terminal in the distributor cap in relation to the rotor revolving on the shaft). If
you don't understand this concept, with the
engine off remove the distributor cap, loosen
the nut at the base of the distributor (see
the following steps) and turn the distributor.
Notice that you are turning only the distributor, not the rotor and shaft. Thus you are
changing the location of the plug terminals
in the distributor cap in relation to the
rotor. This will change the time when current

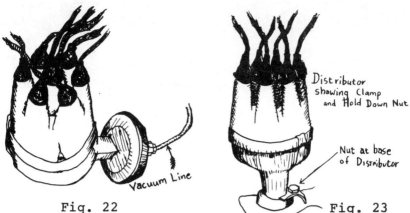

Distributor
showing Clamp
and Hold Down Nut

Vacuum Line

Nut at base
of Distributor

Fig. 22   Fig. 23

is delivered to the #1 plug terminal and thus
the firing of the #1 spark plug.

To change when the #1 plug fires:

1) Loosen the nut at the base of the distributor where the distributor shaft goes into
the engine (Fig.23).

2) If the distributor will turn fairly freely,
then use the vacuum unit to turn it one way
or the other. If it doesn't turn freely, then
it is better to grab the distributor around
the cap below the wires and turn it that way,
so there is no chance of bending the vacuum
unit. Be careful not to touch the plug wires
or the primary wire coming from the coil to
the side of the distributor.

3) With the engine running, turn the distributor and watch the timing mark on the pulley
with the timing light. Turning the distributor will cause the marks to move. Turn the
distributor until the two timing marks line
up.

4) Tighten the nut at the base of the distributor and then recheck the timing marks to
make sure they are still lined up. Reconnect
the vacuum lines to the distributor.

5. ADJUSTING THE CARBURETOR

If your car seems to be idling well and at the correct speed (see Information Needed), then I wouldn't
try to adjust the carburetor. However, if it is

idling too fast or too slow and you think the fuel
mixture might be incorrect (if it is running poorly
and using a lot of fuel) then you should probably
adjust the carburetor.

There are two adjustments on the carburetor - idle
speed and fuel mixture (the proportion of gasoline
to air) at idle speed. Both of these adjustments
are controlled by turning screws in or out. The
hardest part of adjusting a carburetor (and also of
explaining how to do it) is locating the screws.(Fig.24)

First, remove the air filter. The idle speed
screw is usually located somewhere near the
top of the carburetor on the linkage. It will probably go through a small spring. The fuel mixture
screw is located near the bottom of the carburetor
and screws directly into the carburetor. It will
also probably go through a small spring. If you
can find a picture of the carburetor on your car,
then you should be able to locate the screws using
the picture.

Fig. 24

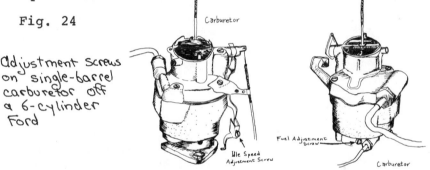

Adjustment screws
on single-barrel
carburetor off
a 6-cylinder
Ford

Carburetor

Idle Speed
Adjustment Screw

Fuel Adjustment
Screw

Carburetor

To adjust the idle speed:

  a. Hook up a tachometer (usually a dwell tach).
     The tachometer is hooked up the same way as
     the dwell meter.

  b. Let the engine warm up so it is not on fast
     idle. Turn the idle speed screw in to in-
     crease the idle speed and out to lessen the
     idle speed. Watch the rpm reading on the
     tachometer as you turn the screw. Set the
     idle speed at the proper number of rpms (see
     Information Needed).

To adjust the fuel mixture:

  a. First set the idle speed using the idle speed
     screw at about 800 rpms.

  b. Turn the fuel mixture screw in until the rpms
     start to drop. Turn the screw back out about
     a turn and a half from where the rpms started
     to drop.

c. If there are two fuel mixture screws, adjust each one in turn, trying to turn them approximately the same amount.

d. Adjust the idle speed screw so it reads the proper idle rpms.

OTHER JOBS THAT MAY BE PART OF A TUNE UP

A. COMPRESSION TEST

If you are having engine problems - missing, loss of power, backfiring or making a popping sound when accelerating, then you should do a compression check on your engine. A compression check tests the compression in each of the cylinders - the compression that is created when the piston comes up on the compression stroke. The compression needs to be a certain number of pounds per square inch (psi) in order to create a powerful enough explosion on the power stroke.

If the engine is in good condition then the compression will be high (100-170 psi) and consistent among all cylinders (within 10-15 psi of each other). If the compression of a cylinder is low it could mean burned valves, bad compression rings on the piston, scored cylinder walls, etc. - anything that would prevent the combustion chamber from being sealed and thus allowing the compression to leak out. If you have a bad compression reading for 2 cylinders right next to each other, that could mean a bad head gasket, which would allow the compression to leak out between the two cylinders. A low compression reading in 1 or more cylinders means you have problems with your engine and need to do (or have done) some engine work.

1. Tools Needed

Compression gauge (Fig.25)

There are two kinds of compression gauges - one kind you push in the spark plug hole and hold there; the other kind has a long hose that screws in the hole like a spark plug. I would advise using the kind that screws in if you have a choice because it is real hard to hold the gauge in the hole and seal it well enough so no compression leaks past the gauge.

2. Supplies/Parts Needed

None

push pin to release compression

Screw into spark plug hole

2 Kinds of Compression Guages

Hold in spark plug hole

Fig. 25

3. Information Needed

None

4. Steps

a. Remove all spark plugs

b. Prop the throttle wide open. To do this have a friend get in the car and push her foot all the way down on the gas pedal. While she does this, look under the hood and see where the accelerator linkage moves and then stick a screwdriver or something somewhere in the linkage to keep it in that position. The reason for doing this is that while cranking the engine to do the test, if the throttle is closed you are pumping gasoline into the cylinders, which could eventually wash the oil off the cylinder walls, thus giving a falsely low compression reading.

c. Standard transmission - put the car in neutral.

d. Pull off the large wire in the center of the distributor cap (the coil wire) and using a piece of insulated wire with alligator clips on each end clip one end to the metal end of the coil wire and the other end to a metal part of the engine - this grounds the coil wire so that sparks won't be coming out of the plug wires.

e. Insert the compression gauge in the first spark plug hole (you can test the cylinders in any order that you want - just keep track of what reading is for what cylinder).

f. Have your friend turn the ignition key on and start the engine (the engine won't start because the plug wires are all off). Allow the engine to turn over 4 times. The compression of the cylinder will register on the gauge as the engine is turning over. If a loud hissing sound occurs, that is air blowing out past the compression gauge and that means the gauge isn't in the plug hole correctly. Write down the reading on the compression gauge and then push the pin on the gauge to release the pressure, and unscrew the gauge.

g. Test each cylinder in the same way. If you have a low reading in one cylinder, test it a couple of times more to make sure it just wasn't a faulty reading for some reason.

h. How high all the cylinders read is not so important (as long as it is at least 100 psi) as is the consistency of the readings. All of the cylinders should have readings within 15 psi of each other.

Condenser

Fig. 26

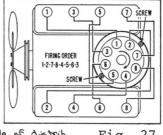

Example of distrib. wiring diagram   Fig. 27

B. CHANGING CONDENSOR, DISTRIBUTOR CAP & ROTOR

1. Condensor (Fig.26)

When the points open and the electrical current is broken a small arcing is produced at the points. The purpose of the condensor is to absorb this electrical arcing so it doesn't burn the points. It is not usually necessary to change the condensor when doing a tune up, unless the points are burning out frequently - this is a symptom of a bad condensor. Changing the condensor is fairly easy, depending on where it is located in the distributor. Some condensors are mounted on the outside of the distributor. The condensor comes with a bracket, so to replace it, unscrew the screw holding the old condensor and bracket. Disconnect the wire leading from the condensor to the points and remove the condensor and bracket. Install the new condensor and bracket and rehook the wire. If it is easier not to remove the bracket, but to just loosen it and slide out the condensor, then don't use the new bracket.

2. Distributor Cap

The distributor cap should be replaced anytime there are cracks in it. Replacing the distributor cap is just a matter of taking the wires off the old cap and putting them on the new cap. The only important thing is to not get the wires mixed up. It is best to draw a diagram of where the wires go before taking the old ones off. Also, you can usually find a diagram of the wires on the distributor cap in the

section for your make of car in a Chilton's manual,
etc. (Fig.27). If after replacing the distributor
cap, you start the engine up and get a lot of back
firing or firing up through the carburetor, then
you probably got some of the plug wires mixed up.
Recheck their locations according to the diagram.

3. Rotor

Rotors don't usually need to be replaced unless
cracked or badly corroded, though you might want to
replace the rotor when replacing the distributor
cap.

Air Filter or Air Cleaner

Fig. 28

C. AIR AND FUEL FILTERS

1. Air Filter

The air filter should be replaced about every 12,000
miles or more often if you drive on a lot of dusty
roads (Fig.28). The purpose of the air filter is
to filter out dust, bugs, etc. from the air before
it enters the carburetor. If you have access to
compressed air, you can blow out the filter periodically to clean it, but I would still replace it
every 12,000 miles. Replacing the filter is very
easy: Remove the top of the air filter container,
take out the old filter, put the new one in, and
replace the top of the filter container. Air filters can be bought at discount stores and they have
charts to tell which filter to use for your car.

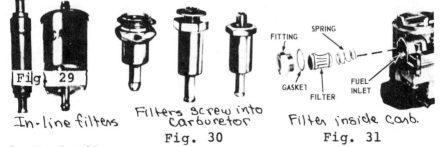

In-line filters   Filters screw into carburetor   Filter inside carb.

Fig. 29   Fig. 30   Fig. 31

2. Fuel Filter

Fuel filters should also be replaced every 12,000
miles or so. Not all cars have fuel filters. The
purpose of the fuel filter is to filter the gasoline before it reaches the carburetor to get out
any dirt or other nitsies. There are two kinds of

filters - in line and in the carburetor. The first kind, in line (Fig.29), is located on the gas line, most often between the fuel pump and carburetor. Many of them are small, clear plastic containers. By shining a flashlight through them you can see whether dirt has accumulated on the bottom of the filter. If so, it should be changed. To replace the filter, remove the lines going into the filter and coming out of the filter. Then connect the lines up to the new filter. The new filter should be marked with an arrow to indicate the direction of fuel flow, so be sure to hook the filter up in the correct direction.

Another kind of in line filter, found on most Ford carburetors, screws directly into the carburetor (Fig.30). These are also fairly easy to replace. Disconnect the fuel line, and then using a large wrench, unscrew the filter (the filter has a hexagon nut built into it). Screw the new filter into the carburetor and reconnect the fuel line. Don't screw the filter in too tight or it will strip out and ruin the carburetor.

Some carburetors have a small fiber filter located inside the carburetor where the fuel line goes into the carburetor (Fig.31). To replace this type of filter, disconnect the fuel line at the carburetor and then unscrew the large nut on the carburetor at the place where the fuel line goes into the carburetor. In the opening behind the nut, the fiber filter is located. It sort of looks like a small sparkly cork. Replace it with a new filter, making sure it goes in the opening in the same direction as did the old filter.

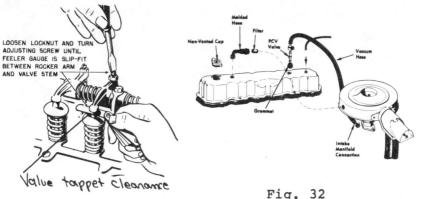

LOOSEN LOCKNUT AND TURN ADJUSTING SCREW UNTIL FEELER GAUGE IS SLIP-FIT BETWEEN ROCKER ARM AND VALVE STEM

Valve tappet clearance

Fig. 33

Molded Hose

Non-Vented Cap

Filter

PCV Valve

Vacuum Hose

Grommet

Intake Manifold Connection

Fig. 32

D. PCV VALVE

PCV stands for positive crankcase ventilation. The
purpose of pcv is to take the gas fumes from the
combustion of the engine and to recirculate them
back into the engine to be burned again. Older
model cars (before 1965 about) don't have pcv, but
rather vent the gas fumes to the air through a road
draft tube. If you have an older car, and have
ever wondered what the tube you see underneath the
car coming from the engine is, that is the road
draft tube.

The introduction of pcv eliminated a large percen-
tage of the air pollution of earlier cars. The
purpose of the pcv valve is to regulate the flow of
the ventilating air that carries the gas fumes. The
pcv valve is located in the valve cover (Fig.32).
The gas fumes travel up to the valve area and out
the pcv valve and through a rubber hose to the
intake manifold where they are sucked into the
engine and burned again. To find the pcv valve on
your car, locate the large rubber hose going to the
valve cover and pull it off at the valve cover.
Either inside of the hose or in the hole in the
valve cover where the hose goes will be the pcv
valve. The valve should be replaced everytime you
do a tune up, because if it gets clogged up it will
cause the engine to run poorly. It usually will
pull out of the rubber fitting on the valve cover
that holds it, and then you can push a new one into
the fitting. Sometimes they are hard to get out
and take a little work. Make sure you notice in
what direction the old valve fits into the valve
cover, so you will install the new one in the right
direction.

E. VALVE ADJUSTMENT

If you have a foreign car, then you probably will
need to adjust the valves when you do a tune up or
every 12,000 miles. Valve adjustment refers to
adjusting the amount of space between the part of
the rocker arm that hits the valve and the top of
the valve stem (this space is called the valve
tappet clearance, Fig.33). Valve adjustment isn't
necessary on most american cars, especially '66
models on, because american engines have hydraulic
lifters which adjust the clearance automatically.
I am not going to explain valve adjustment, because
every foreign car seems to have a slightly different method of adjusting valves. Most manuals will
explain how to do a valve adjustment fairly thoroughly - try Chilton's imported car manual, or a
specific manual for your car.

128

Chapter 7

BRAKE REPAIR

Brake repair is one of those things that every car is going to need at some time or another, and probably more than once. It is also one of those jobs that you really get socked for at a mechanics' garage. Doing brake work isn't all that hard, though, and it also has the added advantage that it is one job where you don't have to crawl underneath the car and have dirt fall into your eyes. Not that you don't get dirty when working on brakes.......

What I want to do in this chapter is to explain simply how brakes work and what the difference is between drum and disc brakes. Then I will go through the steps of doing a complete brake job on your car. However, it is important for you to keep in mind that brake shoe assemblies all have a little different set up depending on the type of car, so you may not be able to follow the steps verbatim, but they should offer some sort of guideline to follow. Also, if you haven't ever done brake work, then I hope the work explanation will give you the sense that brake work is one more area of your car that you can get to know.

HOW BRAKES WORK

All brakes in automobiles are what is known as hydraulic brakes, meaning the braking action is done through the use of fluid. There are 2 types of brakes - drum brakes and disc brakes. Up until a few years ago, practically all american made cars had only drum brakes. Now, many newer american cars have disc brakes in the front and drum brakes in the rear. Many foreign cars have had front disc brakes for a long time, and now a lot of foreign cars have disc brakes on both the front and rear.

The difference in how the two types of brakes work is that drum brakes have two shoes that, when the brakes are applied, press out on a drum to which the wheel is attached, causing the wheel to stop. Disc brakes work like bicycle caliper brakes: When the brakes are applied two pads press together on either side of a disc to which the wheel is attached, causing the wheel to stop (Fig.1). Drum brakes are self-energizing. This means that once the shoes start putting pressure against the drum, they generate their own force, multiplying the original force applied. Disc brakes, on the other hand, have no self-energizing action, and thus the force or pressure applied to the disc is not multiplied beyond the original pressure applied. Because of this, most cars equipped with front or both front and rear disc brakes, have some sort of power assist unit (power brakes) attached to the master cylinder. Of course, many cars with only drum brakes may also have a power assist system. One of the main advantages of disc brakes over drum brakes is that disc brakes will operate even when wet, whereas drum brakes won't, as you might have discovered if you've ever driven through a deep puddle and then tried to apply your brakes.

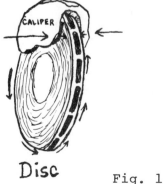

Disc

Fig. 1

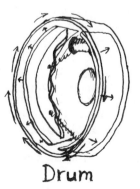

Drum

The hydraulic system carries the fluid to and from the brake shoes or pads. This movement of fluid is what actuates the brakes. Whether the brakes are disc or drum, the hydraulic system is essentially the same. In the hydraulic system, there is a master cylinder, wheel cylinder for each wheel, brake assembly for each wheel (containing the brake shoes and springs), and the fluid lines, connecting the master cylinder with each wheel cylinder. The brake pedal that you step on is connected directly to the master cylinder by way of a push rod, which is connected to a piston in the master cylinder. When you step on the brake pedal the rod is pushed forward into the master cylinder, moving the piston, and thus pushing the fluid in the master cylinder out into the brake lines. The fluid in the brake lines is then pushed into the wheel cylinder at each brake assembly. Wheel cylinders consist of two pistons in the case of drum brakes. These two pistons are connected to the brake shoes - one piston to each brake shoe. The fluid moving into the wheel cylinders from the brake lines forces the fluid in the wheel cylinders to push the pistons outward, thus pushing the brake shoes against the drums and stopping the wheels from turning (Fig.2). Disc brakes work the same way, except that the pistons push the pads against the disc, instead of shoes against the drum. Also in some disc brake assemblies there is only one large piston, or there may be as many as four pistons in one disc brake assembly. Drum brakes, however, always have just two pistons in each wheel cylinder.

When the foot is taken off of the brake pedal, powerful springs hooked to the shoes bring the shoes away from the drum and back to their original position, forcing the pistons back into the wheel cylinder. This action pushes the excess fluid in the wheel cylinder out into the brake lines and then back into the master cylinder. If there is any obstruction in the brake lines - dirt particles in the brake fluid, air bubbles in the lines - the movement of the fluid will be hindered, resulting in little or no braking pressure.

All automobiles from the late 1960's on have what is known as a dual braking system, with a dual master cylinder. What this means is that the master cylinder has two pistons instead of one and that there are a separate set of brake lines for the front and rear brakes. As a result, if for some reason the brakes fail (line breaks, etc.) in the rear, you would still have front brakes, and vice versa.

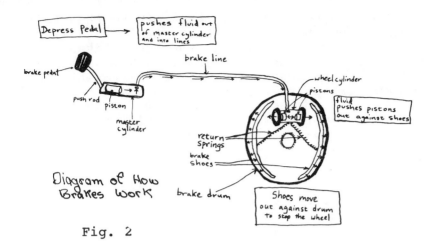

Depress Pedal → pushes fluid out of master cylinder and into lines

brake line

brake pedal

wheel cylinder

pistons

push rod   piston

fluid pushes pistons out against shoes

master cylinder

return springs

brake shoes

Diagram of How Brakes Work

brake drum

Shoes move out against drum to stop the wheel

Fig. 2

WHEN TO DO A BRAKE JOB

Automobiles <u>normally</u> need brake work done somewhere
around 50-60,000 miles, though that certainly is no
steadfast rule, especially if your car is equipped
with disc brakes. If your car has that many miles
on it and no brake work has been done on it, then
I would check the brake linings (drum brakes) or
brake pads (disc brakes) to see what kind of condition they are in. I'll explain how to do that
in the repair section following. Actually the
brakes should be checked regularly - at least once
a year.

There are also certain symptoms of the braking
system that would indicate a need for brake work.
I am going to go over a few of the more common
symptoms here and what trouble they usually indicate:

A. BRAKE PEDAL IS LOW TO THE FLOOR

This generally means one of two things. If your
car has the types of brakes that have to be manually
adjusted (a lot of foreign cars and earlier american
cars), then the brakes may be in need of adjustment.
The other possibility is that the brake linings are
worn and need replacing - check the linings.

B. THE BRAKES MAKE A SCRAPING NOISE WHEN APPLIED

Hopefully, you won't have to deal with this symptom
if you check your brakes regularly. A scraping
noise usually indicates that the brake linings or

pads (disc brakes) are completely worn so that the
metal to which the linings/pads were attached is
pressing against the drum/disc when the brakes are
applied. If such a noise develops, I would check
your brakes right away. Any prolonged braking with
badly worn linings or pads will ruin the drum or
disc, and they are pretty expensive to replace.
Also, eventually the braking action will be lessened
and you won't have very good brakes.

C. WHEN YOU APPLY THE BRAKES, THE CAR PULLS TO ONE
   SIDE OR THE OTHER

When you have this problem, before suspecting the
brakes, check the tire pressure. Uneven tire infla-
tion can cause a car to pull to one side or the
other. Braking problems that could cause pulling
to one side or the other are: uneven adjustment if
the brakes are the kind you adjust; the self adjusting mechanism on one side or the other may not be
working; or there may be problems in the wheel
cylinder on one side or the other. Whatever the
reason, I would pull off the wheels and check the
condition of the brakes and possibly rebuild the
wheel cylinders if you don't see anything obviously
wrong, (like loose springs, etc.).

D. BRAKE PEDAL GOES ALL THE WAY TO THE FLOOR AND
   THERE IS VERY LITTLE OR NO BRAKING PRESSURE

A symptom like this indicates trouble with the
brake fluid - that it is leaking somewhere. Check
the master cylinder and see if the fluid level is
low. Pull off the wheels and check the wheel cylinders to see if they are leaking. If none of the
wheel cylinders are leaking, then there is probably
trouble in the master cylinder and it should either
be rebuilt or replaced.

If the brakes go to the floor suddenly and there is
no braking pressure being applied, then probably a
brake line broke somewhere. Crawl underneath the
car and have a friend pump the brakes and see if
fluid is squirting out from a line somewhere.

E. BRAKE PEDAL IS SPONGY - HAS TO BE PUMPED UP
   AFTER APPLYING THE BRAKES

This symptom can also indicate leaking wheel cylinders. Air in the brake lines would be another
reason for spongy brakes. Try bleeding the brakes
and see if that helps to 'harden up' the brake
pedal.

HOW TO DO A COMPLETE BRAKE JOB (DRUM BRAKES)

This explanation will be about drum brakes, because they are the most common braking system and also the one I know the most about. At the end of this section, I will explain replacing pads in disc brakes.

Doing a complete brake job involves these steps:

1. REPLACING THE BRAKE SHOES AND CLEANING THE BRAKE ASSEMBLY

2. REBUILDING THE WHEEL CYLINDERS

3. TURNING THE DRUMS

4. BLEEDING THE BRAKES

5. ADJUSTING THE BRAKES

All of these steps are not always done. If you are just interested in correcting one braking problem, then you might want to do the step(s) that involves just that problem. For example, rebuilding a wheel cylinder that is leaking. However, at some time, a complete brake job should be done on your car that would include all of these steps. So, if you have leaking cylinders and the shoes are looking pretty worn, then that would probably be a good time to do all of the brake work involved in a complete job.

In going over the steps, I am going to refer to just one wheel, though you would perform the same procedures on all the wheels you are working on. There will be a slight difference in brake assemblies between the front and rear wheels, mainly because the rear assemblies have a parking (emergency) brake cable hooked up to them. However, if you understand the procedure for one wheel then you should be able to work on all the wheels.

Brake work should always be done in pairs. If you replace the shoes or rebuild the wheel cylinder on one rear brake assembly, then you should do the same thing for the other rear brake assembly. The same applies to the front brakes. If this isn't done, an uneven braking action can occur between the right and left sides of the car.

Brake Adjusting Tool
Fig. 3

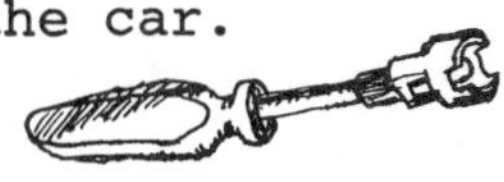

Hold-down Spring
Fig. 4

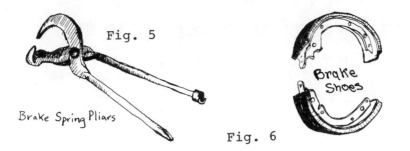

Fig. 5

Brake Spring Pliars

Brake Shoes

Fig. 6

A. REPLACING THE BRAKE SHOES AND CLEANING THE BRAKE ASSEMBLY

1. Tools Needed

    a. Lug nut wrench

    b. Screwdriver or brake adjusting tool (Fig.3)

    c. Ball peen or blacksmith hammer (rear brakes)

    d. Hold down spring tool (Fig.4) or pair of slip joint pliers

    e. Brake spring pliers (Fig.5)

    f. Vise grips (rear brakes)

    g. Large screwdriver to pry with

    h. Rubber mallet

    i. Rubbing alcohol (possibly)

2. Supplies/Parts Needed

    a. Brake shoes

You don't replace just the linings. You replace the whole shoe with the linings. You usually get money refunded if you return the old shoes to where you get the new ones. The brake shoes come in axle sets - 4 shoes, 2 for each wheel of the axle, front or rear. Be sure and compare the new shoes with the old ones to make sure they are the right shoes (Fig.6).

    b. Solvent and brush

    c. Rags

    d. Grease

There is a special brake lubricant, but if you don't want to put out the money, wheel bearing grease or something like it should suffice.

3. Information Needed

Though not absolutely necessary, a diagram from Chilton's or some other manual showing the brake

assembly for your car would be very helpful. I
will say more about that in the Steps section.

4. Steps

    a. Jack up the car, put it on stands and remove
    the wheels.

       1) Front wheel - The front wheel can be re-
       moved according to the procedure in repacking
       the front wheel bearings (Part II, Chapter 4).
       Once the wheel is removed, you can separate
       the wheel from the drum by unscrewing the lug
       nuts.

       2) Rear wheel - First, take off the lug nuts
       and remove the tire and rim, leaving only the
       drum to be removed. Put the car in neutral
       and make sure that the emergency brake is off.
       Back off the brake adjustment (this might also
       have to be done for the front wheels - see the
       Brake Adjustment section in this chapter for
       procedure). After backing off the adjustment,
       hopefully the drum will be able to be pulled
       off by hand. The lug nut studs are not part
       of the drum - the drum has holes in it that
       the studs fit through. (When looking at the
       drum it might appear that the studs are a
       part of it, but they really aren't.)

       Frequently the drums are stuck on pretty tight
       and you won't be able to remove them easily.
       One method for getting them off is to spray
       some penetrating lubricant around the lug nut
       studs and then hit the drum on its side with
       a hammer, turn it a bit and hit it again and
       do this working all the way around the drum
       (Fig.7). This should help loosen up the drum
       so it can be removed. Sometimes hitting it
       on the front near the outer edge of the drum
       will also work as it will tilt the drum and
       thus loosen up the shoes so the drum can be
       removed. Don't be afraid to hit it too hard.
       Also a larger type of hammer like a blacksmith
       hammer would be helpful. Sometimes you have
       to pound them quite a bit to get them off.

       If you can't get the drum off by the above
       method, you can rent a drum (wheel) puller and
       use it to remove the drum. Before using one,
       I would check with a garage, etc. that works
       on your type of car and make sure it is okay
       to use a wheel puller on the drums. Some
       drums aren't strong enough and a wheel puller
       will bend them.

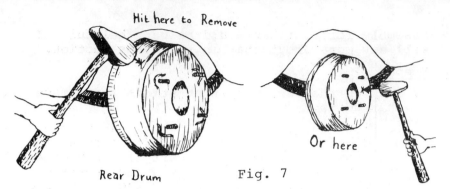

Hit here to Remove

Or here

Rear Drum   Fig. 7

Wheel pullers vary in their construction and
use, so I would ask the people where you rent
one to show you how to use it.

Once the rear drum is off, the rear axle with
the lug nut studs will be in front of the
brake assembly. Don't attempt to remove the
rear axle. You have to work around it when
working with the brake assembly.

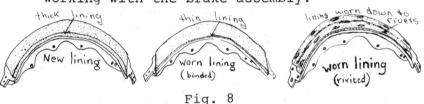

thick lining   thin lining   lining worn down to rivets

New lining   Worn lining   worn lining
                    (bonded)   (rivited)

Fig. 8

b. Inspecting the brakes

With the wheels off, you will be able to
inspect the brake linings. Brake shoes have
either bonded or riveted linings (Fig.8).
Bonded linings are attached to the shoe by a
gluing process and are smooth with no visible
means of attachment to the shoe. Shoes with
bonded linings should be replaced if the
linings are worn to about 1/32 inch thick or
less. Examine all along the shoe for wear,
as the linings will wear more rapidly in
different parts of the shoe. Riveted linings
are attached to the shoes by means of rivets
that go through holes in the linings. If the
linings are worn down to within 1/32 inch or
less of the rivets, then the shoes should be
replaced. If anywhere along the shoe the
lining is worn flush with a rivet, be sure to
replace the shoes.

c. Disassembling the brake parts

Before going any further, find a diagram in
Chilton's or the shop manual for your car that

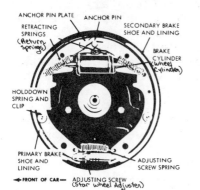

ANCHOR PIN PLATE   ANCHOR PIN

RETRACTING
SPRINGS
(Return
Springs)

SECONDARY BRAKE
SHOE AND LINING

BRAKE
CYLINDER
(Wheel
Cylinder)

HOLDDOWN
SPRING AND
CLIP

PRIMARY BRAKE
SHOE AND
LINING

ADJUSTING
SCREW SPRING

◄ FRONT OF CAR ─ ADJUSTING SCREW
(Star Wheel Adjuster)

a Typical Brake
Assembly.
Does not have
self-adjusting
brakes or an
emergency brake
cable and lever.

Fig. 9

shows the exact brake assembly that you're
working on (Fig.9). If you can't find any
diagram, then I would do one assembly at a
time so you can use the other assembly for
reference. Once you tear down the assembly
and have a pile of assorted springs and other
paraphernalia before you, I find it difficult
to know what goes where no matter how hard I
studied the assembly before dismantling it.

1) Remove the hold down springs - Hold down
springs are the little round springs in the
middle of the shoes that hold them down.
They fit onto a nail that comes through a
hole in the shoe and in the backing plate.
To remove the springs, there is a special
tool made called (you guessed it) a "hold
down spring tool". This isn't a very expensive tool and makes the job a whole lot
easier. However, if you can't, or don't want
to get one, then a pair of slip joint pliers
will work - it just makes the job more of a
hassle.

To remove the hold down spring, put your
finger or thumb on the head of the nail behind
the backing plate. Holding the nail so it
won't turn, depress the spring with the hold
down spring tool or pliers and turn it until
the slot in the round keeper on top of the
spring lines up with the end of the nail (Fig.
10). Remove the tool you are using and the
spring and keeper will pop off the nail.

Fig. 10

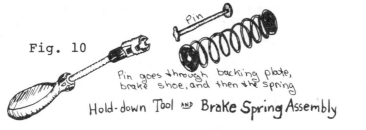

Pin

Pin goes through backing plate,
brake shoe, and then the spring

Hold-down Tool AND Brake Spring Assembly

2) Remove return springs - These are the long springs that hook from the upper part of the shoes to the anchor pin, a nob usually located above the wheel cylinder. They return the shoes after the foot is removed from the brake pedal. There is also a special tool to remove the return springs called brake spring pliers. One end of the pliers looks something like a socket with an extra edge to it. Hook this end of the pliers over the anchor pin and turn the pliers, catching the spring with the edge, and by turning it, remove the spring off the anchor pin (Fig.11). Remove both springs this way.

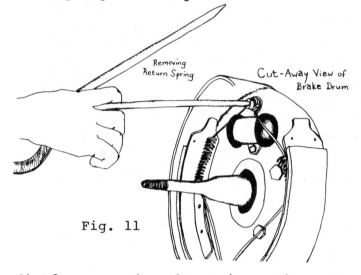

Removing Return Spring

Cut-Away View of Brake Drum

Fig. 11

3) After removing the springs, the rest of the brake assembly should come apart fairly easily. You may have to pry the upper part of the shoes out of the wheel cylinder. Take off the adjuster mechanism, lower spring, star wheel adjuster, etc. Remove all of the parts, leaving only the wheel cylinder remaining on the backing plate. If you are working on rear brakes, it will be necessary to disconnect the parking brake cable from the piece that hooks on to the shoes. Usually you can do this by grabbing the spring around the cable with a pair of vise grips and pulling the spring back and then slipping the cable out of the part it is attached to. This part then will have to be separated from the old shoe so it can be attached to a new shoe. Some sort of clip will be holding it to the old shoe - remove the clip and separate the two parts.

4) Wheel cylinder - If you are planning on rebuilding the wheel cylinder, it should be dismantled and rebuilt now (see Rebuilding the Wheel Cylinder). Otherwise leave the wheel cylinder intact and take care not to get dirt in it.

5) Brake drum - the drums should be turned at this point if you are planning on doing that (see Turning the Drums).

6) Clean the backing plate (where the brake parts are attached) with solvent and brush off the springs and other brake parts with solvent. If you don't have any solvent, you can use a stiff wire brush to remove all the excess dirt, though it is better to use solvent.

7) Assembling brake parts

a) Lay all the brake parts out on the floor in the position that they go on the backing plate, so you know where everything goes and don't forget some part. Make sure you have the shoes in the right position. Usually there is one shoe that has more lining along it. This shoe almost always goes to the rear of the assembly, but compare it with the diagram of the assembly or the brake assembly on the other wheel.

Make sure that the adjuster is clean and that the star wheel turns freely - put a little grease on it to keep it lubricated. If the brake assembly you are working on doesn't have a star wheel adjuster, then just make sure that whatever moveable parts there are in the adjustment mechanism move freely and are lubricated.

b) It is up to you how to reassemble the brake parts on the backing plate. There is no correct order as far as I know. I will tell you how I do it, but you might find an easier way. The important thing is that you end up with correctly assembled brakes.

Assemble the two shoes on the floor with the bottom of the shoes fitting into the adjuster and attach the bottom spring to both shoes. Then, trying to keep the parts all together, put this assembly on the backing plate, fitting the top of the shoes into the places provided for them on the wheel cylinder. Attach all the rest of the brake parts except for the return springs that hook to the anchor pin. You install the hold down springs the same way that you take them out. To put the return springs back on, first hook one end of the spring (be sure it is the correct end) into the hole provided for it in the brake shoe. Then hook the other end of the spring around the curled end of the brake spring pliers and place the curled end over the anchor pin. Pry outward, stretching the spring until it slides downwards on to the anchor pin (Fig.12). Do the same thing for the other spring.

Because all of the brake springs are pretty powerful springs, getting the brake parts back together can be a bit of a hassle. Try not to get too discouraged - just remember that the next time you do a brake job on your car you'll know how to go about getting things back together and it won't be as much of a hassle.

c) If you have self adjusting brakes, you can check to see if everything is assembled correctly by seeing if the self adjuster is working. Hook the end of a fairly large screwdriver into the top of the rear brake shoe and pry the shoe outwards a bit and let it back in. This should cause the part that is hooked up to the star wheel to turn the wheel, thus adjusting the brake (Fig.13). If the wheel isn't being turned, then somewhere something isn't hooked up right. Compare the brake assembly with a diagram or the other wheel assembly.

d) Make sure there is no grease on the shoes. If there is some, then clean it off with a clean rag and alcohol solvent (something like rubbing alcohol works okay).

e) Replace the drum and adjust the brakes. If the wheel cylinder was rebuilt, then the brake line should be bled and the brakes then adjusted again (see Bleeding the Brakes).

If you have trouble getting the drum back on, be sure that the adjustment is in as far as possible, meaning that no threads would be showing on the star wheel adjus-

ter. Also, you can hit the brake shoes
with a rubber mallet (not too hard) to
move them around in different positions
which might help in getting the drum on.
If the drum still won't go on over the
shoes, then there might be a ridge on the
outer edge of the drum from the old shoes.
Feel the inside of the drum to see if it
is smooth and level all the way out to the
edge. If it does seem to have a high spot
at the edge, then have the drum turned
(see Turning the Drums).

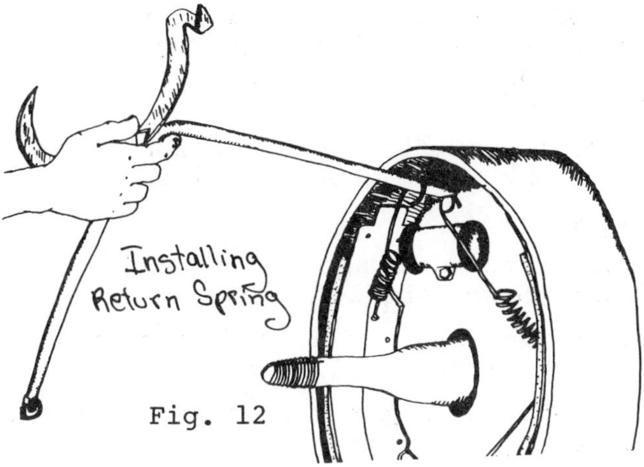

Installing Return Spring

Fig. 12

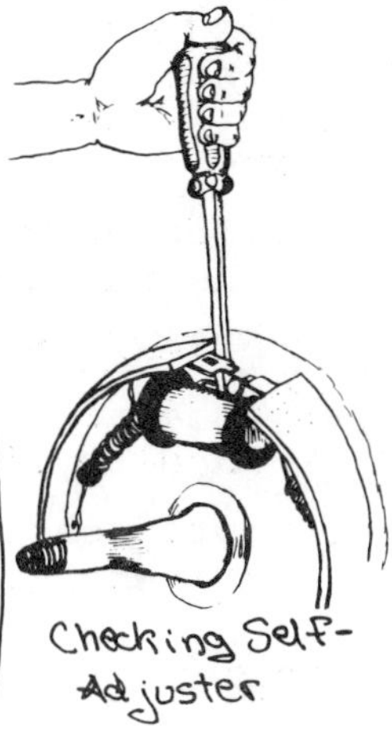

Checking Self-Adjuster

Fig. 13

B. REBUILDING THE WHEEL CYLINDER

It is a good idea to rebuild the wheel cylinders
when you are replacing the brake shoes, and it is a
must if the wheel cylinder is leaking. Sometimes
leaking is obvious as there will be brake fluid all
over the brake shoes and backing plate. If there
isn't any obvious leaking, then turn back one of
the dust caps on the wheel cylinder and see if
there is any fluid in it. If so, it is leaking and
it is only a matter of time before the fluid leaks
out past the dust cap and on to the rest of the
brake assembly.

1. Tools Needed

    a. Electric drill (Fig.14)

    b. Brake hone (Fig.15)

    A brake hone is a Y looking piece that fits into

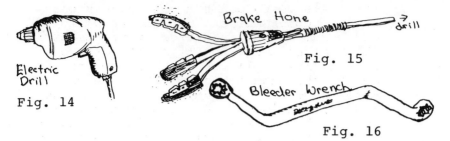

Fig. 14 Electric Drill

Brake Hone drill
Fig. 15

Bleeder Wrench
Fig. 16

an electric drill and has a sanding stone on the
end of each fork (some hones have three branches
instead of two). The branches of the hone have
spring tension and thus push out against the
cylinder walls while the drill is turning the
hone. The stones can be replaced when they wear
down.

   c. Bleeder wrench to fit the bleeder screw on
      the wheel cylinder to be rebuilt (Fig.16)

2. Supplies/Parts Needed

   a. Wheel cylinder rebuild kits, one for each
      wheel cylinder to be rebuilt

   b. Spray carburetor cleaner or alcohol cleaning
      solvent (rubbing alcohol will work)

   Do Not use any gasoline or kerosene base solvent.
   It must be alcohol based.

   c. Plenty of clean rags, as lint free as possible

   d. Pan to catch dripping brake fluid

3. Information Needed

   None in particular, though a diagram of the
   wheel cylinder would be helpful. It isn't so
   necessary as with the brake shoe assembly.

4. Steps

   a. Tear down the brake assembly until only the
      wheel cylinder remains on the backing plate.
      You do not have to remove the wheel cylinder
      to rebuild it.

   b. Remove the dust caps from both ends of the
      cylinder. You should be able to peel these
      off fairly easily.

   Inside the cylinder there will be two pistons,
   two rubber seals, and most likely a spring in
   the middle (Fig.17) (not all wheel cylinders
   will have a spring). What you see at both ends
   of the cylinder are the pistons. Push inward
   on one of the pistons, thus popping the other
   piston out. The spring might cause the pis-

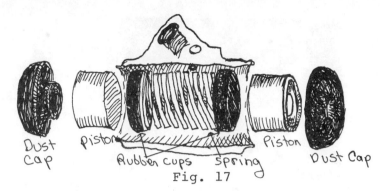

Dust Cap   Piston   Rubber cups   Spring   Piston   Dust Cap

Fig. 17

ton to pop out with some force, so try to
catch it when it comes out. Brake fluid will
come out with the pistons and will continue
to drip out, so have a pan under the wheel to
catch the dripping fluid. If the pistons are
stuck and won't come out, use a piece of
broom handle as a punch so as not to hurt the
piston, and tap the piston out. Remove the
other piston, seals and the spring.

Wheel Cylinder

a. Bleed screw in
   wheel cylinder
b. Bleed screw with
   protective rubber
   cap
c. Bleed screw without
   rubber cap

Fig. 18

c. At this point, I would make sure you can
   loosen the bleed screw (Fig.18). Sometimes
   they are very corroded and you end up twisting them off. If this happens, I would
   replace the entire wheel cylinder, as it is
   difficult to bleed the cylinder through the
   brake line and also, sometimes it doesn't work
   because air gets trapped in the bleed screw
   and won't bleed out.

   The bleed screw is located behind the backing
   plate where the brake line goes into the
   backing plate (Fig.19). To loosen the bleed
   screw, it is best to use a 6 point wrench
   that will fit on the screw snugly and not
   round it off. Special bleeder wrenches are
   made that are offset so they can fit down on
   the bleed screw (Fig.16). Remove the bleed
   screw by unscrewing it all the way. Make
   sure it isn't clogged - blowing compressed
   air through it is the best way, but you can
   also work a small wire through it to clean it
   out, and spray some carburetor cleaner in the

Fig. 19

hole. Replace the screw and screw it in all
the way, making it tight.

If you do break off the bleed screw, it isn't
too difficult to remove the wheel cylinder
and replace it (the difficult part is in your
pocketbook - they are pretty expensive).
Loosen the fitting on the line where it goes
into the cylinder behind the backing plate
using a line wrench (a 6 point open end
wrench - Fig.26) and then remove the bolts
that hold the wheel cylinder to the backing
plate. Pull the cylinder a little forward
and then unscrew it from the brake line.
Brake fluid will drip out of the line so have
a pan ready to catch the fluid. To put a new
cylinder in, reverse these steps, but you
probably will have to remove the bleed screw
from the new cylinder before bolting it to
the backing plate. The cylinder will come
complete with pistons, seals and dust caps,
so you won't have to rebuild the cylinder.

d. Honing the cylinder

Honing is a sanding process - the sanding
stones are turned at a high speed inside the
cylinder to remove old fluid deposits, burrs,
pits, etc. To hone:

1) Squirt penetrating lubricant or some old
brake fluid into the cylinder.

2) Squeeze the arms of the hone together and
insert them into the cylinder.

3) Turn on the drill and move the hone back
and forth through the cylinder with a smooth
continuous motion. Be sure not to push the
hone so far that the stones leave the cylinder, because it is likely that the stones
will come flying off the drill.

4) After honing for about 30 seconds, turn the drill off and remove the hone. Wipe the cylinder out with a cloth and inspect the walls for pits, light grooves, etc.

5) Continue to hone and inspect until the cylinder walls are smooth and shiny. If you can't get all the nicks and grooves out and they seem pretty deep, then you might have to replace the wheel cylinder. Indentations in the cylinder walls will allow fluid to leak past the seals. You can pretty much ignore grooves, etc. in the middle of the cylinder because the pistons and seals do not travel back and forth there.

If you are uncertain whether or not to replace the cylinder, then I would go ahead and use the old cylinder and see if leaking occurs. Wheel cylinders are so expensive that it would be a shame to replace one when it wasn't really necessary.

e. Rebuilding the cylinder

A rebuild kit contains two rubber seals, two dust caps, and often the spring (though not always). The essential thing to remember when rebuilding the cylinder is cleanliness - you must not get any dirt into the cylinder. When you are ready to put the new seals in, make sure that your hands are clean.

1) Clean out the cylinder with alcohol or the carburetor cleaner that comes in a spray can. DO NOT use gasoline solvent. Wipe excess moisture out with a clean, lint free cloth. Clean pistons in the same manner.

2) Coat cylinder parts - new spring and seals, pistons, and inside of the cylinder - with fresh brake fluid.

3) Insert the spring into the cylinder. Push the seals into each side of the cylinder so the flat part of the seal faces outward towards you. Be sure not to pinch or twist the seals.

4) Push the pistons into the cylinder so the flat part of the piston rests against the flat part of the seal.

5) Put the new dust caps over each end of the cylinder, making sure that they fit into the grooves provided for them. An easy way to get the dust caps on is to turn them inside

out, put the center of the cap around the piston, and then turn the edges of the cap out over the cylinder into the grooves.

worn down and gouged surface

a brake shoe

An old brake drum which needs turning

Fig. 20

C. TURNING THE DRUMS

Drums should be turned if there are any grooves or ridges in the surface of the drum (Fig.20), or if they are out of round. Out of round drums would be indicated by a vibration action when braking.

If you are replacing the brake shoes but not turning the drums even though there are grooves in them, the brake linings will wear uneven and faster. The braking action, however, won't be affected unless the drums are severely scored.

Turning the drum refers to cutting a thin layer of metal off the surface of a drum so it is smooth and has no ridges or grooves in it. The most that can be removed is .060 inch - otherwise the drum becomes too thin. If your drum has very deep grooves in it, it might have to be replaced. A drum can be turned more than once - just so long as it doesn't exceed the .060 limit. Have drums turned at an automotive machine shop. If you need a new drum, the best place to look for one would be a salvage yard, as new drums are very expensive.

D. BLEEDING THE BRAKES

Bleeding the brake lines refers to pumping brake fluid through the lines to push any air in the lines or wheel cylinders out through the bleed screws in the wheel cylinders.

Bleeding the brake lines is necessary any time you think there might be air in the lines or if the lines have been opened for any reason. If you rebuild wheel cylinders, then you have to bleed the lines at those wheel cylinders.

147

Though not absolutely necessary, it is a good idea to adjust the brake shoes (if you just put in new shoes) before doing the bleeding. Adjust the shoes again after bleeding (see Adjusting the Brakes).

1. Tools Needed

Bleeder wrench or wrench to fit the bleed screw (Fig.16)

2. Supplies/Parts Needed

a. Brake fluid - a pint container should be plenty

If you have disc brakes, be sure to get fluid that is made for disc brakes. A word of caution about brake fluid - it will ruin the finish on a car, so be careful not to get any on your car.

b. Rags

3. Information Needed

None

4. Steps

a. All the drums should be on, as the wheel cylinder pistons will pop out if there isn't the drum to stop the movement of the brake shoes. Make sure the master cylinder reservoir (where you put the brake fluid) is filled with fluid and the cap is on. As you bleed the brakes, you should check the reservoir periodically and keep it filled with fluid.

Locate the bleed screws (in back of the wheel next to the brake line where it goes into the backing plate - Fig.19). Make sure you are able to turn all the bleed screws at the wheel cylinders you are going to bleed. Leave the screws tightened after seeing if you are able to loosen them.

b. Bleed the wheel cylinder farthest away from the master cylinder first and then work in progression towards the master cylinder. If you are doing both front and rear brakes, then you would first bleed the right rear wheel, then the left rear wheel, then the right front wheel and finally the left front wheel (the wheel cylinder closest to the master cylinder)(Fig.21).

c. Have a friend pump the brake pedal about four to six times, making sure she allows the pedal to come all the way up each time. On the last pump, hold the pedal down.

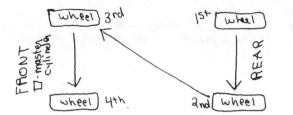

Order in which to bleed brakes

Fig. 21

d. While the pedal is being held down, loosen
slightly the bleeder screw until fluid starts
coming out. Press down on the pedal as the
fluid comes out of the bleed screw, forcing
the fluid out with the maximum pressure. If
you just rebuilt the wheel cylinder, then you
may not get any fluid out on the first few
tries. Once pressure is built up in the line,
fluid and air will come spurting out of the
screw.

e. Tighten the bleed screw while the pedal is
still being held down, and then pump the
brakes up again, hold down, and loosen the
bleed screw, bleed and tighten the bleed
screw. Bleed each line as many times as
necessary to get the air out. A sign that
there is no more air in the lines is when the
fluid comes out of the bleed screw in a steady
clear flow. If you are doing more than one
line, bleed the first line a few times and
then bleed all the other lines a few times,
and then go back to the first line and bleed
all the lines again to make sure all the air
is out.

When pumping the brake pedal, pump slow and
easy so as not to churn up the brake fluid
too much. If it gets churned up, you get
bubbles in the fluid and then sometimes it
is hard to tell when there is air still left
in the fluid coming out of the bleed screws.

f. When you are done bleeding the brakes, make
sure all the bleed screws are tight. Test
drive the car - the brake pedal should feel
hard when the brakes are applied. If you
have to pump up the pedal, or if the brakes
fade when the pedal is applied hard, then
there is probably still air in the lines and
they should be bled again.

E. ADJUSTING THE BRAKES

Most american cars and some foreign cars have self-adjusting brakes. Self-adjusting brakes adjust themselves when the car is braked while backing up. Most foreign cars have non self-adjusting brakes, so they need to be adjusted periodically. If you have just replaced the brake shoes, then be sure to adjust the brakes if your brakes don't have self-adjusters. Self-adjusting brakes can be adjusted by backing up and stopping a lot or they can be manually adjusted using the same procedure as for non self-adjusting brakes.

What you are doing when you adjust the brakes is moving the brake shoes out so they just barely touch the drum. That way the brake pedal will only have to go down a little ways before engaging the brakes which produces a quicker stopping action.

Most adjusters, self-adjusting and non self-adjusting, are of the star wheel type, so the steps will be based on that kind of adjuster (Fig.22). All brakes have some sort of adjustment mechanism usually located at the opposite end of the backing plate from the wheel cylinder. Access to the adjuster is provided at the back of the backing plate (so you don't have to take the wheel and drum off to adjust the brakes).

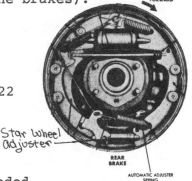

Fig. 22

Star Wheel Adjuster

REAR BRAKE

AUTOMATIC ADJUSTER SPRING

1. Tools Needed

a. Brake adjusting tool (Fig.3); there are different varieties of adjusting tools, smaller ones for foreign cars

b. A medium size screwdriver will usually work well as an adjusting tool

2. Supplies/Parts Needed

Flashlight

3. Information Needed

None

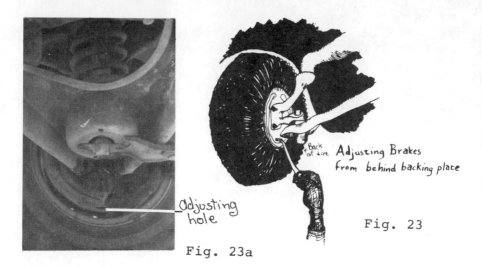

Adjusting Brakes
from behind backing plate

Back of tire

Adjusting hole

Fig. 23a

Fig. 23

4. Steps

a. The wheels you are adjusting have to be off the ground, so jack up the car and put it on jack stands. Brakes should be adjusted in pairs - don't adjust the brakes at one of the rear or front wheels without adjusting the brakes at the other rear or front wheel. Adjusting only one wheel will cause the car to pull badly to the side of the adjusted wheel when the brakes are applied.

b. In the back of the drum (behind the wheel) usually at the bottom, though not always, there will be one or two holes through which you adjust the brakes (Fig.23a). Some brakes have two adjusters per wheel, some just one. Sometimes these holes are covered by a rubber cap - if so, remove it.

c. Spray lubricant into the hole to loosen up the adjuster. If you have just rebuilt the brakes, then this shouldn't be necessary, as the adjusters should already be loose. Sometimes the adjusters are really frozen up and you have to remove the drum and remove the adjuster to free it up (a lot of work if all you had planned on doing was to adjust the brakes).

d. Lay on your back under the wheel and shine a light into the hole so you can see the star wheel. With a brake adjusting tool or a screwdriver, turn the wheel one way or the other by prying either up or down with the screwdriver (Fig.23). Some adjusters have a clip that fits into the star wheel. With this kind of adjuster you have to pry up on

the clip with a screwdriver and turn the star
wheel with another screwdriver or adjusting
tool. I never can figure out which way to
turn the wheel, so I just turn it one way and
see if I am loosening or tightening the drum.
Turn the wheel to get a sense of how freely
it turns. Then turn the star wheel for a few
turns and then spin the wheel and see if it
spins more freely (which means you are backing off the brake shoes) or less freely (which
means the brake shoes are moving closer to
the drum).

e. Turn the adjuster until the drum is so tight
   that you can't turn it. Then back the adjustment off until the drum turns freely with a
   slight drag on it.

f. If the drum has two adjusters do the same
   procedure for both adjusters - usually the
   two star wheels turn opposite ways to tighten
   or loosen the drum.

g. Adjust all the brakes as evenly as possible,
   so you won't have braking pull to one side or
   the other.

h. Remember to put the rubber caps back on.

F. BRAKE WARNING LIGHT

Some cars have a dash light that comes on when the
brakes are bad (as indicated by the movement of
brake fluid). If you have rebuilt the brake assemblies and wheel cylinders, then this light will
probably be on. It doesn't mean something is wrong
with your brakes, but just that the switch for the
light needs to be reset. How to do this varies
with the make of car, so check with a manual for
your car to see how it is done.

WORKING ON DISC BRAKES

I am going to go over doing work on disc brakes in
a fairly limited way because disc brake assemblies
seem to vary so much, and I haven't worked with
enough different kinds to be able to generalize
very much. One nice thing is that replacing disc
brake pads - the main repair work done on disc
brakes - is pretty easy and quickly done, much
easier than replacing brake shoes.

If you don't know whether or not your car has disc
brakes, then look at the back of the wheels, particularly the front wheels. Only the newer cars,
foreign mostly, have disc brakes on both the front
and rear wheels. Most cars with disc brakes have
them only on the front wheels with drum brakes on
the rear wheels. If you look at the back of the
wheel and you have drum brakes then you will see an
enclosed plate or pan with the brake line going
into it and the bleed screw somewhere nearby. However, if you have disc brakes then you will see a
large clumpy-looking part on one side of the back
wheel. This is the brake caliper and it
will have the brake line leading to it (there will
also be a bleeder screw, though possibly not located
near the brake line like it is with drum brakes).
The brake caliper fits over the side of the disc.
You may be able to see the disc, though some disc
brakes have sort of a protective plate behind the
disc.

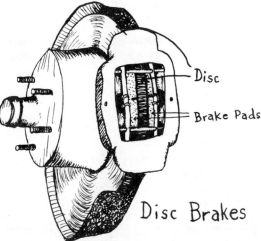

Fig. 24

Disc

Brake Pads

Disc Brakes

A. REPLACING THE BRAKE PADS

Jack up the car and take the tire off. You should
now be able to see the disc and the brake caliper
with the pads in it. The pads are little metal
plates with lining attached to them, like with brake
shoes. There will be two pads in the caliper, one
on either side of the disc. Look down in the caliper with a flashlight and try to see the amount of
lining left on the pads (Fig.24) (don't confuse
the metal that the linings are attached to with
the linings themselves). If either one of the linings
has worn down to about 1/16 inch or less, then
replace the pads.

As with brake shoes, replace the pads on both front wheels at the same time. This is also the only way you buy the pads, in what are called axle sets.

Usually you don't have to remove the calipers to replace the pads. The pads are held in the calipers by long pins - one on each side of the caliper- that go through both pads and both sides of the caliper. Remove these pins using a punch and hammer. Pull the pads out of the calipers - I usually have to grab hold of the top of the pads with a pair of vise grips and then wiggle the pads back and forth to get them out. Remove both pads in the calipers before putting either of the new pads in.

To put the new pads in the caliper, you have to push the pistons all the way into the caliper to make room for the thicker pads. One way to do this is to use a long screwdriver and pry against the disc and piston, pushing the piston in until it is flush with the caliper. If the calipers aren't too big, another way to push the piston in is to use a pair of channel lock pliers. Put one jaw of the pliers on the piston and the other jaw on the outside of the caliper and then squeeze the jaws together. I find this method works particularly well if the pistons appear to be frozen and won't move when pushed with a pry bar.

Put the new pads in the caliper, making sure the lining side of the pads goes against the disc. Replace the pins and any other parts you had to remove to get the old pads out.

After you have put the wheels back on and let the car down on to the ground, pump the brake pedal a few times to move the pistons back out into contact with the pads. Do this before driving the car, or you won't have any brakes the first time you put your foot on the brake pedal.

As with drum brakes, the brake indicator light might appear on the dashboard after replacing the pads. See a manual about how to reset the switch for the light.

B. OTHER DISC BRAKE WORK

1. If the pistons are sticking in the calipers, or if fluid is leaking out of the calipers, then the calipers should be removed and rebuilt. The rebuilding process is similar to rebuilding wheel cylinders, though the calipers are somewhat more complicated and also vary a lot among different

makes of cars. Rebuild kits can be gotten for the
calipers at an auto parts store. Removing the
calipers is usually fairly easy - the brake line
has to be disconnected and then there are two large
bolts that hold the calipers on. These have to be
loosened (a breaker bar helps) and removed and then
the caliper can be removed and rebuilt on the bench.
After putting the rebuilt caliper back on the discs,
be sure to bleed the brakes at the calipers.

2. As with the brake drums, if the discs are scored
or have ridges in them, they should be turned. To
remove the disc, first remove the caliper, and then
remove the bearing assembly holding the disc on (see
Part II, Chapter 4, Repacking Front Wheel Bearings).
The disc then will come right off. This would be a
good time to repack the front wheel bearings, since
you wouldn't normally remove the disc to repack the
inner bearings on disc brakes. If you are removing
the rear discs to be turned, then usually you have
to remove the caliper and there will be some keeper
mechanism (screws, etc.) to hold the rear disc on.
Remove these and then the disc can be taken off.
Discs can be turned at an auto machine shop.

With both the front and rear brakes, if you aren't
planning on removing the caliper to rebuild it then
sometimes the brake line can remain connected and
just the bolts holding the caliper removed. Pull
the caliper off the disc and hang it up somewhere
out of the way. Use wire to hang the caliper up so
the weight of the caliper doesn't pull on the brake
line.

3. Adjustment - there is no adjustment to make with
disc brakes.

REBUILDING THE MASTER CYLINDER AND
REPLACING BRAKE LINES

A. REBUILDING THE MASTER CYLINDER

The same procedure for rebuilding the master cylinder would be used for both disc and drum brakes.
Rebuilding the master cylinder is essentially the
same as rebuilding a wheel cylinder, except the
master cylinder is removed from the car and rebuilt
on the bench. To remove the master cylinder, the
push rod that comes out of the cylinder must be
disconnected from the brake pedal (sometimes it is
held on by a pin that goes through both the pedal
and the push rod). Disconnect the brake lines on
the master cylinder and then remove the bolts that

hold the master cylinder onto the fire wall and
take the cylinder out of the car.

Remove the insides of the cylinder - be sure you
know where and in what direction all the springs,
pistons and seals go. A diagram would be helpful
(Fig.25). To get the seals and pistons out, first
remove the snap ring and then blow compressed air
through one of the holes where a brake line goes.
This should cause the pistons, etc. to pop out of
the cylinder. The inside of the cylinder is honed
out, and the parts are cleaned. Coat the new seals
and all the parts with brake fluid and put them
back in the cylinder. Reinstall the cylinder in
the car and bleed it at the brake lines coming out
of the cylinder.

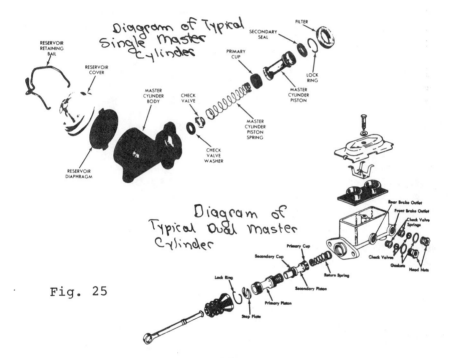

Fig. 25

Master cylinder rebuild kits can be purchased at an
auto parts store. Sometimes rebuilding a master
cylinder isn't always successful. It might be
wiser to replace the cylinder with a factory rebuilt master cylinder, rather than going through
the hassle of rebuilding the cylinder yourself.
However, rebuilt cylinders are pretty expensive.
Not many garages rebuild master cylinders anymore -
it is a lot easier for them to just put an already
rebuilt cylinder on the car. Try to check around
and see if you can get any information as to the
success rate in rebuilding the master cylinders on

your make of car. On some cars it just isn't worth
the hassle, because rebuilding rarely seems to fix
the problem with the cylinder.

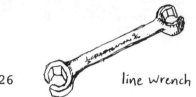

Fig. 26   line wrench

B. REPLACING THE BRAKE LINES

Brake lines should be replaced if they break. Brake
lines are really not too hard to replace, though
sometimes the fittings on the old lines will be
rusted and not turn easily. Brake lines come in
sections, so you only replace that section where
the break is. To unscrew the fittings use a line
wrench (Fig.26) that fits securely on the fitting
and won't round it off. If the fitting does get
rounded off then use a pair of vise grips to unscrew
the fitting. The line should not turn, only the
fitting. If you are replacing the line it actually
doesn't matter whether the line turns or not, but
if you are just removing the line from a wheel cylinder, say, then it is very important the line
doesn't turn for it will twist and kink and then
you will have to replace it.

You can buy brake line in different widths and
lengths at a parts store with the fittings already
on it. Brake line is flexible and won't kink when
you bend it normally, so you can shape the line to
have the same shape as the old line.

After replacing the line, be sure to bleed the
wheel cylinder or cylinders that the line feeds, to
get the air out of the line.

Chapter 8

HINTS ON
GENERAL REPAIRS

This chapter is sort of an overlap between Part II
covering Repairs, and Part III covering Troubleshooting. I will be talking about a little of both
in this chapter. The specific areas I will cover
are: shocks; exhaust system; universal joints; the
front end; the transmission; and the clutch. I
won't be going into detail in the repair explanations because the parts of these systems vary a lot
from car to car. Rather, I will just try to give
you some pointers when replacing certain parts.

SHOCKS

A. SYMPTOMS

The symptoms of bad shocks are a looseness in the
steering and a general feeling of instability when
the car hits bumps, etc. For example, if every
time you go over railroad tracks the steering wheel
jerks around a lot in your hands, then the car
might have bad shocks. Or if the passengers are
jostled real badly when driving over a bumpy road.

Extreme jostling and bumpiness could be attributed
to a broken spring. Park the car on level pavement,

and get out and take a look at it and see if it is
sagging noticeably somewhere. If so, then probably
the spring on that side is broken and should be
replaced.

B. CHECK

The best way to tell the condition of the shocks is
the "bounce" test. Park the car on level pavement.
Bounce each corner of the car up and down as hard
as you can. Bounce it a few times and then let go
of the car. If the shock is good, then the car
will return to its original position right away and
stop moving. If the shock is bad, then the car will
continue to bounce up and down a few times after
you let go of the car. Also, as you push on the
car, look along the side of it and see if it moves
in a straight up and down line. If it jostles back
and forth while you are pushing on it, this is
another sign of a bad shock. Bounce each corner of
the car, checking the shock at each wheel. Shocks
should be replaced in pairs, so if one of the rear
shocks is bad but the other rear shock seems okay,
then you should still replace both rear shocks.
Same for the front shocks. Shocks normally have to
be replaced about every 24,000 miles on american
cars.

Another way of checking for bad shocks is to crawl
underneath the car and look at the shocks to see if
they are leaking. Most shocks operate hydrauli-
cally and are filled with oil (there are also what
is known as air shocks that operate on air pressure,
though these aren't real common). If the shocks
are leaking, there will be old oil deposits on the
shocks where the upper part of the shock goes over
the lower part of the shock (Fig.1). Even though
the shocks are leaking, they may still operate
okay. However, eventually the leaking will lessen
the cushioning ability of the shock and it will
have to be replaced.

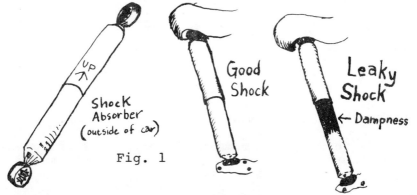

Shock
Absorber
(outside of car)

Good
Shock

Leaky
Shock

← Dampness

Fig. 1

There are different designs of shocks, but they all
fasten to the car in some manner at the top of the
shock and at the bottom of the shock. Removing
shocks is fairly easy - sometimes you don't even
have to jack up the car. Removing the shock is a
matter of loosening and unscrewing the bolts that
hold the shock on the car. Shocks don't support
the weight of the car, so you don't have to worry
about anything happening when you take the shock
out. Sometimes the bolts holding the shock on the
frame are hard to get loose. A 1/2 inch drive
breaker bar is the best tool I have found to loosen
the shock bolts.

When installing the new shock, be sure to install
the shock with the right side up. Most shocks have
an arrow on them indicating which way is up. The
shock can be pulled out to the length it needs to
be to install it. When tightening down the bolts
that hold the shock on, only tighten them until the
rubber mountings are squeezed to about even with
the washer or cup next to them (Fig.2). Directions
as to how to assemble the rubber mountings and how
much to tighten the shock bolts usually come with
the new shock.

Fig. 2

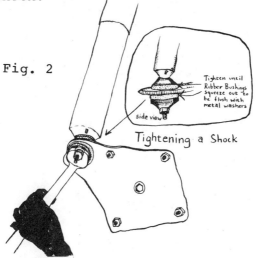

Tighten until
Rubber Bushings
squeeze out to
be flush with
metal washers

side view

Tightening a Shock

EXHAUST SYSTEM

A. SYMPTOMS

The most obvious symptom of trouble in the exhaust
system is, of course, a lot of noise coming from
the exhaust. When you are driving along and can't

talk to the woman sitting next to you, then you
know you have problems with the exhaust system.
Another not so obvious symptom is a rumbling or
knocking coming from under the car, particularly in
the rear. Though this could be a symptom of other
difficulties, it could also indicate an exhaust
part that has come loose from its hanger and is
banging against the body or some other part of the
car. Also, if the exhaust system was just repaired,
then such a noise would indicate that the exhaust
system is positioned wrong - it should not be
banging on anything. If you had the work done at a
garage, be sure to take your car back and get them
to fix it, because they should have made sure that
the exhaust system didn't rattle in any way. The
smell of exhaust fumes while driving or getting
headaches, feeling dizzy, etc. is a third indication of possible exhaust system troubles.

B.CHECK

Checking out the exhaust system is a matter of
crawling underneath the car and looking the pipes
and muffler over for any holes or places where one
piece has broken off from another piece. If your
exhaust system has been real loud, then the holes
or breaks are probably going to be pretty obvious.
However, if you are just checking the general condition of the exhaust system, then look for tiny
pinholes in the muffler and pipes (an easy way to
detect pinholes is to hold a rag over the end of
the tail pipe with the car running and see if smoke
is coming out of the exhaust pipes anywhere). Also
look for soft and/or badly rusted sections of the
muffler and/or pipes. Any condition like this would
indicate that that part of the exhaust system will
probably need replacing soon. If you are going to
be replacing a part - like if there is a hole in
the muffler - then be sure to check the condition

161

of the pipes that are connected to it. If they
look like they are going to have to be replaced
soon anyway, then it would be a lot easier to replace them at the same time you replace the muffler.

C. REPAIR

To repair the exhaust system, you only have to
replace those parts that need replacing - you don't
have to replace the whole exhaust system. The
hardest part of doing exhaust work, I think, is to
get the old exhaust parts off. First, remove the
clamps where the parts come together. You should
replace the clamps, so it is okay if they break off
while you are trying to unscrew them. A lot of
mechanics tighten the nuts on the clamps instead of
loosening them in order to twist the nuts off.

Getting the pipes apart can be a real chore. Garages
use either an air chisel - a chisel driven by compressed air, or an oxy-acetylene torch to get the
rusted pipes apart. Not having access to either of
these tools, the best way I know to get the pipes
apart is to use a sharp chisel and a hammer. Catch
the edge of the old pipe where it is split, and try
to peel back the pipe with the chisel and hammer
(Fig.3). If the outside pipe is good, and you are
just removing the inside pipe, then bend the edges
of the good pipe out a little, and chisel a hole in
the old pipe and then try to cut the inside pipe
apart. Once the pipes have been slit all the way
to the end of the pipe, then usually you can pull
the pipes apart from one another.

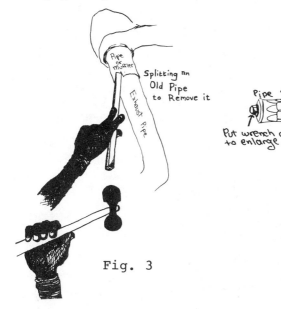

Splitting an
Old Pipe
to Remove it

Pipe or muffler

Exhaust Pipe

Pipe Spreader   Piece of pipe

Put wrench on here
to enlarge spreader

Fig. 4

Fig. 3

Before putting the new pipes on, scrape off any paper labels that might be on them. I've heard of fires starting from these labels heating up.

When you start to put the new pipe on the old pipe you might discover that the new pipe won't fit very well onto the old pipe. Try bending the edges of the outer pipe out a little bit using a pair of channel lock pliers. Also, bend in any edges that stick out on the inner pipe. If the inner pipe is the old pipe and is rusted, then sanding it a bit might help. If you still can't get the new pipe on, then there is a tool known as a pipe spreader that is made for this problem (Fig.4). The pipe spreader is inserted inside the outer pipe and then tightened, spreading the parts of the tool outward, and thus the pipe. Usually you can rent a pipe spreader at a rental place.

Make sure you put the muffler on going in the correct direction for the exhaust flow. The in and out pipes should be marked on the muffler.

Once you get all the pipes and muffler together, put the new clamps on and barely tighten them. Check the positioning of the entire exhaust system to make sure it won't bang against something when the car hits a bump - bounce the exhaust system up and down with your hand to get an indication of whether or not it will be hitting something.

When you are sure the system is positioned correctly, then tighten all the clamps real tight. Start with the clamp nearest the engine and work back to the tail pipe.

One other word about exhaust systems: If you replace the pipe that comes from the exhaust manifold on the engine, then be sure to replace the gasket where the pipe bolts on to the exhaust manifold. Also, after putting in a new muffler, you may get a strange smell when you first drive the car - don't worry about it, new mufflers always give off a strange odor when they are first used. It goes away after a bit.

Fig. 7

See page 169 for Figure 5

UNIVERSAL JOINTS

A. SYMPTOMS

Universal joints are another one of those parts on
your car that will have to be replaced at least
once in the life of the car if not more often.
U-joints are the cross-looking pieces on the drive
shaft that allow the drive shaft to adjust to different angles of the car (Fig.5). There is a u-
joint located at the beginning of the drive shaft
and at the end of the drive shaft. Some cars have
a split drive shaft with a universal joint located
in the middle of the drive shaft in addition to the
u-joints at each end of the shaft.

One of the most common symptoms of a bad u-joint is
a clunking noise when the car changes gears. A way
to check for that kind of noise is to open the car
door, and back up and then go forward a few times,
and see if you can hear any clunking sound when the
car changes direction. Another symptom of a bad
u-joint is a vibration in the car, especially in
the rear, when driving at any speeds. Vibration
could be caused by other problems, also, but bad
u-joints are one major cause of vibration.

Fig. 5

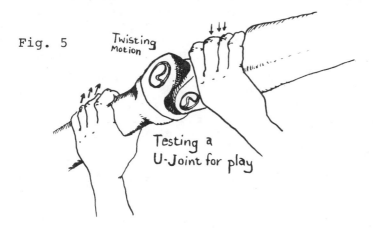

Twisting
Motion

Testing a
U-Joint for play

B. CHECK

To check for a bad u-joint, first jack up the rear
of the car so both wheels are off the ground and
put the car on jack stands. The transmission should
be in neutral and the emergency brake off. Crawl
underneath the car and look at the drive shaft. You
should be able to turn it by hand. Locate the u-
joints on the shaft. Put your hands on either side
of the u-joint and try to twist it - like wringing
out a wet towel (Fig.6). If the u-joint is bad,

then you will feel some play and movement when you try to twist the joint. If the joint is really bad, then the movement will be very obvious. If the u-joint is good, there won't be any movement in the joint at all; it should be just like trying to twist a solid piece of metal. Test all the u-joints in this manner. If may be harder to test the u-joint at the front of the shaft because it will be lower to the ground than the rear and thus you might find it hard to get your hands on it. If necessary you can jack up the front of the car so you can get to it (leave the rear wheels off the ground).

C. REPAIR

Replacing universal joints is sort of my downfall at work. I don't think they are all that hard to do - I just have a problem with them for some reason. Anyhow, I don't think I should attempt to tell you how to replace one, because I might pass on some of my bad habits.

If you don't want to replace the u-joint yourself (you almost have to have a bench vise to do it), then you can take the drive shaft out and take it to a machine shop with the new u-joint, and have the shop take out the old joint and put the new one in. Doing that would be a lot cheaper than taking your car to a garage and having them do the whole job. I don't want to discourage you from replacing the joint yourself - maybe you can find someone to show you how to do it.

To remove the drive shaft, jack up the rear of the car so both wheels are off the ground and put the car on jack stands. The drive shaft is bolted to the differential right at the rear u-joint (Fig.7). Some joints have U bolts that go around the universal joint and the differential flange - remove the nuts from these bolts. The drive shaft with the u-joint will then come away from the rear flange. You can then pull the drive shaft out of the transmission. Stuff a rag or something in the hole in the transmission where the drive shaft comes out to prevent transmission fluid from leaking out of it.

Once you have the drive shaft out of the car, you can replace the bad u-joints in it (or take the shaft somewhere to have the joints replaced).

Installation of the drive shaft is the reverse of these steps. Be sure to get the bolts that hold the shaft on at the rear good and tight.

FRONT END — STEERING LINKAGE, BALL JOINTS

A. SYMPTOMS

Symptoms of front end problems are the car pulls to
one side or the other when you are driving down the
road; looseness in the steering wheel; noises in
the front part of the car when you make a sharp
turn; and shimmy and shakes in the front part of
the car. All of these symptoms could indicate
troubles with the steering linkage or ball joints
or that the front end is in need of a wheel alignment. If you think your car needs alignment, I
would first check over the front end parts, because
it is of little use to have an alignment done with
bad front end parts, as the wheels will quickly go
back out of alignment. Also, if you do end up
replacing one or more of the front end parts, then
the car will have to be realigned.

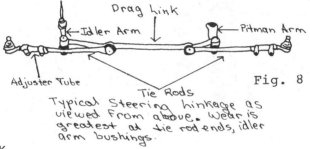

Fig. 8

Typical Steering linkage as
viewed from above. Wear is
greatest at tie rod ends, idler
arm bushings.

B. CHECK

What you need to check for is any sort of looseness
in the steering linkage or ball joints. To check
the steering linkage, jack up the front end of the
car and put it on jack stands. First, grab hold of
the different parts of the linkage and try to move
them back and forth, seeing if there is any play in
any of the parts. They should feel tight and
strong. Next, have a friend hold one front wheel
while you try to turn the other front wheel (like
twisting both ends of the u-joint). Look at the
joints where the linkage is hooked together and see
if there is any up-and-down or excessive movement
in the joints (Fig.8). If the joints are worn, they
move up and down or twist when you try to turn the
wheel.

To test the ball joints, jack up one side of the
front of the car directly under the spring. Just
jack the car up until the wheel on that side is
about 2 inches or so off the ground. Jacking the
car up under the spring takes the weight off the
ball joints so they can be checked for looseness.

Put a long pry bar underneath the wheel and pry it up and down (Fig.9). There shouldn't be more than about 1/2 inch movement of the wheel up and down. Excessive movement of the wheel up and down means that the ball joints are loose and need to be replaced.

C. REPAIR

I am not going to get into talking about front end repair because I have done very little of it, and don't really know a whole lot about it.

Fig. 9

TRANSMISSION

A. SYMPTOMS

In an automatic transmission, symptoms of transmission troubles are: difficulty in shifting; the transmission will shift only when you take your foot off the gas pedal; and slipping out of gear.

Manual transmission difficulties are also indicated by inability of the transmission to change gears, slipping out of gear, and a grinding noise when the transmission changes gears.

B. CHECK

About the only easy thing to do when you think you have transmission problems is to check the fluid level in the transmission and make sure it is at the proper level. Any investigation beyond that requires taking out the transmission and taking it apart to see what the problems are. Both checking out the transmission and repairing it are beyond the scope of my knowledge and this book.

CLUTCH

A. SYMPTOMS

Clutch problems are indicated by the clutch slipping or vibrating (having to double clutch when you change gears), the transmission slipping out of gear (driving down the road and all of a sudden the engine races like you put the clutch pedal in), and no free play on the clutch pedal (the clutch engages when the pedal is almost all the way out).

B. CHECK

As with the transmission, there is no way to check the clutch without removing the transmission and then taking the clutch out and inspecting it. However, you can check the clutch adjustment to make sure it is adjusted properly. There are different methods of doing this, depending on the make of car, so check with a manual for your car or Chilton's. I would be sure to check the clutch adjustment before deciding you have a bad clutch, because sometimes problems with the clutch are just a matter of it being out of adjustment.

C. REPAIR

Replacing a clutch is not too difficult. The difficult part is getting to the clutch. You have to first take out the drive shaft and then remove the transmission with the bell housing (the part that covers the clutch) attached to it. The transmission on an american car is pretty heavy, so you would need a transmission jack to support the weight of the transmission as you remove it. After removing the transmission and bell housing, the clutch can be unbolted from the flywheel. The clutch is made up of the clutch disc, a round disc with lining material similar to brake shoe lining riveted to it; and the pressure plate and clutch cover, a heavy metal disc with a spring loaded cover attached to it(Fig.10). Sometimes you just need to replace the disc, though it is probably a good idea to replace both the disc, pressure plate and cover as long as it's out. It will minimize the need to do the job again in the near future.

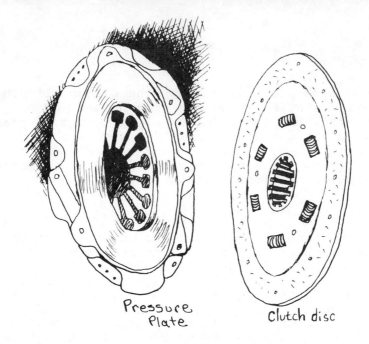

Pressure Plate

Clutch disc

Fig. 10

what a u-joint looks
like out of the drive
shaft and dismantled

Fig. 5

PART III

TROUBLESHOOTING

Troubleshooting is one of the hardest and also one
of the most important tasks of working on cars.
Troubleshooting is mostly based on experience, I
think. The more problems you encounter with cars
then the more you build up a backlog of experience
to determine possible causes for different problems.
I have been doing mechanic work for about three
years and only now am I beginning to get any confidence in my ability to troubleshoot. Because most
women haven't had the experience that men who have
grown up working on cars have had, a lot of times
we have to depend on men to figure out what is
wrong with our cars, even when we are doing the
work on them ourselves. What I want to do in this
part of the manual is to try and transfer some of
the knowledge I have accumulated in troubleshooting
to you to give you a start on determining what is
wrong with your car. I will only be dealing with
the most common causes of the most common problems
with cars. In using these troubleshooting chapters,
check out possible causes for a problem in the
order that they are listed. The lists start with
the most likely solution and end with the least
likely solution.

There is a manual that Chiltons or Motors puts out
on troubleshooting that lists every possible cause
of a problem in the order of what is most likely to
be the cause. It might be of further help to you
in trying to determine what is wrong with your car.

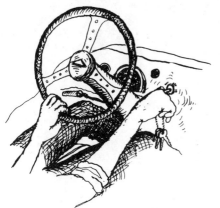

Chapter 1

WHEN YOUR CAR
WON'T START

All of us at one time or another have had the
experience of not being able to start the car and
then having to pay a terrific amount for a gas
station person to come out, jiggle some wires, and
have the car start right up. He goes away feeling
the smug man of knowledge and we are left feeling
the stereotypical dumb female. In this chapter I
hope to prevent that from happening to you in the
future. I am going to go through the standard
trouble shooting procedures mechanics use when
trying to start a car. I will go through all the
procedures in the order that they should be fol-
lowed, starting with the most common cause for a
problem or the simplest thing to check, and ending
with the least common cause for a problem.

First, you need to determine one of three things:

1. the engine doesn't crank at all

2. the engine cranks slower than normal

3. the engine cranks at normal speed but won't
   start

By engine cranking, I mean the engine turning over
what it does when you start the car before it
"catches" and begins to run. Cranking is just the
starter motor turning the crankshaft.

In going through all these troubleshooting procedures, you should keep in mind the weather. The
colder it is, the harder your car is to start. I'll
talk more about the effect of cold under specific
problems.

ENGINE DOESN'T CRANK AT ALL

(You turn the key on and all you hear is a click
or nothing. Or you might hear sort of a whirring sound - see step D.)

When the engine doesn't crank it means that for
some reason the starter motor isn't functioning.
Most frequently, this is not trouble with the
starter motor, but rather with electrical connections preventing current from getting to the
starter.

1. DEAD BATTERY

The first thing to consider is whether or not you
left the lights or some other electrical accessory
on for a long period of time that would cause the
battery to be totally dead. However, if the car
was just running, or nothing was left on, then this
wouldn't be the cause of no cranking action.

2. BAD CONNECTION AT THE BATTERY

The most common cause for no cranking action would
be a bad connection at the battery that is preventing electrical current from getting to the starter.
Frequently it is the negative cable connection that
is at fault, though a bad connection at either
battery post would cause no cranking action. Remove
the battery cables and clean both clamps and posts
and reinstall them, making sure the clamps are tight
on the posts (see Battery Care under Winterizing
chapter). If the engine still won't crank, then
check the positive battery cable connection at the
starter motor to make sure it is clean and tight.
If you have a Ford, check the connection of the
positive cable at the relay switch (small box
mounted on fender near the battery that the positive
cable goes to) (Fig.1). Also, if the negative cable
goes to the body of the car somewhere, not the
engine, then there should be a ground strap (looks

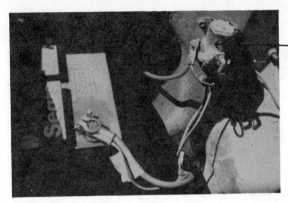

Magnetic relay switch (commonly called a solenoid) on a Ford

Fig. 1

like the negative battery cable--Fig.2) going from
the car body to the engine. Sometimes the ground
strap is located underneath the engine. If the
connections on the ground strap are dirty or loose,
then this could cause a break in the electrical
connection. (I explain the idea of ground and what
it means in terms of a continuous electrical current
in Chapter 3 of this section.)

If your car doesn't start and you think it is the
battery connections, one thing you can do if you
don't have access to tools is to stick a nail
between the battery post and clamp or anything else
that would make a good metal to metal connection
between the post and clamp (Fig.3). Hopefully, such
a temporary measure will provide enough electrical
connection to get your car started, and then you
can clean the posts and clamps later.

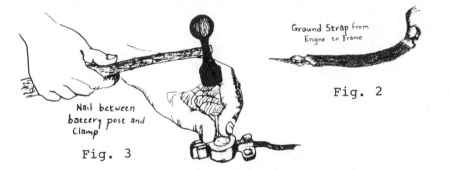

Ground Strap from Engine to Frame

Fig. 2

Nail between battery post and Clamp

Fig. 3

3. FAULTY IGNITION SWITCH

Another possible cause of no cranking action at all
is a faulty ignition switch or loose electrical
connections to the switch. Check the electrical
connections at the ignition switch to see that they
are tight.

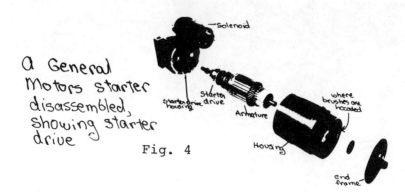

a General Motors starter disassembled, showing starter drive

Fig. 4

(Labels on figure: Solenoid, starter drive housing, starter drive, Armature, where brushes are located, Housing, end frame)

4. FAULTY STARTER MOTOR

If the engine doesn't crank, but you do hear sort of a whirring sound, then you possibly have problems with the starter motor. Most likely the trouble is in the starter drive (or bendix it is called) (Fig. 4). The starter drive is the part of the starter motor that moves forward to engage the flywheel and start turning it, and thus the engine. (The flywheel is bolted to the back of the crankshaft.) Sometimes the starter drive fails to move forward, and just spins where it is, causing the whirring sound you hear. If you think you have starter motor problems, then the starter motor would have to be removed to do any repairs on it. To remove the starter, first disconnect the negative cable at the battery, and then disconnect the positive cable at the starter and any other electrical wires leading to the starter. There should be two or three bolts holding the starter to the engine. Remove these and then you can take the starter out of the engine. Once you have it out, you might want to take it to an automotive electrical shop to have the trouble diagnosed and repaired if you don't want to get into pulling the starter apart. Starters are fairly simple and easy to work on, however. Find a diagram of your starter before you take it apart.

Push Starting Your Car....

5.   PUSH-STARTING YOUR CAR

If you have starter motor problems, you can push-start your car to get it going so you can move it somewhere to work on it. You can only push-start standard transmission cars - don't try it on an automatic. To push-start a car, put the car in second gear, put your foot in on the clutch, and turn the key on so the ignition lights come on. Have another car push your car. When you get going at a fair rate of speed, bring the clutch out real fast (known as popping the clutch), and give the engine some gas at the same time, and the car should start. This will only work if your problem is a bad starter. It won't work if it is an electrical connection problem. If you don't have anyone around to push you, and you are lucky enough to have parked on a hill pointing downhill, then you should be able to start the car as it rolls down the hill.

ENGINE CRANKS SLOWER THAN NORMAL

This refers to when the engine cranks slowly the first time you try to start it. If you are having trouble starting the car and keep cranking it a lot, then eventually the battery will wear down and the engine won't crank at normal speed:

1.   RUN DOWN BATTERY

The most common reason for the engine cranking slowly is a run down battery. This could be caused by a number of problems.

a. A problem with the battery itself that would cause it not to have a full charge could be some-thing as simple as the battery being low on water, in which case the battery should be filled with water and recharged at a service station. Or it could be a bad cell in the battery, meaning the battery would have to be replaced (to check for a bad cell, see the testing procedures under Battery Care, Part II, Chapter 5).

b. A problem in the charging system could cause run down battery. The charging system is what keeps the battery charged up so it can start the car. The simplest thing that can be wrong with the charging system is a loose fan belt that is slipping on the alternator pulley and not turning it. Test the

tension of the fan belt (Part II, Chapter 5) to make
sure that it is correct. Other charging system
problems are a bad voltage regulator, bad brushes or
faulty diodes in the alternator. A charging system
problem is usually indicated by the dashboard "amp"
light being on all the time or the "amp gauge"
reading discharge. It isn't very difficult to work
on the charging system - the hard part is diagnosing
what is wrong with it. If you are planning to do
the work yourself, then I would take the car to an
automotive electrical shop and have them diagnose
the problem using their instruments, and then you do
the repairs. If you are removing either the voltage
regulator or the alternator/generator, be sure to
disconnect the negative cable at the battery first.
This is so you won't have any hot wires going to any
of the charging system parts.

c. If your car has a run down battery, then the car
can be started by jumping it off the battery of
another car. What you are doing is using the other
car's battery to start your car.

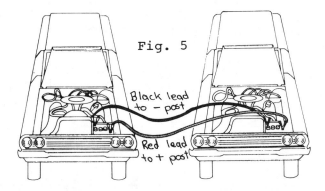

Fig. 5

Black lead to - post

Red lead to + post

JUMP STARTING YOUR CAR

<u>Steps</u>:

    1) To jump start a car, you need jumper cables,
two long thick insulated cables with large
clamps at both ends. One cable should have red
clamps, the other cable should have black clamps.
Hook the black clamps to the negative posts on
each battery. Hook the red clamps to the positive
posts on each battery.(Fig.5) Be sure to get the
right clamps on the right posts.

    2) Once the batteries are hooked up, start the
car that you are jumping your car off of. Push
down on the accelerator so the engine is racing
at a moderate speed.

3) Try and start your car. Once your car starts, disconnect the cables from the other car and then from your car. Be sure to not touch the clamps to each other while still hooked up to one of the batteries. That would be like touching a screw driver from one battery post to another, and would cause a large spark, and also possibly damage the alternator.

2. STARTER MOTOR PROBLEMS

A starter motor problem could also cause the engine to crank over at a slower than normal speed. Particularly if the bushings where the starter drive spins are worn badly, they will prevent the starter drive from turning at a normal speed. Any repair on the starter motor would have to be done after removing it from the car.

3. ENGINE PROBLEM

A final possibility for the engine cranking at slower than normal speed would be a problem within the engine itself that would prevent the crankshaft from turning at normal speed. Overly tight or worn crankshaft bearings would, for example, cause the crankshaft to turn slowly. Any internal engine problem would mean extensive engine work, of course. However, remember that this is the least likely cause for an engine to crank at a slower than normal speed. All other possibilities should first be eliminated before you start thinking about internal engine problems.

4. WEATHER

In extremely cold weather (sub zero temperatures), the oil in the engine will thicken to a point that it might hinder the turning over of the engine. This is why in the winter it is very important to have the battery fully charged and with good connections, so the starter will have full electrical strength to turn the engine over at a normal speed.

ENGINE CRANKS AT NORMAL SPEED BUT WON'T START

BEFORE you follow the troubleshooting procedures in
this section, check the gas gauge and make sure you
haven't run out of gas. To start a car that has
run out of gas, pour most of the gasoline that you
get into the gas tank, but save about 1 ounce to
prime the carburetor with. Take off the air cleaner
and pour the ounce of gas down into the carburetor.
This gives the carburetor some gas to get the car
going. Otherwise you will have to crank the engine
until the fuel pump pumps enough gas into the carburetor to start the engine.

The three most common reasons for an engine to crank
at normal speed but not start are:

1. a problem in the fuel system so the engine
   isn't getting any fuel or the right mixture of
   fuel

2. a problem in the ignition system preventing
   spark from getting to the right cylinder at
   the right time

3. an internal engine problem

1. PROBLEM IN THE FUEL SYSTEM

a. If the engine won't start when it's cold, check
to see if your automatic choke is working. Before
starting the car in the morning, take the air
cleaner off and look down into the carburetor. The
flap at the top of the carburetor, known as the
choke, should be closed so you can't see into the
carburetor.(Fig.6) The reason for this is to cut off
air supply to the carburetor and thus give the
engine a richer fuel mixture (meaning more fuel
proportionate to the amount of air) to help start
and run the engine when cold. If working right, as
the engine warms up the choke should gradually open
until it is wide open - you can see straight down
into the carburetor when the engine is fully warmed
up (Fig.6). If you have sticky linkage or a faulty
bimetal spring (located in the choke housing - round
box on the side of the carburetor) then the choke
won't close when it gets cold. If this is your
problem try spraying the linkage with choke cleaner.
It also might be necessary to remove the carburetor

Choke
open
(engine is warm)

choke
linkage

choke
housing

Choke
closed
(engine is cold)

Fig. 6

and take apart the linkage to free it up. You also might need to replace the bimetal spring (it pulls the choke closed when cold).

b. Another problem might be that the car is flooded. This could occur if you are pumping the gas pedal a whole lot to get the car started. A lot of times you can smell the gas when a car is flooded. To start a flooded car, hold your foot all the way down on the gas pedal while starting. This provides the maximum amount of air for the fuel mixture. Another way to start a flooded car is to just sit a few minutes allowing the gas to evaporate and then try starting it again. As a last resort, for a very badly flooded engine, you can pull the spark plugs out, squirt engine oil down each plug hole. Flooding causes the oil to be washed off the cylinder walls thus keeping the engine from building up any compression. Squirting oil into the cylinder restores the oil.

c. If you don't think you have a choke or flooding problem, check to see if the carburetor is getting any fuel. To do this, remove the fuel line where it goes into the carburetor. Put a rag loosely around the end of the line and crank the engine over to see if any fuel comes spurting out of the line. If no fuel comes out, then the next place to check would be the fuel pump. Take the fuel line off at the fuel pump on the side going to the carburetor, and crank the engine over again to see if the pump is pumping out fuel. If no fuel comes out, either the pump itself is bad, or no fuel is getting to the pump. To determine which is the case, pull the fuel line off that goes into the pump. If there is gas in the line, some should come dribbling out when you take off the line. You might try sucking

on the line a little (careful not to swallow) to
see if any gas comes out of the line.

If there is gasoline in the line before the fuel
pump, but not after, then the problem is a bad fuel
pump. One way to check for a bad fuel pump is to
remove the engine oil dipstick and see if the oil
smells like gasoline. A bad fuel pump will leak
gasoline into the crankcase where it mixes with
engine oil. Fuel pumps are pretty easy to replace.
Usually it is just a matter of disconnecting the
fuel lines and unbolting the old pump from the
engine and reversing the steps to install the new
pump.

If there is fuel coming out of the pump but not
getting to the carburetor, then the problem is most
likely a clogged fuel filter located either on the
fuel line between the pump and carburetor or where
the fuel line goes into the carburetor. Replace
the fuel filter (Part II, Chapter 6).

If no gasoline is getting to the fuel pump, then
one of three things has probably occurred:

1) Dirt has gotten into the gas line. Dirt in
the gas tank and line can clog the line and
prevent the flow of gasoline. To clean out the
line, disconnect the line at the fuel pump and
at the gas tank and blow through the line with
compressed air. It is important to disconnect
the line at the gas tank even though it might be
a hassle to get to it because you can balloon
out the gas tank by blowing compressed air into
it. A preventive measure to keep dirt out of
the tank and lines is to never let the gas tank
get real empty. Sediment and other junk in the
gasoline settles down to the bottom of the tank,
and if the tank gets real low the gasoline in the
bottom of the tank will carry the sediment, etc.
into the gas lines and possibly clog them. Now,
I drove a car for 4 years never putting more than
a $1 worth of gasoline in it at a time and never
had that happen, but other folks I know haven't
been so lucky.

2) A second reason for no gas getting to the fuel
pump is that the water in the fuel line has
frozen, blocking passage of the gasoline. Obviously, this is only a winter time hazard. Add a
can of "Heat" to the gas tank to thaw the line
(it takes a while). Two preventive measures are
to put gas antifreeze ("Heat") into the gas tank
to prevent frozen gas lines and to try and keep
the gas tank as full as possible during really

cold weather. If the tank isn't full, moisture
can collect inside the tank and lines and freeze.

3) A final reason for no gas getting to the fuel
pump is vapor lock in the gas line. Vapor lock
occurs when the gasoline heats to such a point
that it changes from a liquid state to a gas
state (vapor), thus producing air bubbles in the
gas line which block the flow of gasoline. Vapor
lock occurs most often on real hot summer days,
though it can also occur in the winter if the gas
line is touching the exhaust manifold (the hot-
test part of the engine). About the only thing
you can do for vapor lock is to wait for the
gasoline to cool down and turn back into liquid
form. If the line is located next to the exhaust
manifold, then it should be relocated somewhere
else. Vapor lock usually occurs only after the
car has been running, not when you are first
trying to start it.

2. PROBLEM IN THE IGNITION SYSTEM

a. If you have problems starting your car on wet
days, the problem might be moisture in the ignition
system. Check the inside of the distributor cap
and the top of the coil for any cracks (Fig.7). Old
spark plug wires can also sometimes be affected by
moisture getting on them. Have a friend turn the
engine over and look for any arcing from any of the
ignition parts. Arcing is electrical current jumping an air space, thus producing a spark. With a
cracked plug wire, the current going through the
plug wire can come out the crack and jump to the
nearest metal on the engine. If possible, check for
arcing at night - it is much easier to detect. If

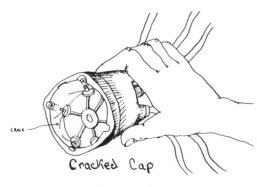

Cracked Cap

coil tower
crack

Cracked Coil

Fig. 7

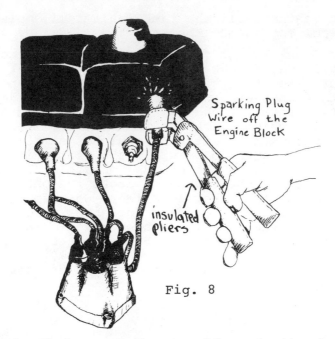

Sparking Plug Wire off the Engine Block

insulated pliers

Fig. 8

you can't find any obvious problems in the ignition
system, you might try replacing all of the spark plug
wires. They are frequently at fault when an engine
won't start on wet days.

b. If it's not a wet day and your car isn't starting
and you've checked out the fuel system, then you
should check to see if the ignition system is producing any spark. The best way to do this is to
take off one of the spark plug wires (it doesn't
matter which one) and hold it close to the engine
block and crank the engine (Fig.8). If the ignition
system is producing spark, a small arcing will come
out of the end of the wire - the arcing is the electrical current jumping to the metal ground of the
engine. You shouldn't hold the wire with your hand
as you might get a shock. The best tool to use is
a pair of insulated pliers, but if you don't have
such a tool, you can sort of prop the wire close to
the engine somewhere. Be careful not to put the end
of the wire near the carburetor because the arcing
could ignite any gas deposits on the carburetor. If
no spark comes out of the wire when you crank the
engine, try the same thing with another wire in case
that wire happens to be faulty. If you still don't
get any spark, then there is a problem somewhere in
the ignition system that is causing it not to produce any spark. Problems to check for are:

    1) If the points are burned badly, they won't
    open and close properly. Also, check the little

pigtail wire that leads to the points inside the distributor and make sure it isn't shorting out - sometimes the wire will get pinched by the distributor cap. You might also check the small wire that leads from the coil to the distributor to make sure it isn't broken.

2) A bad coil could also cause the ignition system not to produce spark. About the only way I know to determine this is to replace the coil with a good one and see if the car will start.

3) A bad rotor terminal in the distributor cap or a bad rotor could be the cause of the problem.

4) A bad ignition switch could also be a cause of no spark in the ignition system.

c. If the ignition system is producing spark, then check the tune up settings of the car - the dwell and the timing. (See Part II, Chapter 6.) If the timing is way off, then the spark won't be getting to the right cylinder at the right time and the car won't start. The timing shouldn't change from when it was set while doing a tune up. If it has changed, reasons for it changing might be that the distributor wasn't tightened down sufficiently or that the gear on the distributor shaft where it runs off the camshaft is stripped. If the distributor gear is stripped, then the distributor would have to be replaced.

3.   INTERNAL ENGINE PROBLEM

If you have thoroughly checked out both the fuel and the ignition systems and can't find anything wrong, then there might be a problem in the engine somewhere that would cause it not to start. The most likely possibility would be that the timing gears or the timing chain have slipped causing the valve timing of the engine to be off. The timing gears govern when the valves open and close and if they aren't opening and closing at the right time the engine won't start or run. You can determine if the valves are opening and closing at the correct time by taking off the valve cover and observing the action of the rocker arms while turning the engine over by hand. You would need some help from someone familiar with your type of engine to determine if they are opening and closing properly.

If the timing gears or timing chain is at fault,
they can be replaced without taking out the engine.
They are located in the front part of the engine
and can be gotten to by removing the radiator, fan,
water pump and the front timing cover. A Chilton's
or Motors manual would give the procedure for your
car if you want to do the work yourself.

HOW TO START YOUR CAR WITHOUT AN IGNITION KEY

Though not exactly a troubleshooting procedure, I
want to explain how to start your car if you lose
the ignition key. This method only applies to cars
that don't have the steering wheel lock system (you
have to turn the key to unlock the steering wheel).
To start the car without a key you need to do two
things - bypass the ignition switch and activate
the starter motor. To bypass the ignition switch,
use a piece of insulated wire (12 or 14 gauge automotive wire is fine) with an alligator clip on each
end. Hook one end of the wire to the positive terminal on the coil and the other end of the wire to
the positive post on the battery (Fig.9). This will
bypass the ignition switch. To start the car, you
need to jump from the positive battery cable at the
starter to the solenoid winding terminal (one of the
smaller wire terminals on the starter). On Fords
this is pretty easy to do, because you can do it at
the relay switch (small box on the fender near the
battery). Pull off the insulated wire from the
small post nearest the positive cable coming from
the battery. With a screwdriver or other long
metal object, touch across the battery cable terminal
and the small terminal (Fig.9). This will cause
the starter motor to activate and turn over the
engine. The wire from the coil to the battery will
provide a circuit for the engine to start and keep
running.

On starter motors where the solenoid is mounted on
the starter (almost all cars except Fords), you have
to touch a screwdriver from the battery cable terminal to one of the two small terminals on the
starter (Fig.10). You can try both to see which is
the right one - you won't hurt anything. Sometimes
the starter terminals are difficult to get to, but
usually not impossible.

You can't drive a car any long distance (probably
not more than 100 miles) with it wired this way
because it will burn out the points. If you want to
drive the car a long distance, then the wire going
from the coil to the battery should be replaced with
a wire that has a resistor hooked into it (you can
buy simple porcelain resistors at a parts store).
The resistor cuts down on the flow of current through
the points, thus reducing the chance of burning them.

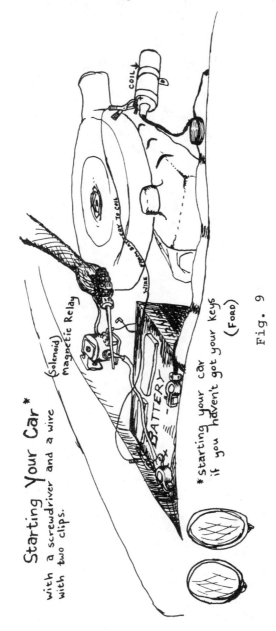

Starting Your Car *
with a screwdriver and a wire
with two clips.

* starting your car
if you haven't got your keys

(FORD)

Fig. 9

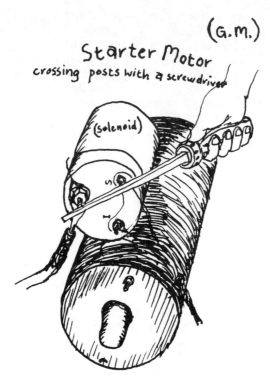

Fig. 10

Chapter 2

WHEN YOUR CAR
WON'T RUN RIGHT *

In this chapter I am going to cover things like lack
of engine power, engine running poorly, engine overheating, noises in the engine and other general
symptoms of a sick engine. Most engine problems are
caused by something relatively simple. Major engine
problems that would necessitate extensive and expensive engine work are the exception, not the norm.
When anything starts going wrong with my car, I
always immediately think the worst - that it is some
huge problem that is going to take a lot of time and
money to fix. However, the problem almost always
turns out to be a relatively little one not worth
all the anxiety it caused me. The reason I am
telling you this is to try and get you to learn from
the errors of my thinking and not do the same thing.
A lot of our "hysteria" about cars comes from the
fact that as women the knowledge about what makes
a car run has been denied us. As we gradually claim
that knowledge, we will be able to determine the
cause of a sick engine and fix it, and not let the
broken down car panic overtake us.

*or when the golden chariot falters

GENERAL ENGINE PROBLEMS

A. ENGINE MISSING OR LACK OF ENGINE POWER

If the engine is missing, meaning the engine doesn't run smoothly and occasionally cuts out, or if it has little power and won't accelerate very quickly, then there is probably one or more cylinders not firing for some reason. A cylinder not firing could also cause the engine to vibrate a great deal. If you are having these kinds of problems I would first check to see if the car is due for a tune up. An engine that is badly in need of a tune up will run very poorly, if at all. Even if you aren't going to do a tune up, I would take out the spark plugs and do a compression test on the engine (see Compression Test, Part II, Chapter 6). The compression test will determine the general condition of the engine and indicate any cylinder that has low compression.

Besides checking to see if the engine is due for a tune up and doing a compression test, there is one test that you can perform on the engine that will determine if any cylinder(s) is missing or not firing, and if so, which one(s). To test for a missing cylinder, you need a pair of insulated pliers, and a tachometer, if you have one, though it isn't absolutely necessary. Hook the tachometer up to the engine (as described in Part II, Chapter 6) and let the engine warm up so it is idling at normal speed. Leave the engine running, and with the insulated pliers, pull the first spark plug wire off the spark plug (Fig.1). Watch the tachometer to see if the engine rpm's drop. If that cylinder is firing, then pulling off the plug wire should cause the rpm's to drop slightly. If pulling off the wire seems to have no effect on the engine, then that cylinder is probably not firing. Test each cylinder in this manner. If you find two cylinders that aren't firing, it might be that the plug wires going to those two cylinders got reversed for some reason (this would be if a tune up or other work was done recently that would necessitate removing the plug wires from the spark plugs). Try reversing the wires and see if that has any effect.

Besides reversed plug wires, common causes for a cylinder not firing are a bad plug wire that isn't delivering the spark to the spark plug, or a spark

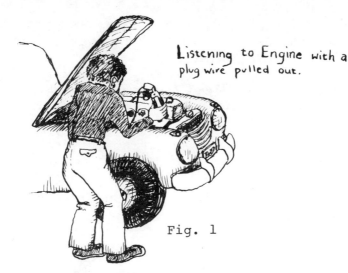

Listening to Engine with a
plug wire pulled out.

Fig. 1

plug with a carbon bridge, meaning that carbon
deposits have closed the gap in the plug so that
the plug doesn't fire. Check the condition of the
plug (see Part II, Chapter 6). If the plug seems
okay, then replace the plug wire. You can usually
buy single plug wires; you don't have to buy the
entire set.

If the engine in your car is cutting out at high
speeds, then the problem is most likely a faulty
fuel pump. Take the engine oil dipstick out and
see if the oil on the stick smells like gasoline -
it should be a pretty distinctive smell. A bad
fuel pump will leak gasoline into the engine crankcase and thus into the engine oil.

B. ENGINE OVERHEATING

If you are having problems with the engine overheating, first I would check the water level in the
radiator to make sure it isn't low. If it is low,
check for water leaks (explained further on in this
chapter). Also, check whether or not the thermostat is operating correctly (see Part II, Chapter
5). One quick way to do this without removing the
thermostat is to start the engine when it is cold
and let it run until the temperature gauge shows
normal or the cold light goes off. Shut off the
engine and feel the top of the radiator. If it is
cold, then the thermostat is probably defective.
The radiator should be very hot to touch.

A faulty water pump can also cause the engine to
overheat. To test the water pump squeeze the upper
radiator hose in your hand while the engine is

running. Speed up the engine and see if there is pressure on the hose - if so, the water pump is operating properly.

Another reason for an engine to overheat is lack of lubrication. Check the level of the engine oil and its condition - dirtiness and how thick it is.

C. ENGINE NOISES

I find engine noises very difficult to diagnose. It takes a whole lot of experience to distinguish one engine noise from another and know what it is. It is also sometimes hard to tell what is a loose part rattling and what is an actual noise within the engine somewhere. Given all these hesitations, I will try and describe to you some common engine noises that I am most familiar with.

Fig. 2

where Tapping noise comes from - adjusting valves to correct clearance

1. Valve tapping

Valve tapping is a light metal tapping sound that occurs in time with the engine - as the engine speeds up, the sound speeds up. Valve tapping indicates the clearance between the valve stem and the rocker arm is too great and should be adjusted (Fig.2). On foreign cars and older american cars the valve tappet clearance can be adjusted - see a manual for your car. On newer american cars, the tappet clearance is adjusted automatically through the use of hydraulic lifters. If an engine with hydraulic lifters develops valve tapping noise, one or more of the lifters are malfunctioning and should be replaced. This can also occur if not enough oil is getting to the lifters - be sure to check the level of engine oil.

2. Knocking or clattering

Any loud knocking or clattering sound within the engine is an indication of some sort of engine trouble. I would take the car to a mechanic that you trust and have her or him diagnose the noise. Do this as soon as the noise develops, because an engine with serious internal problems won't last long if it is continued to be driven in that condition.

3. Screeching

A screeching noise when you start the car most often indicates a loose or worn fan belt. Check the tension and condition of the fan belt. A screeching noise while the engine is running could indicate worn bearings in the alternator/generator or possibly the water pump. Bad water pump bearings will sometimes make more of a clattering sound coming from the front of the engine than a screeching sound.

To check for worn water pump bearings, grab hold of either side of the fan (this is with the engine shut off, of course). Try to rock the fan towards the engine and away from it (Fig.3). If the water pump bearings are bad, you will feel a movement in the fan. When the bearings are good, the fan should feel tight with no play in it.

If the water pump is bad, it should be removed and replaced. Replacing a water pump isn't usually too difficult of a job. First, drain the radiator and remove it. Then unbolt the fan from the pump. The pump can then be removed by unbolting it from the engine. When installing the new pump, be sure to scrape all the old gasket off the engine block and to seal the new gasket to the pump with gasket sealer. After installing the pump and replacing the hoses, fan, and radiator, fill the radiator with water and start the engine and check for leaks around the water pump gasket.

4. Popping sound

A popping sound when the engine is accelerated usually is caused by the combustion firing up through

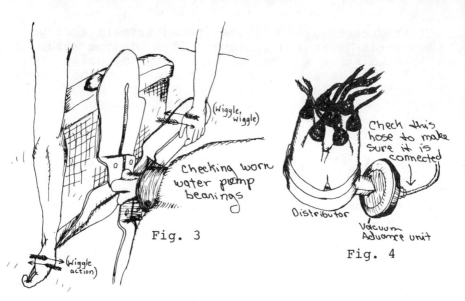

(Wiggle, wiggle)

Checking worn water pump bearings

Fig. 3

(Wiggle action)

Chech this hose to make sure it is connected

Distributor

Vacuum Advance unit

Fig. 4

the carburetor. This means that either the spark plug is firing in the cylinder at the wrong time or that the intake valve is not opening or closing at the correct time. Causes for these problems could be incorrect ignition timing (check tune up), incorrect valve timing (timing gear or chain slipped), a burned intake valve (should show up in a compression test as low compression in that cylinder), or the distributor advance unit is not working properly to advance the spark.

To check for a bad advance unit, shine your timing light on the timing marks; accelerate the engine and watch to see if the timing mark on the pulley moves. If it doesn't, then the advance unit on the distributor is faulty. Check the hose going to the advance unit and see that it is connected properly and is in good condition (Fig.4).

D. EXCESSIVE FUEL CONSUMPTION

A car using too much gas is another common car complaint. In-town driving in the winter will cause the car to use more gas then highway driving or in-town driving in the summer. This is because the carburetor choke will constantly be going on as the car is stopped and started. If excessive fuel consumption is occuring at a time when it shouldn't be happening, first check the operation of the choke and make sure it is opening all the way (see Part III, Chapter 1). If the choke is opening all the way, then the problem could be an improperly

adjusted carburetor. Check the adjustment on the
carburetor (Part II, Chapter 6). A missing cylinder
will also cause the engine to use an excessive
amount of gas.

OIL AND WATER LEAKS

A. OIL LEAKS

1. Engine

If your car is using an excessive amount of oil,
then the engine is either burning the oil or the oil
is leaking out somewhere. Burning oil is indicated
by a bluish exhaust smoke and/or oil on the spark
plug electrodes. Burning oil results from oil
getting into the combustion chamber of the cylinders.
Worn oil rings on the pistons, scores in the cylinder walls, or bad oil seals on the valve stems could
all cause oil to leak into the combustion chamber.
To correct an engine that is burning oil would
require major engine work.

Excessive use of oil is usually due to the oil
leaking out somewhere. Some oil leaks are fairly
easy to repair, others require more extensive work.
I find it pretty difficult to detect where oil is
leaking from, especially if the car is old and is
all covered with oil and dirt from years of being
on the road. One way to determine where the oil is
leaking from is to look for the cleanest spot on
the engine. The oil from the leak will clean away
the grit and dirt immediately around the leak.
Also, remember that the oil will flow towards the
rear of the car because of the force of the wind
passing by the engine, so look for leaks in front of
any excessive accumulation of oil. Common places
for oil leaks to occur are:

a. Oil drain plug

A leak at the oil drain plug can usually be re-
medied by adding a copper washer to the plug the
next time you change the oil.

b. Oil filter

Sometimes leaks will occur around the oil filter
due to a bad gasket on the filter. Usually
replacing the filter will fix the leak.

c. Valve cover gasket

Oil leaking from the valve cover will appear on the spark plugs or down the side of the engine. To correct a valve cover gasket leak, remove the valve cover and replace the cover gasket. Sometimes the old gasket will cause the cover to stick to the engine even after all the bolts are removed. If you have that problem, hit the cover lightly with a rubber mallet. This will usually jar the cover loose. Be sure to clean all of the old gasket off the valve cover and the engine. Any remaining bits of old gasket can cause the new gasket to not seal and thus to leak oil. If the new gasket doesn't quite fit the cover, soak it in water for a few minutes - the water will cause the gasket to stretch out. Apply a thin coat of gasket sealer to one side of the gasket and to the valve cover. Allow the sealer to dry for a minute or so until it feels tacky to touch. Put the gasket on the cover, lining up the bolt holes. Put the cover and gasket back on the engine, making sure to not disturb the gasket. Replace the bolts holding the cover to the engine; tighten them securely but be careful not to over-tighten them.

d. Oil sending unit

The oil sending unit is the part that registers the oil pressure in the engine and transmits it to the oil pressure gauge or oil light on the dashboard. The oil sending unit is usually located on one side or the other of the engine a little below the middle of the engine (Fig.5).

Close-up of oil sending unit

Showing location of oil sending unit on engine

Fig. 5

It is a small roundish part that screws in to the engine and has one or more electrical wires leading to it. If the unit is leaking, then it should be replaced. Remove the electrical wires and using a large wrench, unscrew the unit from the engine. When you install the new unit, be sure it is started straight in the hole as you don't want to crossthread the threads in the engine. Screw the unit in until it gets tight - it may not be all the way next to the engine, but that is okay. Reconnect the wires, and turn the car on and check for oil leaking around the unit.

e. Oil pan

Like the valve cover, the oil pan gasket could also be leaking oil. Check the bolts holding the pan on and make sure they are tight. The oil pan gasket is replaced using the same method as replacing the valve cover gasket. Sometimes oil pans can be real difficult to get off because of their positioning underneath the engine. You might try to eyeball it before you start the job to see what difficulties you may encounter. Sometimes it is easier to put up with oil leaks than to do the job necessary to correct them.

f. Front timing cover

The gasket around the front timing cover could also sometimes leak oil. Replacing the gasket necessitates removing the radiator, fan, water pump and finally the timing cover. See a Chilton's or Motors manual for more explicit instructions for your type of car.

g. Front and rear main seals

These are the seals located at either end of the crankshaft where the crankshaft hooks up to parts outside the crankcase. The front seal is located behind the crankshaft pulley and the rear seal is located behind the flywheel (see Fig.2, Part I, Chapter 2). There are different methods for changing these seals according to the type of car. Leaks from these seals usually show up as oil coming out around the crankshaft pulley (front main seal) or oil coming out where the engine hooks up with the clutch (rear main seal). Sometimes a leak from the rear main seal is hard to distinguish from a leak from the front seal of the transmission, since the oil would leak out in approximately the same area. There is an additive you can buy to put into the engine oil to color it so you can distinguish between leaking engine oil and transmission fluid.

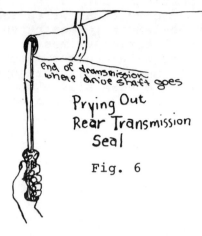

end of transmission
where drive shaft goes

Prying Out
Rear Transmission
Seal

Fig. 6

2. Transmission

The two places the transmission - automatic or standard - usually leak oil are the front seal and the rear seal. To replace the front seal, the transmission would have to be removed from the car. The rear seal, however, can be replaced without removing the transmission. Jack up the rear wheels and remove the drive shaft (see repairing u-joints, Part II, Chapter 8). The seal fits around the hole that the drive shaft goes into. Pry the seal out with a long screwdriver (Fig.6) and tap the new seal in. Replace the drive shaft.

3. Differential

If the differential is leaking fluid, it would probably be coming from the pinion seal where the drive shaft flange is (the part of the differential that the drive shaft bolts on to). I'm not real sure how to replace the pinion seal as I have only done one on a foreign car. A Chilton's or Motors manual would probably be of some help.

A General Word about Oil Leaks

Some oil leaks are fairly simple to repair and some aren't, as should be obvious from this discussion about oil leaks. I think that if the leak would require major work to repair the leaking part, I would just learn to live with the leak, unless it became excessive. If you have a leak in the transmission or differential, be extra careful to check the fluid levels in these two parts on a regular basis.

B. WATER LEAKS

If every time you check the water level in the radiator it is down quite a bit, then there is a water leak in the engine somewhere - the water is either leaking outside of the engine, or it is leaking internally into the engine oil. Water leaking internally is normally a sign of a blown head gasket (the head gasket is the large gasket between the crankcase and head of the engine). To detect a blown head gasket, look for oil in the radiator (oil slicks floating on top of the water), water deposits in the oil which will appear as a whitish substance inside the oil filler cap (though this could also be caused by moisture forming inside the crankcase in the winter), and water streaks (whitish deposits) down the side of the engine coming from the area of the head gasket. A blown head gasket would also cause the engine to lose power and have poor compression. To repair a blown head gasket, the head of the engine has to be removed and a new gasket installed.

Places to look for <u>external</u> water leaks are:

1. Radiator and heater hoses, especially around the clamps

2. Radiator - three places radiators commonly leak are (Fig.7):

    a. Around the flanges where the hoses fit on

    b. From the top and bottom seams of the radiator

    c. Through the veins - greenish or bluish deposits will appear on the veins (the color is caused by antifreeze)

    A temporary repair (or longer if you are lucky) for a radiator leak can be made by adding some stuff known as Stopleak, which will stop up the leaks for a period of time. Permanent repair of the leaks requires removing the radiator and taking it to a radiator shop and having them repair the leaks (this can be kind of expensive). If you need to replace the radiator, try a junk yard - that would be a lot cheaper than buying a new radiator.

3. Thermostat housing - leaking from the gasket on the thermostat.

    Remove the housing and replace the gasket.

4. Water pump gasket

    Remove the water pump and replace the gasket.

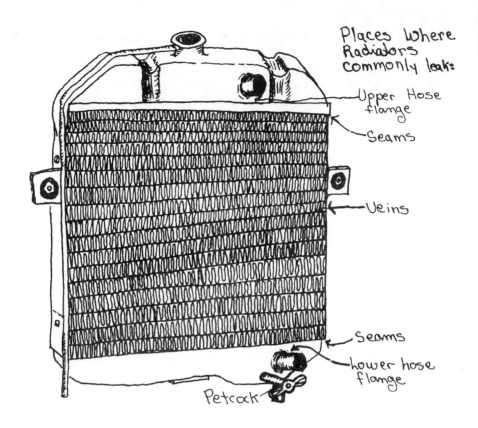

Fig. 7

Chapter 3

WHEN YOUR CAR'S LIGHTS, HORN, WIPERS DON'T WORK

In this chapter I am going to talk about what to check for when one or more of the electrical accessories on your car isn't working. Before getting into step by step troubleshooting procedures, however, I want to talk in general about the electrical system of the car.

Automotive electricity is the Direct Current (DC) type. Electricity flows to the electrical accessory and then returns to the source, thus completing the circuit. The source for electricity in the car is the battery. The current flows out of the positive side of the battery (via the alternator or generator) and returns to the negative side of the battery (Fig.1). The current gets back to the negative side of the battery because the negative cable of the battery is bolted to the engine or frame, thus "grounding" the engine and frame. The metal of the engine and frame serves as a conductor for the electrical current. This means that whenever the electrical current comes into contact with any metal part of the engine or frame that isn't insulated, the current travels through the engine and frame and through the negative cable. All electrical parts of the car have to be grounded - either by the part touching the metal of the car or by a wire that goes to the metal of the car - in order for the electrical circuit for that part to be completed.

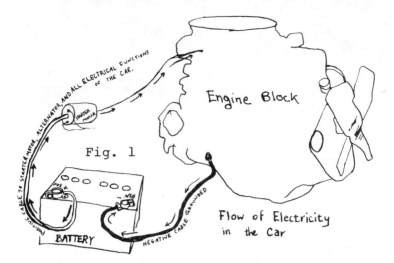

Engine Block

Fig. 1

Flow of Electricity
in the Car

BATTERY

It is important to keep this simple explanation of
automotive electricity in mind when trying to determine why lights or other accessories aren't working.
For instance, if a light isn't grounded sufficiently
so that the current to the light can complete the
circuit back to the battery, then the light won't
work. In the following steps, I'll explain how to
check for sufficient ground and other causes of
accessories not working. First I'm going to go over
the different types of electrical connectors and how
to work with them.

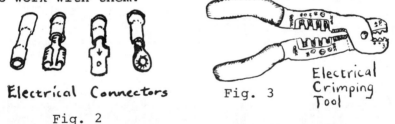

Electrical Connectors

Fig. 2

Fig. 3

Electrical
Crimping
Tool

Automotive electrical wire is mostly 14 or 16 gauge
wire. Gauge refers to the thickness of the wire -
the larger the gauge the smaller the wire. A different variety of connectors are available according
to what is needed (Fig.2).

It helps in doing automotive electrical work to have
a crimping tool (Fig.3), though it isn't absolutely
necessary. When putting a connector on a wire,
first strip about one half inch of insulation off
the end of the wire. Then put the connector over
the exposed part of the wire. With a crimping tool
or a pair of pliers smash the part of the connector
that is over the wire. The connector then should be
tight on the wire and ready for use (Fig.4). There
are different size connectors for different gauges

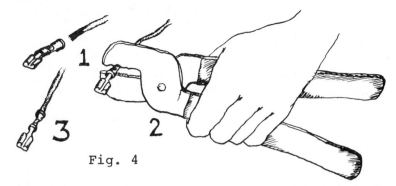

Fig. 4

of wire. If you have a very small wire that is too
small for the connector, you can strip an extra
amount of insulation off the wire and fold the end
of the wire over so it will be thick enough to
insert in the connector and hold it when smashed.

LIGHTS NOT WORKING

A. GENERAL CAUSES (APPLIES TO ALL LIGHTS)

1. BLOWN FUSE

When any of the electrical system isn't working, the
first thing you should always check for is a blown
fuse. This is particularly true if a group of items
quit working at the same time. However, even if it
is just one light that is out, I would check the
fuse box first. Older Volkswagens, for example,
have a separate fuse for each of the hi and low
beams of the headlights.

Find the location of the fuse box with help from
your owners' manual if you don't know where it is.
Frequently they are under the dashboard someplace,
but that isn't always the case. Sometimes there
will be a chart in the owners' manual or on the
fuse box telling which fuse is for which accessories.
Check the fuse for the accessory that is out and see
if it is blown. If you don't have a chart, then
just check all the fuses for a blown fuse.

A car fuse works on the same principle as a house
fuse. It is a strip of metal inserted in an electrical circuit so that if something goes wrong with
a circuit and it gets overloaded, the strip of metal
will burn and break the connection, rather than the
circuit wire overheating and possibly burning. You
can tell a blown fuse by whether or not the metal
strip or wire in the fuse is broken. If you have
glass tube fuses, the glass tube will become dark
and clouded (Fig.5).

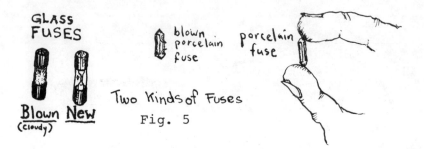

GLASS FUSES

blown porcelain fuse

porcelain fuse

Blown **New**
(cloudy)

Two Kinds of Fuses

Fig. 5

Always replace a blown fuse with a fuse of the same amperage. The amperage will be written on the old fuse, or else it would probably be listed in your owners' manual. It is important that the fuse be the correct size, because if it is of too high an amperage, then an overload in the circuit may not cause it to blow, and will burn out circuit wires instead. If the fuse is too low amperage, then the circuit might carry too high amperage for the fuse and constantly blow out the fuse.

If the fuse isn't blown, but the holder where it fits in looks corroded or the fuse itself looks corroded (green deposits usually), then clean the holder, scraping the deposits off with a knife, and replace the fuse.

FUSE KEEPS BLOWING OUT

If you keep blowing a fuse (the same fuse) then you probably have a short somewhere in that circuit. A short is when instead of the electrical current following the course of the wires, it makes a short-cut to the engine (ground) via an exposed part of wire touching metal. Look all along the circuit for any frayed or exposed wire that could be touching metal or that is touching an exposed part of another circuit. That is probably your problem.

double filament light bulb

Single filament light bulb

Sealed Beam

Fig. 6

2. BULB BURNED OUT

If you don't have a blown fuse or corroded fuse and/
or holder, then try checking the bulb that is out.
There are basically three different kinds of bulbs
in cars in the main lights (headlights, taillights,
turn signals, back up lights, brake lights):
a. sealed beam headlights; b. single filament bulb;
c. double filament bulb; (Fig.6).

a. Sealed beams

If a headlight is out, then you have to replace
the whole light, glass cover and all - this is
called a sealed beam. It is impossible to tell
if the beam itself is burned out, so before
replacing the beam I would check to make sure
the wires to the beam are good (see Step 3). In
sealed beams, you either have a combination high
and low beam (2 headlight system) or a separate
beam for high and low (4 headlight system). When
replacing a sealed beam, be sure to get the
correct one.

To remove a sealed beam, first take off the outer
chrome piece around the headlight - this piece
will usually be held on by two or more small
sheet metal screws. After taking the chrome
piece off, loosen (don't remove) the three little
screws that hold the metal retaining ring around
the beam. Turn the retaining ring so the holes
on the ring line up with the little screws and
remove the ring. You should then be able to
unplug the beam from the two or three prong plug
in the back of it. Installation is the reverse
of these steps. Be sure not to loosen or remove
the two larger screws that aim the beam. One is
located at the top or bottom of the beam, and the
other one is located to one side or the other of
the beam. They can be distinguished from the
retaining ring screws in that they are much
longer - at least an inch or so.

After installing the beam, turn the headlights on
to make sure it works. If the beam is dim, check
the plug to see if it is plugged into the beam
correctly.

Single Filament

Fig. 7

Burnt out (Broken Filament)

b. Single and double filament bulbs

You can usually tell if the small bulbs used in
turn signals, taillights, etc. are burned out by
seeing if the filament inside of the bulb is
broken or if the glass of the bulb is dark
looking (Fig.7). With double filament bulbs,
sometimes one filament will burn out, but not
the other. You would still have to replace the
whole bulb.

Even if you can't tell if the bulb is burned out,
you might want to try replacing the bulb anyhow
to see if that works. The bulbs are fairly cheap
and are easy to take in and out. To replace a
bulb, first remove the lens cover over the bulb.
On some cars, you get to the rear lights through
the trunk instead of removing the lens cover.
If you don't see any way to remove the cover,
then that is probably the case. With that kind
of set up, you pull the socket out of the lens
area to the inside of the trunk and then take the
bulb out. With any socket, to get the bulb out
you push the bulb in and turn it to one side or
the other. There is a little nob on the side of
the bulb that fits into a groove in the socket.
The bulb has to be turned so it lines up with
the groove and then it will come out. When you
replace the bulb, look at the new bulb and the
socket and note the nob on the bulb and where it
should go to line up with the grooves in the
socket (Fig.8). Double filament bulbs have two
nobs, one higher than the other. Look in the
socket where the bulb goes so you know which side
of the socket has the higher groove in it.

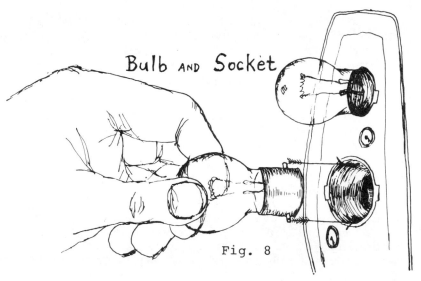

Bulb AND Socket

Fig. 8

Sometimes a socket will be corroded and the bulb might stick in the socket or be broken off. If this is the case, grab hold of the remainder of the bulb with a pair of needle nose pliers and twist the bulb until you can get it out. Clean out the corroded socket as much as possible with sandpaper.

3. BROKEN WIRE OR BAD ELECTRICAL CONNECTION

A third cause of a light not working might be a broken wire or a bad connection at some point along the circuit to the light. First, check the electrical connections at the light socket to see that they are good and tight. If there are any sort of connection boxes along the wire, check to see that they are tightly plugged into one another (Fig.9).

To check for a broken wire, you need a test light. A test light looks like an ice pick with a wire and clip attached to it and a light in the handle (Fig. 10). When you hook the metal clip to a ground and

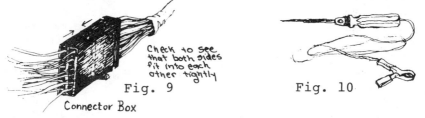

Check to see that both sides fit into each other tightly

Fig. 9

Connector Box

Fig. 10

touch the end of the probe to an electrical wire, the light in the handle will light if the wire the probe is touching is hot (meaning there is electrical current going through it).

To use the test light, first attach the clip to a metal part of the car somewhere to provide a ground for the light. If you are working with front lights, then you might be able to attach the clip directly to the negative post of the battery. Any part of the engine, bumpers, bolts on the body are good places to attach the clip. Make sure the ground is good by testing a light that is working first. If the test light lights up, then you know the ground is good. Leave the clip where it is so you will have a good ground to test the light that isn't working. Touch the probe of the test light to the terminal of the light you are testing (remove the bulb and touch the probe to the socket, Fig.11). The light you are testing needs to be turned on, and also the ignition key would have to be on if it is a light that only works when the car is running (such as turn signals). Turn the ignition key on until the oil and amp lights on the

204

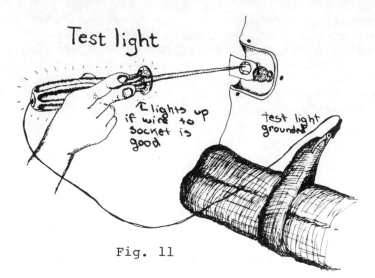

Test light

I lights up if wire to socket is good

test light grounded

Fig. 11

dash light up. Do not leave the ignition key on
for a very long period of time, as it will cause
the points in the ignition system to burn out. If
you are testing brake lights, then someone needs
to be stepping on the brake pedal and the car needs
to be in reverse to test back up lights.

If the wire is hot, then the test light should
light up. If it doesn't, then the wire is broken
somewhere along the circuit or some other problem
is causing the wire not to be hot (see Specific
Causes). Trace the wire back and push the test
probe into it at different intervals to see if it
is hot (test light will light up). Replace the
wire from the point where it doesn't light up the
test probe to where it does. A lot of time the
trouble is in the connector blocks, so test them
first. If you do have problems in a block, then
bypass the block by splicing a piece of wire into
the circuit that you are testing that takes the
circuit around the box.

4. POOR OR NO GROUND

Symptoms of a bad ground are dim lights or no
lights at all, lights that go on and off periodically, or lights that generally do weird things,
like if the turn signals go on when you step on
the brakes.

If the test light lights up where the bulb is but
you don't have a bad bulb, then test the ground.

Lights on cars are grounded (the ground completes
the electrical circuit back to the battery) either
through another wire or through metal to metal
contact with the body of the car. To test for a

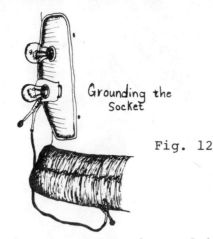

Grounding the Socket

Fig. 12

bad ground, you need a piece of insulated wire
with clips on both ends. Put the bulb back into
its socket. Clip one end of the wire to the bulb
and the other end to a good ground (Fig.12). If
the bulb lights up (once again the light you are
testing has to be on) then your problem is a bad
ground. If the light is grounded through a wire
(if that is the case you would have two wires
leading to a single filament bulb and three wires
leading to a double filament bulb; sealed beams are
always grounded through a wire) then remove the
ground wire from the light socket (usually the
black wire) and connect a new wire from the socket
to a metal part of the car (a sheet metal screw
somewhere would probably work). If the light is
grounded through metal to metal contact, clean off
the part of the light socket that touches the metal
of the car. If you can't get a good enough metal
to metal contact to provide ground for the light,
then you can run a ground wire to the light socket
and ground it that way.

B. SPECIFIC CAUSES

1. TURN SIGNALS

If you are having trouble with your turn signals or
emergency flashers - particularly if the lights
come on but don't blink - then you might have a bad
flasher. The flasher is what makes the turn
signals go on and off. Usually there is a separate
flasher for the turn signals and for the emergency
flashers. The flasher is a small rectangular or
round metal box with either 2 or 3 prongs for wires
(Fig.13). In most cars it is located in the maze
of wires under the dashboard. To replace it, just

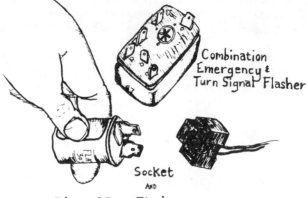

Combination
Emergency &
Turn Signal Flasher

Socket
AND
Fig. 13   Flasher

unplug the wires from it and plug them into a new
flasher. You can get flashers at local discount
stores pretty cheap.

2. HI LOW BEAMS

If the headlights won't switch to high or low, then
there probably is a bad dimmer switch (Fig.14).
Dimmer switches are pretty easy to replace, at
least the ones located on the floor are. Take the
bolts or screws holding the old switch out, disconnect the wires and remove the switch. If the
screws holding the switch in place are impossible
to get out, you might be able to drill them out and
then use a bolt and nut to hold the new switch to
the floorboard.

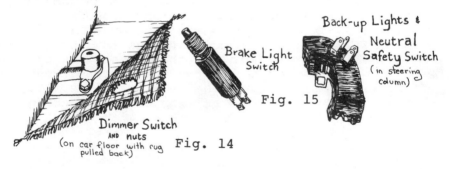

Back-up Lights &
Neutral
Safety Switch
(in steering
column)

Brake Light
Switch

Fig. 15

Dimmer Switch
AND nuts
(on car floor with rug   Fig. 14
pulled back)

3. BACK UP LIGHTS AND BRAKE LIGHTS

Both back up lights and brake lights have some sort
of switch that channels the current when the light
is supposed to go on.   If this switch is
faulty, then the lights won't work. The back up
light switch is located either in the transmission
(looks like the oil sending unit) or in the steering column (Fig.15). The brake light switch might

be either located at the brake pedal or on a
brake line coming from the master cylinder. It
will have one or two electrical wires leading into
it.

Test the switches using a test light. The wires
coming into or out of the switch should be hot when
the light is on, except for the ground wire (a wire
leading from the switch to the car frame). If the
wire coming out of the switch leading to the brake
or back up lights is not hot, then the switch is
bad and should be replaced. If the wire coming
into the switch is not hot, check for a broken
connection.

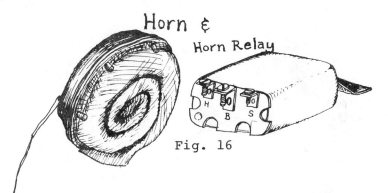

Horn &
Horn Relay

Fig. 16

HORN NOT WORKING

If the horn on your car isn't working, then you
should go through the troubleshooting procedure
that is used for the lights (with the exception of
the burned bulb step). Special things to look for
with a nonfunctioning horn are the connections at
the horns (the horns are located somewhere between
the engine compartment and the front grill usually)
and a bad ground in the horn lever on the steering
wheel. Horns also sometimes have a relay switch
that relays the current from the horn lever (what
you press to activate the horn) to the horns. The
relay looks like a flasher, though larger, and is
usually mounted somewhere in the engine compartment, on the fire wall or a fender (Fig.16). If
the relay isn't functioning then the horn won't
work. Test both sides of the relay when the horn
is activated to see if current is going into the
relay and then coming out again. If the wire
coming out of the relay that goes to the horns
isn't hot, then the relay is probably bad and
should be replaced.

WASHERS/WIPERS NOT WORKING

First, check the fuse. If the fuse is okay, then
check the wire at the wiper and washer motors
to see if it is hot when the washer or wipers
are turned on. If the wire is hot, but there isn't
any motor action, then check the ground wire to
make sure it is providing a good ground. If the
fuse, wires, and ground all test okay, then the
motor is bad and will have to be replaced. Sometimes you can get used washer or wiper motors at a
junkyard. New ones can be pretty expensive, especially wiper motors.

Reading a Wiring Diagram

Reading a wiring diagram isn't all that difficult.
First, find the correct wiring diagram for your
make and year of car. The owners' or shop manual
for your car would have the correct diagram. Locate
the part that you are working with (turn signals,
for instance) on the diagram using the numbered
list that comes with the diagram. Then trace the
wires from the part to their sources. The wires on
the diagram are usually marked with a letter indicating color of wire: R for red, Y for yellow, etc.
Other symbols are:

Ground

Connector

Light Bulb

Switch

Fuse

Glossary

This glossary is not intended to be a general glossary of automotive terms. Instead, I tried to make it a glossary of terms that are used a lot by mechanics when talking about cars--terms that are frequently hard to find a definition of in dictionaries, repair books, etc. If you have terms you would like to see in the glossary of a revised edition of The Greasy Thumb, please send them to me. I'm sure in dealing with cars and mechanics, we've all come across words that are baffling.

AC: Air conditioning

AIR COOLED ENGINE: An engine that is cooled by air instead of water; the volkswagen bug engine is the most common automotive air cooled engine

ALIGNMENT: Setting the angle of the front wheels so the car will steer and hold the road properly; also helps minimize tire wear

AT: Automatic transmission

BACKFIRING: The explosion in the combustion chamber takes place when the valves aren't fully closed thus causing firing out either through the carburetor(intake valve isn't closed) or the exhaust system (exhaust valve isn't closed)

BALANCING OR WHEEL BALANCE: Putting small weights on the tire rim so the weight of the tire is even all around the rim; unbalanced tires wear faster and put greater strain on front end parts and shock absorbers

BAY: Service stall at a garage

BEARINGS: A part in which a shaft turns (usually a round flat metal piece like a ring); any part of the car that has a turning shaft will have a bearing

BENDIX: The starter drive of the starter motor--a gear that moves forward and meshes with the flywheel to turn the engine over

BLEEDING THE BRAKES: Pumping fluid through the brake lines by means of the brake pedal in order to push any air out of the lines

BLOCK: Also called the cylinder block; the main part of the engine--the basic structure that forms the cylinders; the crankshaft, pistons, and camshaft all are housed in the block

BURNED VALVE: The edges of the valve has been burned from wear and overheating so the valve no longer seals the combustion chamber; results in compression escaping out and loss of engine power and means the engine needs a valve job

BUSHING: Thin piece of metal that serves as a bearing liner; replaceable when wears out

CARBON: Black powdery stuff that gets on engine parts--spark plugs particularly-- as a result of engine combustion and sometimes too rich of a fuel mixture

CATALYTIC CONVERTER: A part of the exhaust system of new cars that converts harmful exhaust gases into harmless gases (supposedly); looks like a small muffler

CELL: Unit of the battery; each cell (indicated by the hole where you add water) has 2 volts--thus, a 12 volt battery has 6 cells

COMPRESSION: Engine compression--the squeezing of the fuel mixture in the combustion chamber to make it highly explosive; the amount of compression determines the power of the engine; if the combustion chamber doesn't seal properly, then the compression will be low and the engine will be lacking in power

CRANK: The crank--short for the crankshaft

CRANK THE ENGINE: Turning the engine over by turning the ignition key on; what the engine does before it starts running

CRANKCASE: Lower part of the enging that houses the crankshaft--a combination of the cylinder block and the oil pan

DIESELING: Refers to when the engine keeps running after you turn off the ignition key; also called running on

DRIVE TRAIN: The parts of the car that transfer the power of the engine back to the differential--consists of the transmission, universal joints, and the drive shaft

DUALS: Usually refers to a dual exhaust system on a V-8 engine, meaning the engine has two separate exhaust systems, one coming off each exhaust manifold; could also refer to dual carbs, meaning an engine with two carburetors--a souped up car

ENGINE REBUILD: Pulling the engine out of the car and overhauling it--usually consists of boring or honing out the cylinders, replacing the piston rings and possibly the pistons, checking the crankshaft and putting in new crankshaft and camshaft bearings, and grinding the valves and valve seats

ENGINE SEIZED: Means that for some reason there was no lubrication in the engine parts, causing the metal to overheat and start scraping and scratching and sometimes fusing together (you got problems)

FIRE WALL: Partition between the engine compartment and the passenger compartment

FOULED PLUGS: Spark plugs that have a build up of carbon and oil deposits on the electrode preventing them from firing properly

FOUR BARREL: Carburetor with four throats, etc. (as in four single barrel carburetors put together)

FOUR WHEEL DRIVE: The power of the engine drives both the rear wheels and the front wheels, not just the rear wheels as in conventional drive cars

FRONT END: Refers to all the steering parts that are located in the front of the car--ball joints, tie rods, pitman arm, idler arm, etc. (the only place where there are steering parts is the front of the car)

FRONT WHEEL DRIVE: The power of the engine drives the front wheels instead of the rear wheels (most cars have rear wheel drive); front wheel drive is an advantage in snowy conditions because the weight of the engine gives the front wheels a lot of traction

FUEL INJECTION: A fuel system that squirts gasoline directly into the combustion chamber or the intake manifold instead of the gasoline mixing with air in the carburetor; a fuel injected engine has no carburetor

FUEL MIXTURE: The mixture of gasoline and air as regulated by the carburetor

GROUND: The negative post of the battery (see pages 198-199 for further explanation of ground)

GROUNDED: The electrical current returns to the battery

HEAD: The part of the engine that is bolted to the top of the cylinder block; houses the valves, valve springs, rocker arms, rocker arm shaft, and forms the combustion chamber

HEADERS: A part that replaces the exhaust manifold to provide a better flow of exhaust gases and
decreases back pressure from the exhaust in the
combustion chamber; another souped up car item

HYDRAULICS: Pertains to a system that operates
through the movement of fluid--such as hydraulic
brakes

INTERNAL COMBUSTION ENGINE: Engine in which the
explosion (combustion) takes place inside the en-
gine--the type of engine in automobiles

LEAN: Refers to a fuel mixture which has too much
air in proportion to gasoline

KNOCKING: Can refer to a lot of different engine
noises, but usually means a noise caused by too
rapid burning of the compressed fuel mixture which
causes an extra explosion against the piston--thus
the knocking sound; also called detonation and
pinging

LIFTERS: Refers to valve lifters, which are small
cylinder pieces of metal that ride on the camshaft
and "lift" the push rods--one for each valve; can
also refer to metal pieces that boys put in the
rear springs of their cars to raise the rear end
higher than the front end

LINKAGE: Series of rods, cables, etc. that transfer motion from one place to another--accelerator
linkage, clutch linkage, etc.

LUGGING: What the engine does when it is in too
high of a gear for the speed the car is traveling--
the engine is being overworked

MAGS: Mag wheels--special spoke rims made of mag-
nesium/aluminum that are seen on a lot of souped
up cars

MAIN BEARINGS: The bearings for the crankshaft

MISFIRING: When one of the cylinders doesn't fire
for some reason while the engine is running--can
happen continuously or intermittedly

MISSING: Same as misfiring

MODIFIED: What the boys do to soup up their cars--
change different parts of the engine to make it
run faster

MPH: Miles per hour

OCTANE: Measures the tendency of a fuel to knock--
gasoline with high octane ratings are resistant
to knocking, low octane gasolines knock very easily

OVERHEAD CAM: An engine with a camshaft located directly above the valves--eliminates the need for lifters, push rods, rocker arms and shaft

OVERDRIVE: An extra transmission gear which allows the drive shaft to turn at a faster rate of speed than the engine; designed to save fuel in high speed driving

PB: Power brakes--The braking action is assisted by a vacuum unit that runs off the engine vacuum

PINGING: A metallic rapping sound from the engine-- same thing as knocking; caused by too low octane rating fuel or the pumping of too much fuel into the cylinders while the engine is under load (being too heavy footed while going up a hill,for example)

POP THE CLUTCH: Bringing the clutch pedal out very rapidly while giving the engine gas in order to make a rapid start (squeeling out) or to get the engine started when the car is being push started

PS: Power steering--the steering is assisted by a pump that runs off the engine

RACK-AND-PINION STEERING: A steering design found in most sport cars and some small foreign cars that allows for a sharper turning radius

REAR END: Common term for the differential and rear drive axles

RICH: A fuel mixture that has too much gasoline in proportion to air

RING JOB: Refers to installing new rings on the pistons; is usually done when oil is leaking past the oil rings into the combustion chamber and the engine has poor compression

RODS: The connecting rods that attach the pistons to the crankshaft

ROTARY ENGINE: Wankel engine--instead of pistons that move up and down, the rotary or wankel engine has three point lobes that turn in an oval chamber

RPM: Revolutions per minute--refers to the revolutions of the crankshaft; it takes two revolutions of the crankshaft to deliver one power impluse

RUNNING ON: Dieseling--see definition of dieseling

SHIMMY: Wobbling or shaking of the front wheels

SHORT: An electrical current taking a shorter path than the path of the circuit; often happens when a bare wire touches metal on the engine so the current grounds before completing the circuit

SLUDGE: Thick, pasty substance that forms when
engine oil gets old and water mixes in with it;
hinders engine lubrication

STROKE: The distance traveled by a piston in a
cylinder

STUD: A headless bolt that is threaded on both
ends--usually screws into the engine block

TAPPET: Can refer to the valve lifters (see lifters)
or to the clearance between the rocker arm and
valve stem (see valve clearance)

THROW A ROD: A term used to describe what happens
when a connecting rod breaks loose while the engine is running causing a lot of internal engine
damage--means a engine rebuild job

TORQUE: Turning or twisting effort

TWO-BARREL: Carburetor with two throats, etc.
(combination of two single barrel carburetors in
one carburetor)

U-JOINTS: Short for universal joints, the cross
like pieces that connect the drive shaft to the
transmission and differential and allow it to
twist and different angles

V-8: An eight cylinder engine with a bank of four
cylinders on each side at a slant to form a V

VALVE ADJUSTMENT: Setting the clearance between
the valve stem and the rocker arm at a specified
amount; needs to be done periodically on cars
with adjustable valves (mostly foreign and compacts)

VALVE CLEARANCE: The space between the rocker arm
and the valve stem

VALVE JOB: Removing the head from the engine and
regrinding the valves and the valve seats in the
head, replacing any necessary parts (bad valves,
worn springs, etc.); usually done when there is
one or more burned valves and/or compression in
one or more cylinders is low

VALVE NOISE: Tapping or clattering in the engine
caused by excessive valve clearance or worn push
rods, camshaft, etc.

VALVE TRAIN: All the parts of the engine that
operate the opening and closing of the valves--
camshaft, lifters, push rods, rocker arms, rocker
arm shaft, valve springs, and the valves

VAPOR LOCK: When the gasoline in the fuel lines
heats to a point where it turns into vapor thus

causing air bubbles which block the flow of fuel in the line; happens most often on very hot days or when the fuel line is located too close to the exhaust manifold

WANKEL ENGINE: Rotary engine (see definition of rotary engine)

WIND OUT THE GEARS: Accelerating the engine to the maximum amount before shifting into a higher gear; occasionally good to do to clean out the carbon on the plugs and in the combustion chamber

INDEX

A

Air filter 47,126
Allen wrench 3
Alternator 37,100,102
Antifreeze 89-94
Antifreeze tester 90
Automotive electricity
   198-200

B

Back up light switch 207-208
Ball joints 44,76,166-167
   testing 167
Battery 36,47,61,184
   battery care 96-99
     cleaning 97-98
     testing 99
   bad battery
     dead 171-172
     rundown 174-175
Battery cable 47,97
Battery clamp puller 97
Battery tester 99
Bell housing 50
Bendix 173
Bleeder wrench 143
Block,engine 28,29
Brakes 45,129-157
   Disc brakes 130,152-155
   Difference between
     disc and drum brakes
     130
   Fluid check 59-60
   How to do brake job
     134-152
     Adjusting the brakes
       150-152
     Bleeding the brakes
       147-149
     Master cylinder 48
       rebuild 155-157
     Rebuild wheel cyl.
       142-147
     Replace brake shoes
       135-142
     Replace brake lines
       157

Symptoms of bad brakes
   132-133
Brake adjusting tool 134
Brake assembly 138,156
Brake hold down spring
   tool 134,138
Brake hone 143
Brake light switch 207-208
Brake shoes 135,137
Brake spring pliers 135
Brake warning light 152
Breaker bar 12
Broken bolt or stud 21
Bulbs 201-204
Buying parts 24-25

C

Camshaft 29,32-33,34
Carburetor 35,48,178
   adjusting 121-123
Charging system 36,37
Chisel 11
Choke 177-178
Clutch 41,50,168-169
Coil 106-108,114
Combustion chamber 30
Compression guages 124
Compression test 123-125
Condensor 125,106,107,115
   change 125
Connecting rods 28,29,31
Cooling system 39-40,
   89-94
   flushing 93-94
Crankcase 29
Crankshaft 29
Crescent wrench 3
Creeper 14

D

Differential 42-43,51,163
   fluid change 68-70
   fluid check 58-59
   fluid leaks 195
Dimmer switch 207

Distributor 47,106,113,
    115,118,121,108
    changing cap & rotor
        125-126
    cracked cap 114
    wiring diagram 125
Drive shaft 42,51,163
Drive train 41-43
Dwell tachometer 109,116-
    118

E

Electrical system, general
    36-38
Electrical connector box
    204
Electrical connectors 199
Electrical crimping tool
    199
Electricity, automotive
    198-200
    testing 204-206
Engine
    how works 28-40
    Types 29-30
Engine oil 56
    change 63-68
    check 56
    dipstick 56
Engine problems, general
    182-183,187-197
    excessive fuel con-
        sumption 191-192
    missing, lack of po-
        wer 187-188
    noises 189-191
    oil leaks 192-195
    overheating 188-189
    water leaks 196-197
    won't start 170-185
Engine support 50
Exhaust manifold 48
Exhaust pipe 51
Exhaust system 40,160-163

F

Fan 39,47,99,102
Fan belts 99-102
Feeler guage 109
Files 12
Fire wall 49

Flasher 207
Fluid drop 55
Flywheel 29
Front end 44,166-167
Front timing cover 194
Front wheel bearings 80-88
Fuel filter 126-127
Fuel pump 35,47
    problems 179
Fuel system 35-36
    problems 177-180, 191-
        192
Fuses 200-201

G

Gasket scraper 70
Gas tank 35,51
Generator 37
Grease fitting 76,77
    removing a fitting 79
Grease gun 75,78
Greasing your car 74-77
Ground, electrical 198-
    199,205-206

H

Hack saw 13
Hammers 10-11
Head, engine 28,33
Head gasket 46
Horn not working 208
Horn relay 208
Hoses 47,48,94-95
Hot wiring 183-185
Hydrometer 99

I

Ignition switch 172
Ignition system 36,105-108
    problems 180-182
Ignition wrenches 109
Impact wrench & screw-
    driver 18-20
Intake manifold 35,48

J

Jack 22-23
Jacking 22-24
Jack stands 23
Jump start a car 175-176

L

Leaf springs 43,51
Lifters 33
Lights not working 200-208
Line wrench 157
Location of parts 46-53
Loosening a bolt, nut,
  screw 16-20
Lubricant changes 63-73
Lubrication system 38-39

M

Magnetic relay switch 172
Main seals, front & rear
  engine 194
Maintenance schedule 55
Mechanic tool kit 11-13
Motor mount 50
Muffler 51,See exhaust
  system

N

Noises, engine 188-191
Nuts 1

O

Oil,engine, type 64
Oil change 63-68
Oil dipstick 56
Oil drain plug 50,65-66,
  192
Oil filler cap 47
Oil filter 47,64,192
  filter change 66-68
Oil filter wrench 64
Oil leaks 192-195
Oil pan 38,50,194
Oil pump 38
Oil sending unit 38,39,
  193-194
Overhead cam engine 34

P

Parking brake cable 51
PCV valve 127,128
Petcock 91-92
Pipe spreader 162
Piston 28-31,34
Pliers 7-10

Points, contact 106,107-
  108
  replace 114-118
Pour spout can opener 64
Pry bar 12
Punch 11
Push rod 32,33,34
Push start 174

R

Ratchet 4-6
Radiator 39,47,90-94,196,
  197
  fluid check 60-61,90
  hoses 47,94-95
Rear axle housing 51
Rings, piston 29
Rocker arm & shaft 32,33,
  34
Rotor 108,126
Rounded nuts 20

S

Safety 22-24
Screwdrivers 6-7
Screws 1
Screw starter 115
Sealed beam 201-202
Service Routines 62
Shock absorbers 44,47,50,
  51,158-160
Sockets 4-6
Solenoid 47,172,184
Solvent 13
Spark plug 106,108
  condition 112
  gaping 113
  replace 111-113
Spark plug gaping guage &
  tool 109
Spark plug socket 109
Spark plug wires 47,108
Springs 43-44
  leaf & coil 51
Starting car without key
  183-185
Starter motor 37,173,176,
  185
  starter drive 173
Steering parts 44-45,50,
  76,166-167
Suspension 44,50

T

Tail pipe 51
Technical manuals 26
Test light 204-206
Thermostat 40,95-96,188
    housing 96,196
Timing 118-121
Timing chain, gears 32,
    182-183
Timing light 109,119
Tire rotation 61
Tools 1-21
    buying 14-15
    description 1-14
    using 15-21
Torque converter 71,72
Transmission 41-42,43,50,
    167,68-73
    fluid leaks 195
    automatic
        fluid check 56-57
        fluid change 70-73
    standard
        fluid check 57-58
        fluid change 68-70
        rear seal replace-
            ment 195
Transmission fluid gun 68
Trouble light 13
Tune up 105-128
    How to do one 109-128
    Theory 105-109
Tune up Specs chart 111
Turn signals 206-207

U

Universal joints 42,51,77,
    163-165,169

V

Valve adjustment 127,128,
    129
Valve cover 47
    gasket 193
Valve tapping 189
Valve train 32
Valves, intake & exhaust
    30
    how they work 32-34
Vise grips 9
Voltage regulator 37

W

Water leaks 196-197
Water pump 39,47,188,190,
    191,196
Wheel bearings 80-88
Windshield washer 61,48,
    103
    not working 209
Windshield wipers 103-104
    not working 209
Winterize 89-104
Wire cutters 9
Wiring diagram 209
Wrenches 2-4
    using a wrench 3